Healing Multicultural America

DEDICATION

Henry T. Trueba dedicates the time and effort invested in this volume to his wife Ardeth L., his children Laura J. and Phillip H. Trueba, and to all the children of Multicultural America.

Cirenio Rodriguez dedicates his efforts to his family: Gloria, his wife, Teresa, Celena, Samuel and Omar, his children; to his parents (especially his father who died 1991), and his nine sisters.

Yali Zou dedicates her work to her daughter Guan Yue, and her professors and mentors, especially Henry T. Trueba, Douglas Minnis and George Yonge.

José Cintrón dedicates his work to his 'queridos padres, Feliciana Vargas Cintrón y José Cintrón'.

The authors offer the fruit of their cooperative labor to the Woodland Mexican community, school board members, and especially educators, whose commitment, hard work and perseverance made possible what is reported in this study.

Healing Multicultural America:
Mexican Immigrants Rise to Power in Rural California

by

Henry T. Trueba
Cirenio Rodriguez
Yali Zou
and
José Cintrón

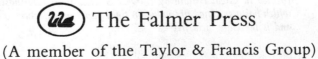

The Falmer Press

(A member of the Taylor & Francis Group)
Washington, DC • London

UK   The Falmer Press, 4 John Street, London WC1N 2ET
USA   The Falmer Press, Taylor & Francis Inc., 1900 Frost Road, Suite 101,
         Bristol, PA 19007

First published in 1993

**A catalogue record for this book is available from the British
Library**

**Library of Congress Cataloging-in-Publication Data are
available on request**

     ISBN 0 75070 150 1
     ISBN 0 75050 151 X

Jacket design by Benedict Evans

Typeset in 9.5/11pt Bembo by
Graphicraft Typesetters Ltd., Hong Kong

*Printed in Great Britain by Burgess Science Press, Basingstoke on paper
which has a specified pH value on final paper manufacture of not less than 7.5
and is therefore 'acid free'.*

Contents

List of Tables and Figures

Tables

Acknowledgments

The research project that resulted in this volume was inspired by members of the Chicano and other ethnic communities in the United States whose lives have demonstrated the intimate relationship between peace within the self and the ability to heal others. There are also many other persons, especially professors and internationally recognized scholars whose written word and personal mentoring have impacted our research directly or indirectly. We want to thank George and Louise Spindler for their personal nurturing, their teaching and mentoring, and for their written word on cultural therapy which is central in this book. Our gratitude to Paulo Freire for his message that generated in us and many others the commitment to pursue historical reflection, educational reform and social emancipation. We wish to thank admired scholars and colleagues whose written and personal word has stimulated our scholarly efforts, such as Joshua Fishman, Larry Iannaccone, George DeVos, Marcelo Suarez-Orozco, Chuck Frake, Eugeen Roosens, Ken Zeichner, Gary Price, Walter Secada, Tom Popkewitz, Roy D'Andrade, and Michael Apple.

The authors also want to thank colleagues and friends for their general support and encouragement over the years, Steve Arvizu, Chris Faltis, George Yonge, Douglas Minnis, Robert Alvarez, Beatriz Arias, Rosemary Papalewis, Mimi Bloch, Luis Moll and Leo Chavez, Concha Delgado-Gaitan, Fred Erickson, Karen Watson-Gegeo, Harold Murai and many others. We feel profound gratitude to the Division of Education at the University of California, Davis, for its generous support of this project, especially to what was called the 'University School Programs' at the time of the research, and more in particular to its then Director, Jon Wagner. His personal support and interest, his theoretical insights and genuine concern for schools and teachers generated in the authors commitment and determination to carry the research and analysis as far as possible.

The authors would like to express their most sincere feelings of gratitude and admiration to the members of the Mexican community in Woodland who generously gave of their time and shared with the authors and readers their personal memories and impressions about their life experience in the United States. Special recognition is given to the school district personnel who provided us important information, to the teachers and administrators who granted interviews with Cirenio Rodriguez and José Cintrón; to the School Board members and their 1991 President, Jesse Ortiz, who played a major role in the study. We thank historian

Shipley Walters for her assistance in editing Chapter 3, and her guidance in interpreting historical events. For their assistance and insights, we are deeply grateful to many members of Mexican organizations in Woodland, especially those of *Concilio* such as Rick Gonzalez, Glen Valenzuela and Antonio Rodriguez, of *Guadalupanas*, *Ballet Folklorico de Beamer School*, *Comite de Beneficencia Mexicano*, Yolo County Hispanic Historical Society, and of the Association of Mexican American Educators.

We want to express our heartfelt gratitude to the administration, staff and resource personnel of Beamer Park Elementary School for their generous cooperation, candor and assistance during the course of the study. We have a special debt of gratitude to the faculty, especially those working in the Immersion/Bilingual program, for sharing generously with us their time, classroom space, personal thoughts and insights, and for their helping us understand their personal experiences in this country. Their continued commitment to a democratic educational philosophy based on equal opportunity for all children, and their passion to the intellectual growth and social adjustment of all children, maintained at a high level our motivation to complete this project.

A special thanks to Professor Michael Apple whose powerful words have articulated for us the many scattered thoughts and dreams we have entertained in our experience as immigrants to the United States. His kind Foreword is a unique gift to us, the authors, but his substantive message will be for readers and authors a treasure to be kept in our hearts for a long time.

In all of the details of final editing, printing, packaging, sending of manuscripts and correspondence, there are many quiet supporters; without them these pages would have never seen the light. Special thanks to Jackie Captain, Carolyn Hackler and Paul Borowsky. Last and most, our gratitude goes to the children to whom we have dedicated our lives. In a very real sense this book belongs to the ethnic children of the world, especially those of Woodland. We express our loving gratitude to all the children of Woodland, particularly those of Beamer Park Elementary School. Their dreams and hopes are ours. Their future role in a world where ethnic and racial groups can search without penalty for an opportunity to become full citizens and active participants in a peaceful world will be most significant.

Foreword

When I began my career as an educator, my first teaching assignment was working in an all African-American and Hispanic school in a decaying east coast city. We were instructed *not* to allow children to use non-standard English or to speak Spanish. Our job was to turn them as quickly as possible into 'real Americans'. The subtle (and not so subtle) racism and the rearticulation of patterns of cultural domination were certainly not invisible either to the students and community members or to many of the teachers who strongly believed that these policies were immensely destructive both to students' senses of self worth and of cultures and histories that needed to be cherished not destroyed.

For years, these and similar policies continued to be common practice. The story of the successful concerted challenges to them is of immense importance. With the growth of the 'English Only' movement and of the rightist assertion of the primacy of the (highly romanticized) western tradition, we are in danger of losing these gains, however. Cultural domination — long a fact of life in many of our institutions (Apple, 1990; Omi and Winant, 1986) — is again coming center stage in the human drama of education as conservative triumphalism spreads out over the landscape.

As I have argued in a series of volumes (Apple, 1985; 1988b; 1990; Apple and Christian-Smith, 1991), it is naive to think of the school curriculum as neutral knowledge. Rather, what counts as legitimate knowledge is the result of complex power relations and struggles among identifiable race, class, gender, and religious groups. Much the same could be said about the ways in which teaching and evaluation are organized, the goals at which they aim, and the manner in which they are carried out (Bernstein, 1977). Thus, education and power are terms of an indissoluble couplet. It is at times of social upheaval that this relationship between education and power becomes most visible.

Such a relationship was and continues to be made manifest in the struggles by people of color, women and others to have their history and knowledge included and/or placed at the center of the curriculum. Driven by an economic crisis and a crisis in ideology and authority relations, it has become even more visible in the past decade or so in the resurgent conservative attacks on schooling. 'Authoritarian populism' is in the air and the New Right has been more than a little successful in bringing its own power to bear on the goals, content and process of schooling (Apple, 1988a). In the midst of the conservative restoration, when many committed educators and community activists are working so hard in increasingly difficult conditions to keep alive the idea of an education that is not simply about creating the 'human capital' needed by economically powerful sectors of our society, examples of educational successes are essential. Here I mean not just successfully carrying out the all too common top-down mandates aimed at making schools 'more efficient and effective' in reaching a limited set of conservative goals. Rather, I am referring to instances where students, teachers, and community members are empowered and where the cultural and political resources needed to make further gains are created.

We have tended to think of the idea of power negatively. Yet, the concept of power merely connotes the capacity to act and to do so effectively. That is, power can mean more than imposing one's will on others; very importantly, it can also be seen much more positively, as connected to a people acting democratically and collectively, in the open, for the best ideals (Apple and Christian-Smith, 1991).

The story told by Henry Trueba and his co-authors is based on this more positive sense of power. It brings together diachronic and synchronic, historical and current, material that allows us to see how a community can succeed in creating educational experiences that dramatically reduce the alienation of 'minority'[1] children and protects the worth of students' language and culture on which so much of one's vision of self depends.

One of the things that is most important in *Healing Multicultural America* is its recognition that lasting changes in schooling are connected to action in other social arenas besides education. The preconditions for a less racist and more democratic experience for the students studied here were laid by organized economic and political activity in the Hispanic community. They were based on an insistance that the language, culture and history of that community would *not* be lost either in schools or in the other institutions that organized people's lives. The volume's account provides ample evidence that it is possible — through long and hard work — for non-dominant groups to make a real difference in their own lives and in those of their children.

Yet, Henry Trueba and his colleagues make a contribution not only by reminding us of such possibilities in educational policy and practice. They also suggest ways in which ethnographic research can assist in this. In many ways, the ethnographic study reported here recognizes that educational research does not stand above the difficult issues of ethics, ideology, and politics. Research reflects and participates in relations of power. This is especially the case with qualitative inquiry, since — as the authors so clearly recognize — it is inherently interpretive. (Roman and Apple, 1990; Carspecken and Apple, 1992). The authors go further than this, however. They propose a role for such research in allowing all of us to step back and examine our own preconceptions and stereotypes and ultimately to heal some of the worst wounds inflicted by the relations of domination and subordination of the larger society. Such healing will not be sufficient by itself to challenge these unequal relations, but it can clearly be one element in dealing with them and in building the coalitions that are necessary in such a challenge.

Of course, what is portrayed here is but one instance of an attempt by a community — acting in its political, economic, and cultural institutions — to protect its youth and culture. One example does not make a movement. Yet, such instances are becoming increasingly more common. In many of our cities and rural areas, ordinary people are discovering that they are not powerless, that change from below is indeed possible. Taken together, these examples stand as eloquent witness to the fact that the vast river of popular democracy still flows in this nation, even in the face of rightist attacks. Raymond Williams, in his book by the same name, calls this process 'the long revolution' (Williams, 1961), the long struggle to transform dominant institutions so that they enhance the possibilities of a more democratic culture, economy and polity (Apple, 1985; 1990). I can think of no better way to interpret what education should be about.

Michael W. Apple
John Bascom Professor
University of Wisconsin, Madison

Note

1 I have placed the word 'minority' in inverted commas for a specific reason. White people are a minority of the world's population, and it would have a salutary effect on social and cultural policy if that was taken much more seriously.

References

APPLE, M.W. (1985) *Education and Power*, New York, NY: Routledge.

APPLE, M.W. (1988a) 'Redefining equality', *Teachers College Record*, **90**, pp. 167–84.

APPLE, M.W. (1988b) *Teachers and Texts*, New York, NY: Routledge.

APPLE, M.W. (1990) *Ideology and Curriulum* (2nd edition), New York, NY: Routledge.

APPLE, M.W. and CHRISTIAN-SMITH, L. (Eds) (1991) *The Politics of the Textbook*, New York, NY: Routledge.

BERNSTEIN, B. (1977) *Class, Codes and Control*, Vol. 3, *Towards a Theory of Educational Transmissions*, London, UK: Routledge & Kegan Paul.

CARSPECKEN, P. and APPLE, M.W. (1992) 'Critical qualitative research', in LE COMPTE, M. *et al.* (Eds), *Handbook of Qualitative Research in Education*, New York, NY: Academic Press.

OMI, M. and WINANT, H. (1986) *Racial Formation in the United States*, New York, NY: Routledge.

ROMAN, L. and APPLE, M.W. (1990) 'Is naturalism a step beyond positivism?' in EISNER, E. and PESHKIN, A. (Eds), *Qualitative Inquiry in Education*, New York, NY: Teachers College Press.

WILLIAMS, R. (1961) *The Long Revolution*, London, UK: Chatto and Windus.

Preface

The research necessary to produce this volume took over two years; we conducted it from the Fall of 1989 to the Winter of 1991, and it was planned and executed with the support from the Division of Education at the University of California, Davis. The researchers, Cirenio Rodriguez, José Cintrón, Yali Zou and Henry Trueba, developed a strong and cohesive team that worked together from the development of the design to its final form as presented in this volume. Frequent team meetings permitted the authors to share information, discuss recent events in Woodland and theoretical issues of common interest, and to provide a clear distribution of labor.

The head of the research project was at the time Director of the Division of Education and Associate Dean for Letters and Science at the University of California, Davis. Trueba was born in Mexico City, obtained an MA in Theology (Woodstock Jesuit College), an MA in Anthropology (Stanford University) and a PhD in Anthropology (University of Pittsburgh). Trueba lived in Mexico until 1962 when he moved permanently to the United States of America. His work has focused on the social and cultural context of education and the role of culture and language in learning; he was the editor of the *Anthropology and Education Quarterly*. He lived briefly in Woodland. In the development of this project, Trueba created opportunities for cooperative work and joint development of research activities, and of the central theoretical thrust evident in the data analysis. Trueba was responsible for writing this preface, introduction and chapters 1, 2, 7, 8, and 9, as well as for revising the entire manuscript. He is currently the Dean of the School of Education at the University of Wisconsin-Madison. Spanish is his mother tongue.

Cirenio Rodriguez is Professor of Education at Sacramento State University. His teaching and research has centered around the politics of education. He is a Chicano who has managed to maintain his home language and culture, and has accomplished important political victories. He obtained his PhD at the University of California, Santa Barbara, where he helped developed La Casa de la Raza (a center for education, legal aid and cultural development sponsored by the Chicano community of Santa Barbara). He served as chair of the Educational Administration Department at Sacramento State University, and was recently elected as a member of the Board of Education in Woodland. Dr Rodriguez was born in California to Mexican parents who worked all their lives as agricultural laborers in the fields of the Southwestern states. Dr Rodriguez was raised in an Spanish-speaking environment and is perfectly fluent in both Spanish and English. He and his family have lived in Woodland for the last eight years. In that community, Dr Rodriguez is seen as an intellectual leader. He has organized a historical society for Hispanics in order to recapture and document the history of Woodland from the perspective of the Mexican and Chicano families. He was responsible for writing chapters 4 and 5, for opening contacts and offering his colleagues feedback and recommendations.

José Cintrón is also Professor of Education at Sacramento State University. He has conducted research in schools and studied bilingual programs and teacher education. He was born and raised in Puerto Rico, transferred to Indiana and to California. He received his PhD in Education at the University of California, Santa Barbara. Cintrón is director of one of the teacher education centers at Sacramento State University; part of his obligations is to prepare, place and visit student teachers. One of the communities in which he has been placing student teachers is Woodland, especially in the Beamer Park Elementary School which is discussed in this book. His parents, both Puerto Ricans, are living in Indiana. The personal accounts and rich data offered in Chapter 6 are important contributions that demonstrate his talents as an ethnographer and his close relationships with the teachers and the principal of Beamer. José is extremely articulate in both English and Spanish, and he is truly bicultural and biliterate.

Yali Zou, the fourth member of the research team was born in Chan Chun City, mainland China and is currently a doctoral student of Education and a lecturer in the Chinese Department at the University of California, Davis. She is an expert in Chinese philosophy and politics, and she has also worked as editorial assistant for the *Anthropology and Education Quarterly*. She spent several years in Shang Hai, working for her government. She received two MAs, one in Metallurgy from Jilin University in China, and the other in Education from the University of California, Davis. Her contribution to the Woodland research project was substantive in the identification and summary of important historical documents dating from the early 1800s, as well as in the writing of Chapter 3. The discussion of the theoretical arguments relative to the political processes in Woodland was clearly enhanced by the contributions of Yali Zou, who presented a cross-cultural perspective and understanding of common events. Furthermore, Yali Zou facilitated the work of the other members of the team with her solicitous assistance in finding references, bringing books, arranging meetings, and providing many other kind services beyond the call of duty. While Yali Zou is more fluent in her mother tongue, Mandarin, and English, Albanian, French and Russian than in Spanish, her comprehension of the Spanish language was sufficient to grasp the key issues during her fieldwork.

In contrast with other books written by mainstream researchers on topics of migration, ethnic conflict, empowerment and healing, the authors know first hand many of the things they write about. What they observed, they had felt in their own flesh during the years of adaptation to American society. Efforts in maintaining the home language and culture, and in acquiring a second language and culture, and feelings of alienation and discrimination, are familiar to these authors. Our research team, in contrast with other researchers, was not looking for failure and incompetence. We started with issues such as: How do we explain the academic success of many Mexican and Chicano children? In contrast with other towns in California, how do we explain the involvement of their families in the Woodland political life and economic life? What is the role of Chicano parents in their children's education? How do we explain the cooperation between Mexican and Chicano families? As the project developed we realized that the lives of Mexican families had not been easy in the past, and that present success had its roots in long-term planning strategies and hard labor.

We struggled with the selection of data, and held debates on whether to use fictitious names for the city and all the people involved. After examining our data very carefully, we decided that it did not make much sense trying to hide the name of Woodland. We just could not make sense of the data if we did not refer to geographic places, proper names of towns, historical persons, etc. But we decided to use fictitious names in Chapter 6 for the teachers, because many of these teachers are still working in the school. There is nothing that is not public. Our sources are mostly newspaper articles and personal observations. We were interested in explaining success where failure was expected on the part of the mainstream population; success of immigrant children, their families and their teachers. The discussion of the politics of success and of the success of politics required careful reading and writing in order to avoid unnecessary disclosures of delicate matters in the life of the people of Woodland. Ultimately, the emphasis was in identifying the steps in the political socialization of Chicanos and other newcomers to Woodland. Obviously, the authors are seriously committed to democracy and to the implementation of equity principles. But we see ourselves as serious scholars, not politicians. Our message is positive. We celebrate the success of Raza, our brothers and sisters who managed to understand and use the democratic system in order to gain access to the American dream, a dream of full participation in the social, political and economic life of Woodland. We particularly celebrate the success of our Hispanic teachers who, retaining their strong commitment to their ethnic identity and their pride in being Hispanic, managed to become empowered as instructors, role models, supporters of the ethnic community, intellectuals, entrepreneurs and Americans committed to the multicultural character of our society.

As it happens in other small cities in California, and most likely in many other cities of the United States, the 'ethnic threat' and the organization of racially motivated groups has intimidated and discouraged many ethnic minority persons. It took a great deal of courage, tact, and faith in the American spirit, but in the end both the mainstream and the ethnic communities won respect for each other, harmony and cooperation. America's leaders for the twenty-first century are already born and many of their faces are not white. We know that by the year 2020 at least 40 per cent of the nation's student population will be children of color, and that today 30 per cent of the total student population is composed of children of color. We also know that today in twenty-five of the fifty largest school districts of America the majority are children of color (Banks, 1991; and Zeichner, 1992). This existing diversity in the public schools is compounded by the increasing segregation, isolation and underachievement of students of color, and by the unwillingness of higher education institutions to diversify their own faculties and student bodies. According to recent studies, 65 per cent of the teacher education faculty are male, and 35 per cent female; 2.9 per cent of the full professors, 6.4 of associate professors, and 9.9 per cent of assistant professors are members of minority groups (Zeichner, 1992:9; Ducharme and Agne (1989:75). From the approximately 45,000 education faculty in the country, less than 5 per cent have taught for one year or more in large urban school districts (Haberman, 1989; Zeichner, 1992:10).

The problems facing the education of future Americans have to do with poverty, alienation, inadequate teacher preparation at the university, interethnic conflict, and the disempowerment of teachers working with minority children (Trueba, 1991).

Michael Apple, discussing the task faced by educational researchers suggests that their audience is not composed only by theoreticians, and that writing for such an audience and using arcane discourse isolates other important audiences — people whose work needs support and attention:

> In a field that has historically shunted theoretical work to the sidelines (sometimes for very good reasons, since educational theory has usually involved male academics theorizing about what is largely women's labor — i.e., teaching), the nearly mystical quality of some critical work, its tendency *not* to take sufficient time to clarify its basic concepts or to write clearly, cannot help but limit is impact (Apple, 1989:200).

Apple urges university faculty involved in teacher education to practice in their own teaching the principles of pedagogy they discuss in class:

> If our job is pedagogic (as I think it is), if our role is to help teach our colleagues at universities and elementary and secondary schools (and enable them to teach us) what kind of society it is that we live in and how schooling now reproduces *and* contradicts the relations of inequality that now exist (for there are some very good things going on now as well that need to be defended), then such pedagogic work needs to be held accountable to particular norms. The 'student' or reader isn't the only one who should be required to do all the work (Apple, 1989:200–201).

This book intends to assist the readers in understanding the significance of the politics of education for ethnic minorities; it illustrates a small success, but perhaps one that can be replicated elsewhere, the success of teachers who found their strength in the community, in the support of parents, and in the support of the principal. The ultimate beneficiaries are the children, all children, and the country whose entire welfare depends on them. Yes, the children of tomorrow are not all white, and we need them all. The future of American society is in their hands.

In conclusion, *Healing Multicultural America: Mexican Immigrants Rise to Power in Rural California*, is a historical and anthropological account of how the low-income Mexicans, who have come to Woodland, California since the turn of the century, have managed to use their Mexican heritage through their language and culture to develop powerful economic and political organizations that pave their way to first class citizenship. Their taking political and economic power, and thus becoming role models of oncoming generations of castelike immigrants is not a trivial accomplishment, but it is certainly one that gives hope to millions of recent comers in the country. The following pages attempt to explain how these immigrants accomplished their goals, and what their contribution is to American society. Their main efforts were directed to reform schools in such a way that their children would not become disenfranchised and isolated. They accomplished that and much more. Indeed, they have shown to mainstream Americans how important is to retain a sense of pride in their cultural heritage, and how ethnic pride can help integrate home culture values and a strong commitment to demo-cratic principles.

This ethnic pride and integration of cultural values is precisely the nuts and bolts, the guts of what is called cultural therapy, that is, the psychological process of healing and strengthening our self-concept. The book focuses on the most serious problems in American, European, former Soviet Union ethnic national-ities, and the highly diversified Asian groups all over the world: interethnic con-flict, cultural conflict, poverty, alienation, violence, and self-rejection. The solution of many of these problems in modern societies is to help people understand what it takes to live in a multicultural democratic society, one in which we must in-tegrate our own ethnic values with those of the mainstream society for the common good. The last chapter of the book illustrates some of the exercises of cultural therapy and applies theoretical knowledge to the practice of healing multicultural America.

Henry T. Trueba
Madison, Wisconsin.

References

APPLE, M. (1989) *Teachers and Texts: A Political Economy of Class and Gender Relations in Education*, New York, NY: Routledge. (First published in 1986).

BANKS, J. (1991) 'Teaching multicultural literacy to teachers', *Teaching Education,* **4**(1) pp. 135–44.

DUCHARME, E. and AGNE, R. (1989) 'Professors of education: Uneasy residents of academe', WISNIEWSKI, R. and DUCHORNE, E. (Eds) *The Professors of Teaching*, Albany, NY: State University of New York Press, pp. 67–86.

HABERMAN, M. (1989) 'More minority teachers', *Kappan*, **70**(10) pp. 771–6.

HABERMAN, M. (1991) 'Can culture awareness be taught in teacher education pro-grams?', *Teaching Education*, **4**(1) pp. 25–31.

TRUEBA, H.T. (1991) 'Learning needs of minority children: Contributions of ethnography to educational research', in MALAVE, L.M. and DUQUETTE, G. (Eds), *Language, Culture and Cognition*, Philadelphia, PA: Multilingual Matters Ltd., pp. 137–58.

ZEICHNER, K. (1992) *Educating Teachers for Cultural Diversity*, National Center for Research on Teacher and Learning, Michigan State University, East Lansing, Michigan.

Introduction

Education? Schooling? What is the nature of these processes, and why are they important for society? Many of us have seen the groups of terrified illegal aliens crossing our Southern borders, running away from the Border Patrol, attempting to escape by zigzagging through dangerous highways in search of safety, with the desperate hope of finding a job and sending money home. We have also seen the hopelessness of young parents dragging their children to the ranks of the homeless, waiting in line for food from a charity, searching for tin cans and usable items to sell, arguing with each other over a small warm spot to protect themselves from the cold at night. Michael Apple commenting on the public attack against democratic principles and on the neglect of the people who suffer, observes:

> So goes America. But the 'conservative restoration' is not only an American phenomenon. In Britain, too, there is an ongoing attempt to a thoroughgoing dismantling of the gains for which the majority of people have struggled for decades. Most educators respond to these conditions in a particular way. They ignore them. The world of capital flight, unemployment, the degradation of labor, disintegrating cities and communities — all of this is not about education, after all. A world in which racism is again on the rise, in which we are attempting to push women both ideologically and economically back into the unpaid labor of the home, in which we warehouse our elderly — these too have little to do with schooling. After all, education is a psychological process, one that is wholly captured by the discourse of learning (Apple, 1989:4–5).

The cycle of despair and failure that Apple describes is, in his view, intimately connected with educational experience, research and philosophy. The role of knowledge and education, and thus the significant role of universities in protecting democratic principles and institutions is most significant:

> We need to remember that there are *educational and cultural preconditions* for a large-scale, or even small-scale, movements and challenges to the conservative restoration. Unless we 'school' ourselves about the unequal realities of this society, how can we make it possible for the students,

teachers, and other with whom we work to have the resources for re-cognizing and acting on these realities as well? (Apple, 1989:179).

Many nations in the world, following the example of the United States, have recently abandoned philosophies and forms of government that for many years had infringed upon people's freedom of speech and movement, upon their rights to privacy, fair competition, search for intellectual excellence and commitment to participate fully in the social and political process associated with the acquisition of goods, prestige and power. This recent tendency to democratize social institutions and governments has recently transformed the Soviet Union into a Common-wealth, has provided the legitimacy for collective intervention of Western countries in Iraq, and has motivated the organization of European and American common markets. The American democratic experiment has succeeded in the United States, and will continue to succeed for as long as there are new believers committed to enjoy their new democratic rights and to face the challenges of cultural adaptation to a new country. Immigrants who come to America with the intent of realizing the American dream often seek low-paying and unwanted jobs citizens do not care for at all. Immigrants who come to large cities are often lost in the crowd and, whether they fail or succeed, they become part of the invisible group of assimilated aliens. One of the areas in which we can document success is in rural small cities. Success, as measured by full participation of immigrant families in politics and in the social and economic life of a city, is the central topic of this book.

It is not often that we can study in detail the dynamics of democratic pro-cesses as they occur in America's small cities. This book will show how several generations of immigrants from Mexico became an integral part of the city of Woodland. It is a story of empowerment of minority groups who immigrated from Mexico and other countries to the rural area of Northern California, going from humble beginnings as underclass agricultural workers to their conspicuous success as politicians, teachers, and members of Education Boards, political committees and other social and religious institutions in Woodland. Eventually, through hard labor and persistant demand for their rights, Mexican Americans learned how to function in American Society, and how to use their political power to pursue the American dream of freedom and economic prosperity.

The presence of what we call minority groups today in Yolo County antedated that of Europeans by many centuries; aborigines of various North American tribes have always lived in Yolo County. Indeed the cultural, linguistic and physical similarities between aborigines in North America and those in Mexico and Central America are remarkable. Frequently, migrant workers from Mexico coming to the United States find support and cultural sensitivity among American Indians. Indian aborigines and Mexican American groups have always made their presence felt in Yolo County, and have left a legacy of hard work and judicious use of natural resources. As in most other regions of America, in Yolo County, the outsiders — the immigrants Europeans — did not discover America, but invaded it and took it by force from the natives. In the course of the last hundred and fifty years the flow of Asian, Hispanic and other immigrant groups created the strong agricul-tural economy of Yolo County, and in particular of Woodland, the county seat.

If we knew in the 1850s, or even in the 1920s, what we know now about the minority populations, their role in rural America, and the formidable changes facing our country, we would have treated them differently, and much of the ethnic conflict, economic distress and prejudice would have not existed. But we were so sure about our judgements and about our psychological instruments. Rewriting history is a unique exercise because it shows not only the myopia and bigotry of social policies and educational practices, but their consequences for a society that has become ethnically pluralistic in ways that are distinct from any other country in the world.

The ethnohistorical account of Woodland gives the reader an opportunity to pursue socioeconomic developments in a rural town, and the impact of minorities on the life of the town. Schools, starting as a mirror of society tend to perpetuate the social order, up to a point. The arrival of several sophisticated minority professionals whose parents have humble origins influenced the educational reform process. Inherent in the ethnic pluralism of school and society is the opportunity for empowerment and success. Empowerment occurs when minorities finally gain power and are recognized as belonging in town. This book is an attempt to document the history of Woodland from the perspective of ethnic minorities, in order to understand the role that these minorities will have in the future of Yolo County and of American society during the next century. American society, with a fundamentally multiethnic and pluralistic democracy, can develop new social and political structures for a peaceful co-existence of diverse peoples, and thus serve as a model to other societies in Europe, Africa, the Pacific Islands, Asia and Latin America.

The Valley in which Woodland is located was the theater of peaceful and not-so-peaceful invasions, first by the Spaniards and Mexicans from the late sixteenth century until the takeover of the Mexican territory of California by the United States in 1848, by virtue of the Guadalupe Hidalgo Treaty. The accounts of the local Indians and their life style, the transition of large haciendas from the hands of the original Mexican and Spanish owners to those of Anglo Americans, the organization of the agricultural industries in the fertile Valley of Sacramento, Yolo and Solano Counties leading to more formal and sophisticated governmental structures, all provide the reader with the historical context necessary to understand minorities in Woodland.

Perhaps the most radical social changes occurred in Woodland from the splendor of the 1920s, through the depression years, until the post-World War II period lasting until the early 1950s. This is the period in which the agricultural basis for Woodland economy was strengthened and the role of minorities redefined. Minority families who lived outside of mainstream society and whose children were not well treated in the public schools, were finally accepted as full participants of the town life.

Equally surprising have been the last two decades, which have marked the rapid mobility of Mexicans to political power through their participation in the School Board, and various political, economic and social institutions. In its own way, Woodland mirrors the quiet but drastic changes in rural California, where minorities took advantage of schooling and have become sophisticated professionals (medical doctors, university professors, government officials, successful business people, etc.) who can play a decisive role in changing the policies and politics of small rural towns. Micro-analysis of sociocultural and political change is like a microcosms of the rest of America. What is happening in large cities, Chicago, New York, Dallas or Los Angeles, is so massive and complex, that the changes cannot easily be observed and analyzed. We study the demographic changes, observe the major political struggles and resulting appointments, follow the realignment of economic power and the share of minorities in the various businesses, but we cannot really have a grasp of the complex phenomena taking place in front of our eyes. An ethnohistorical and ethnographic study of a small rural town gives us the unique opportunity to track down government officials, business owners, educators and citizens who played a key role in the changes affecting current town life. This limited study is only the beginning of several studies in process. It is intended to provide a general theoretical, historical and ethnographic base to pave the way for future studies of Woodland and other similar places. This study is but one example that invites reflection on the central issues of this book: the unique nature of America's ethnic pluralism which seems to contrast with the coexistence of many ethnic groups in other industrial Western societies and Asian societies.

Ethnohistorical and ethnographic methods are presented as methodological tools, which are not only compatible but complementary, in order to follow the historical and current paths of adjustment and acculturation of immigrant, refugee and other minorities in the Woodland area. This study argues that the use of both ethnohistory and ethnography can create a strong methodological combination for the empowerment of educators working with culturally diverse student populations. If educators understand better the history of minority communities from the perspective of these communities, and if they understand also the current sociocultural environment of these communities (their values, traditions and goals), they will truly become empowered to work effectively with these communities. Furthermore, this study presents a view of America as a land of immigrants, in a review of current studies in anthropology and sociology of minorities in this country, their academic achievement, their role, and their adaptation to mainstream societies. It is precisely in this context that the ethnohistory of Woodland makes sense. Ethnohistory is the history of Woodland from the perspective of minority or ethnic populations. In this ethnohistory, it is important to view the reality of Woodland in its economic, historical and educational development, as clearly linked to minority populations. Recent Asian and Hispanic immigrants buy into the American ideals of mass education, political participation and economic opportunity equally accessible to all, because they feel they can belong in the United States. Hispanic and Asian populations feel this relationship particularly for the Southwest, because both populations are historically linked to its growth and development. The question is whether or not these populations can learn how to participate in the democratic process of an America whose very foundations are linked to the recognition of the important historical role played by ethnolinguistic minority peoples (Spindler, 1977; Spindler and Spindler, 1983, 1987a, 1987b).

Given the trauma associated with involuntary migrations (at least not voluntary for all the members of the family, especially children), the adjustment of members of immigrant and refugee families depends much on their ability to recognize their own worth and potential contributions to American society. The conflicts associated with drastic linguistic, social and cultural changes take the form of new beliefs, codes of behavior, communication patterns, and demands to conform with life-style and etiquette that seems to be incompatible with the home life-style. The result of these conflicts is stress from within the newcomer and pressure from without, and often prejudice or intolerance for diversity and racism. It is precisely in this context that schools have special significance; school becomes the institution responsible for transmitting and inculcating American cultural values that keep our society together (Trueba, 1983, 1987a, 1987b, 1988, 1989, 1991). Educators are not only the key persons responsible for transmitting objective academic knowledge to all students, they must also interpret for, and explain to, students the norms of expected behavior, historical accounts, curriculum and the national symbols that provide Americans with a common background for joint efforts in politics, economics, religion, international affairs, etc. At the same time, educators must help culturally diverse students pursue their genuine ethnohistories (or their version of history from their ethnic, cultural and social perspectives) that allows them to appreciate their role in, and contributions to, American society. Educators are the role models for American democracy, and as such they are in charge of helping all children internalize cultural knowledge and values that are pivotal to the existence of democratic institutions. Furthermore, because America is an industrialized technological society, refugee, immigrant, and all newcomers need a high level of literacy in English to succeed and to become active participants in the democratic process. The acquisition of the English language is as important for them as is the retention of their home language, without which their ethnic community and the cultural support system would crumble. Equally important is the maintenance of self respect and pride in one's own ethnic identity. There is no contradiction between their need to maintain their ethnic identity and their need to have a sense of belonging to America, of playing an important role in American society. Indeed, they see America as a unique country in which people can enjoy their right to their language, culture and religion without losing their right to participate fully in the social, economic and political institutions along with many other diverse groups. Furthermore, even the acquisition of English is contingent upon their feeling of belonging in this country. The questions are, therefore: How can one expedite the smooth adjustment to American values and the acquisition of English? What instructional and language policies, what educational philosophy and classroom organization can maximize the learning of English by newcomers?

These questions that have been addressed by recent researchers (Trueba, 1987a, 1987b; Goldman and Trueba, 1987; Trueba and Delgado-Gaitan, 1988; Trueba, 1988, 1989; and by many others) are revisited in this book. The success of Mexican Americans in Woodland is viewed as a proof that the maintenance of the home language and culture produces strong Americans committed to a common good, the education for ALL. By implication, the study intends to show that knowing the role of minorities in American history is an important step in the adaptation of minorities and their achievement in schools.

The first two chapters (written by Trueba) discuss the concepts of culture, cultural transmission, ethnicity and pluralism from a comparative perspective, and in a global context. Intolerance for cultural and linguistic diversity, racial biases and bigotry are part of Western colonial history for the last four centuries. Central concepts to the discussion of diversity, such as race, language, culture, biculturalism, and social class are pursued in these first chapters. The discussion examines historical patterns of the ethnocentrism embedded in the transmission of a culture, and of social structures that result in the abuses of one group over another. The adoption of slavery, the concepts of cultural inequality, the social and economic infrastructure of European societies which were transplanted to the colonies in other countries, the complex accommodation of cast structures in response to economic and social changes in the colonies and other phenomena lead to a better understanding of the differences between American ethnic pluralism, and the pluralism in other parts of the world. Previous sociological and anthropological theories had emphasized the 'castification' process that resulted in disempowering minority groups. The authors have described the conditions under which empowerment was possible. This book deals with the success of groups of individuals who were clearly politically and economically disempowered, excluded from participation in social institutions, and who gradually developed the knowledge and skills to become active participants and leaders in democratic institutions.

Chapter 3 (written by Zou) provides a brief ethnohistory of Woodland from mid-nineteenth century to early twentieth century; it describes the arrival of early European immigrants and the transition from a Mexican territory to a new American state. It offers a rich description of some of the institutions that later became crucial for the success of minorities and their participation in the life of the town, such as businesses, churches and schools. The overall picture of the town and the linkage between historical and ethnographic data carry the reader from the early encounters between Indians in the Putah Creek with European explorers, to today's struggles within the social and political organization of Woodland. From the early manifestations of racism, perhaps better understood as cultural ethnocentrism, transmitted by European and American settlers to recent dwellers of the Central Valley region, to the recognition of the essential role played by minorities in Woodland.

Chapters 4 and 5 (written by Rodriguez) provide a detailed documentation of the process of political socialization of Chicanos. Over several decades of persistent efforts, Chicanos have learned some lessons in politics; they acquired the knowledge and skills necessary to participate in public politics, and they took power in conspicuous positions, especially those related directly to the influence of the school district policy-making system. These two chapters give us a detailed account of numerous political battles related to equity, fair play, appropriate access to information and resources, and finally, to the victory of selected candidates whose constituency was formed by ethnic minority groups. The most important question, in a long-term perspective, is the formation and intervention of political leaders from immigrant groups and the optimal conditions for these leaders to impact ethnic communities in small rural cities. Another set of questions deals with the general theoretical approaches attempting to explain the social, economic and political changes of ethnic minority groups. The ongoing debate in anthropology, sociology, and other social sciences has focused on the role of cultural characteristics in the response of ethnic groups to social abuse (racism, inequity, neglect, and the like). Cultural ecologists adopt theoretical perspectives that attempt to explain the acceptance of 'castelike' by some groups as a response based on cultural values, perhaps on a previous history of abuse that has resulted in values and self-identities conceived in opposition to values and cultural characteristics of the members of mainstream culture (viewed as abusers). In this view, the failure of certain ethnic groups is interpreted as the acceptance of one's own inferiority and low performance as a means to resist acculturation to the life-style of the white oppressors.

Chapter 6 (written by Cintrón) is a description of a school, the Beamer Elementary School, which has become the prototype school supported by political leaders (both minority and non-minority) who advocate the use of home languages and cultures as a means to pursue vigorously the acquisition of the English language. In other words, the philosophy of the school personnel exemplifies the positive role that home languages can play in the development of high achievers who come from ethnic minority groups. This school also illustrates the role of ethnic communities in the pursuit of school academic achievement.

Finally, Chapter 7 (written by Trueba) capitalizes on previous work (Trueba 1992), recognizes the theoretical implications of the Woodland success story and concludes with a strong statement on the need to heal America, to pursue efforts to rescue from public neglect ethnic minority children, and to invest in their intellectual development without forcing them to throw away their personal identities. This chapter examines theoretical issues related to the process of cultural therapy and the adaptation strategies to cope with cultural conflict. The linking of cultural therapy to the empowerment process is based both on the work by the Spindlers and their theory that cultural conflict is partially based on our inability to reconcile our 'enduring self' and to adopt a new 'situated self'. This problem is analyzed as a conflict of cultural values and the need to maintain some cultural continuity within our 'internal self'.

Chapter 8 (written by Trueba) presents three typical scenarios for cultural therapy exercises in the school, community and work settings. This chapter also discusses the methodological strengths and requirements of ethnographic research methods for applied research to the practice of cultural therapy. In brief, we believe that if we better understand small rural cities in their process of democratization, then we can hope to understand better the future of multicultural America. Chapter 9 (written by Trueba) is complementary to the previous chapter. It provides an annotated bibliography on references that can be used to train ethnographers involved in cultural therapy. The comments on the references attempt to link clusters of references that have common theoretical or methodological affinity.

The challenges and opportunities in the last one hundred and fifty years in Woodland can teach us a great deal about ourselves and our democratic institutions. Teacher education reform, the development of adequate services for immigrant and refugee families, the organization of university programs and the very understanding of America's democratic principles can be seen in the microcosms of small rural cities in America.

In the most recent research on the education of teachers who are expected to work among culturally, linguistically and socially diverse student populations, the primary concern of scholars is to explain the reality of diversity in America and the impact of social class, race and economic status on the quality of education received and on the ultimate academic success of students (Zeichner, 1992). It is not only that the social and intellectual climate of teacher-preparation environments disadvantages teachers who work with low-income and racially, linguistically and culturally diverse students. The heart of the problem is that racial, class and ethnic biases are perpetuated through the process of schooling future teachers. There is a strong feeling that in order to prepare future teachers of diversified schools, educators will have to teach future teachers to experience diversity and to acquire knowledge about school children. This is not enough; future teachers will have to learn how to translate this knowledge into pedagogical instruments for effective instruction. Instruction will have to be such that teachers engage ALL students in a two-way communicative learning mode ('reciprocal interaction',

Zeichner, 1992). This mode will result in a joint, cooperative and enthusiastic construction of new knowledge. That is, teachers will learn to inspire and motivate their pupils. It will not be enough to provide future teachers with solid and well-organized subject matter knowledge, or with teaching techniques. Knowledge and techniques must be selected and adapted to context-specific instructional settings in which pupils build new knowledge, with the assistance of the teacher, upon the previous knowledge and experience they bring to class. Furthermore, in order for teachers to become effective in teaching students from diverse ethnic, social and cultural groups, they have to have a strong sense of their own ethnic identity and pride of having such identity. They also must respect the ethnic identity of their pupils, and must use the cultural repertoire of pupils to create high expectations of achievement. Indeed, as Zeichner, based on the work of Cummins (1978, 1986, 1989) has articulated recently (Zeichner, 1992), the teacher must be committed to the academic achievement of ALL pupils and must be able to create cooperative and meaningful instructional activities that teach pupils how to learn and how to function in school, without rejecting their linguistic, cultural and ethnic values.

This book is an illustration of a successful school district that blossomed under the leadership of community leaders (both minority and non-minority), who became strong advocates for minority children's academic achievement. In a very real sense, the teachers described in the book, and the political leaders who supported the school district, are instances of a continued 'struggle for democracy in our educational institutions — for a democratic culture, labor process, and governance' (Apple, 1989:197). The following pages describe how many Hispanics, having experienced the status of underclass were caste-like, and found in their own culture the resources to liberate themselves and participate in the benefits of American society. One of the popular songs one hears in migrant camps and neighborhoods with concentrations of Mexican illegal aliens summarizes the feelings of those struggling to find freedom:

> Here I am established in the United States. It's been ten years since I crossed as a wetback. I never applied for papers, I'm still illegal. What good is money if I am [must live] like a prisoner in this great nation? When I think about it, I cry. Even if the cage is made of gold, it doesn't make it less a prison (Chavez, 1992:158).

These pages describe the long journey to liberation that Chicanos have walked since they crossed the Mexican border; they worked long hours, suffering without complaint poor working conditions, low pay, abuse and segregation. They were proud of being Mexicans and knew that their language and culture, their traditions and values were worth keeping and maintaining. They wanted to become full citizens of Woodland, California, and they accomplished that and more. Many of them have become distinguished citizens of Woodland.

References

APPLE, M. (1989) *Teachers and Texts: A Political Economy of Class and Gender Relations in Education*, New York, NY: Routledge.
CHAVEZ, L.R. (1992) *Shadowed Lives: Undocumented Immigrants in American Society*. In SPINDLER G. and SPINDLER, L. *Case Studies in Cultural Anthropology*, (Eds) New York, NY: Harcourt Brace Jovanovich College Publishers.

CUMMINS, J. (1978) 'Bilingualism and the development of metalinguistic awareness', *Journal of Cross-cultural Psychology*, **9**, 2, pp. 131–49.

CUMMINS, J. (1986) 'Empowering minority students: A framework for intervention', *Harvard Educational Review*, **56**, 1, pp. 18–35.

CUMMINS, J. (1989) *The Empowerment of Minority Students*, Los Angeles, CA: California Association for Bilingual Education.

GOLDMAN, S. and TRUEBA, H. (Eds) (1987) *Becoming Literate in English as a Second Language*, Norwood, NJ: Ablex Publishing.

SPINDLER, G. (1977) 'Change and continuity in American core cultural values: An anthropological perspective', in DERENZO, G.D. (Ed.) *We the People: American Character and Social Change*, Westport, CT: Greenwood Press, pp. 20–40.

SPINDLER, G. and SPINDLER, L. (1983) 'Anthropologists view American culture', *Annual Review of Anthropology*, **12**, pp. 49–78.

SPINDLER, G. and SPINDLER, L., (Eds) (1987a) *The Interpretive Ethnography of Education: At Home and Abroad*, Hillsdale, NJ: Lawrence Erlbaum Assoc.

SPINDLER, G. and SPINDLER, L. (1987b) 'Cultural dialogue and schooling in Schoenhausen and Roseville: A comparative analysis', *Anthropology and Education Quarterly*, **18**(1), pp. 3–16.

TRUEBA, H.T. (1983) 'Adjustment problems of Mexican-American school children: An anthropological study', *Learning Disability Quarterly*, **4**(4), pp. 395–415.

TRUEBA, H.T. (Ed.) (1987a) *Success or Failure: Linguistic Minority Children at Home and in School*, New York, NY: Harper & Row.

TRUEBA, H.T. (1987b) 'Organizing classroom instruction in specific sociocultural contexts: Teaching Mexican youth to write in English', in GOLDMAN, S. and TRUEBA, H.T. (1987) *Becoming Literate in English as a Second Language*, Norwood, NJ: Ablex Corporation, pp. 235–52.

TRUEBA, H.T. (1988) 'Culturally-based explanations of minority students' academic achievement', *Anthropology and Education Quarterly* **19**(3), pp. 270–87.

TRUEBA, H.T. (1989) *Raising silent voices: Educating linguistic minorities for the 21st century*, NY: Harper & Row.

TRUEBA, H.T. (1991) 'Learning needs of minority children: Contributions of ethnography to educational research', in MALAVE, L.M. and DUQUETTE, G. (Eds), *Language, Culture and Cognition*, Philadelphia, PA: Multilingual Matters Ltd., pp. 137–58.

TRUEBA, H.T. (1992) 'Learning and cultural conflict: The role of educational anthropology in healing America', revised version of paper presented at the *Cultural Diversity Working Conference*, Center for Educational Research at Stanford. Stanford, California, October 4–6, 1991 (revised version submitted on January 1992).

TRUEBA, H.T. and DELGADO-GAITAN (Eds) (1988) *School and Society: Learning Content Through Culture*, New York, NY: Praeger Publishers.

ZEICHNER, K. (1992) *Educating Teachers for Cultural Diversity*, National Center for Research on Teacher and Learning. Michigan State University, East Lansing, Michigan.

Chapter 1

The Dynamics of Cultural Transmission

Henry T. Trueba

Cultural values, as transmitted from one generation to another, provide the energy and commitment necessary to act. Whatever we do collectively, we do because, in an effort to enhance a cultural value, we agree upon it. Apple (1990) has noted that liberal educational philosophies ignore fundamental structural issues that determine the overall outcome of schooling (failure of minorities, for example), while at the same time enforcing questionable assumptions about the role of education and the attributes of a liberal education. One of these assumptions is that 'education and the culture it both produces and transmits' are independent and autonomous features of society, and consequently that education is primarily intended to produce 'knowledge and knowledgeable individuals through the sponsoring of academic research and curriculum reform' (Apple, 1990:19). In the context of these questionable assumptions Apple observes:

> In contradistinction to this set of assumptions about education and its relation to a social order, the cultural and educational apparatus are interpreted as elements in a theory of *social control* by those individuals who are concerned with cultural and economic reproduction. Hence, challenges are made to at least three interrelated notions: that the selection processes are neutral; that 'ability' (rather than the socialization of students to socially and economically related norms and values) is what schools actually *do* focus on; and whether the schools *are* actually organized to teach technical curricular skills and information to all students so that each person has an equal chance at economic rewards (Apple, 1990:19).

Culture, as it is transmitted in schools, with the values and assumptions that guide action in everyday life, is one of the most controversial concepts in America. The reason is not only that the concept itself is elusive and difficult, but that the acceptance of a particular concept of culture has implications for the acceptance of American culture, and our own cultural identity as individuals. For several decades the concepts of culture and cultural transmission have been known, and the essential of culture identified: socially shared norms, codes of behavior, values, assumptions, etiquette, and world view. Culture, according to some anthropologists, 'is made up of the concepts, beliefs, and principles of action and organization' (Goodenough, 1976:5). Understanding one's own culture is hard enough, but other peoples' culture is a real challenge. According to anthropologists the test of such understanding is being able to function effectively in other peoples' cultures. Paradoxically, however, it is only in our attempts to understand the culture of others that we come to understand our own culture. Hence, cross-cultural comparisons háve been valued as powerful and insightful methodological instruments in anthropology. Being in another culture and observing unfamiliar behaviors forces us to analyze our own motives and meanings as we act. The problem is not so much 'to state what someone did but to specify the conditions under which it is culturally appropriate to anticipate that he, or persons occupying his role, will render an equivalent performance' (Frake, 1964:112). Knowing another culture is being able to anticipate peoples' observed behaviors; this requires cultural knowledge and an understanding of their cultural values. Yet, the understanding of ongoing cultural changes, processes of adaptation in cultural contact, and adaptive strategies (see Trueba, Cheng and Ima, 1993), requires a better understanding of the process of cultural transmission. Making inferences in order to interpret behavior in another culture is one level of understanding; being able to identify appropriate behavior and to anticipate change requires a deeper knowledge of a culture. Obviously, there are differences among the many cultures of the world; not all are equally complex in terms of their technology, social structure and economy; consequently culture change varies from one culture to another. But some of the cultures, such as the American culture, are particularly complex because they tolerate a great deal of variance and a wide range of adaptive strategies on the part of newcomers.

American society is not easy for newcomers to understand. We have incorporated culturally different populations from all around the world, and people belonging to different social strata. Becoming American can mean many things, and it can occur either in a relatively short time or can take generations. To refugees seeking freedom and economic opportunities, as much as to illegal aliens crossing at great personal risk a busy California highway in their attempts to escape the border patrol, the desire to become American is frequently interpreted as the realization of a 'good education' for their children, and a secure economic future for the entire family. It is an escape from the psychological prison of terrorism and poverty. Unfortunately, the very dreams that bring immigrants and refugees to America are shattered in the first years of their children's experience in schools. Much of the effort to reform schools is focused on the need to meet the learning needs of culturally and linguistically different children. As Apple indicates in his critical analysis of some theories advocated by the pragmatic traditions of American education:

> The pragmatic position tends to ignore the possibility that some theories must contradict the present reality and, in fact, must consistently work against it. These critical inquiries *stand in witness* of the negativity involved in all too many current institutional (economic, cultural, educational, political) arrangements and thus can illuminate the possibility of significant change. In this way, the act of criticism contributes to emancipation in that it shows the way linguistic or social institutions have been reified or thingified so that educators and the public at large have forgotten why they evolved, and that people made them and thus can change them (Apple, 1990:133. Emphasis in original).

At the same time that inquiry and disagreement are defended as requirements of democratic institutions and positive elements to maintain such institutions through needed changes in education, Apple insists that the intent of critiquing scholarship and educational institutions is twofold:

> First, it aims at illuminating the tendencies for unwarranted and often unconscious domination, alienation, and repression within certain existing cultural, political, educational, and economic institutions. Second, through exploring the negative effects and contradictions of much that unquestioningly goes on in these institutions, it seeks to 'promote conscious [individual and collective] emancipatory activity' (Apple, 1990:133).

Immigrants and their children search for the cultural values that permit them to function effectively in American democracy. The pace of cultural adaptation is determined by experiences and perceptions in pre-arrival times of immigrants, refugees and other newcomers. The nature of the cultural shock and conflict resulting from rapid social change is a function of newcomers' ability to understand American cultural values, and to reconcile with their own home values. In turn, immigrants and refugees are pressed to selectively retain those values and patterns they consider essential to their own self-identity and their capacity to cope with cultural conflict in the new country.

Newcomers will ask themselves many times: What is American culture? What is the essence of American democracy? How does democracy lead to freedom of religion, freedom of speech, and to economic success? Will future Americans continue to defend with passion democratic values and respect cultural differences? Culture contact and change are inevitable, and continues to affect all modern societies, especially American and European industrial societies who are attracting large numbers of immigrants and refugees. The conflict faces both newcomers and other Americans. The ideal of a multicultural America has some rough realities attached, such as the slow pace of certain groups to function in American society, and their inability to buy into the core values of working ethic and participation in the political process. Consequently, an important issue here is the need to socialize newcomers into the core values of American society, the need to establish the process of cultural transmission in such a way that it does not violate newcomers' basic rights to their language, culture and privacy. Multicultural America can only be successful if, in addition to the diverse cultural resources and traditions, we all can function as a society. Before the concept of cultural transmission is discussed, however, the notion of culture needs to be revisited.

George and Louise Spindler were among the first anthropologists to use and describe the process of cultural transmission as a dynamic transactional process through which culture is reinterpreted and recreated. This means that culture is not merely passed from one generation to another, with some changes and revisions. Culture is continuously reshaped and reinterpreted, precisely in the context of socializing others, especially the young, to the American way of life. The Spindlers' research resulted in descriptions of schools, academic competition, multiethnic settings, cultural conflict, and of relatively harmonious traditional middle-class instructional environments. What all these various settings had in common was the critical function of passing on cultural values unique to American society. The challenge confronted by the Spindlers in their attempt to map out the behavioral responses of immigrant, refugee and minority persons facing culture change led them to three tasks:

1 The redefinition of culture, cultural transmission, and cultural conflict as interlocking concepts;
2 The demystification of ethnographic (cross-cultural) research methods appropriately used to study culture, cultural conflict and cultural transmission;
3 The construction of a new theoretical model ('cultural therapy') to resolve cultural conflict.

Rediscovering Culture

The process of cultural transmission is readily observable as adult members of a society teach their young to carry on the daily duties necessary for meeting physical and spiritual needs of all members. Different societies have their own ways to carry on the teaching of the young to preserve their life styles and distribution of labor. American Indians were taught to hunt, fish and make pottery; they were also taught to respect nature and protect the environment. Much of their religion and ritual aims at inculcating respect for the natural environment. Many modern societies, who must face war and terrorism on a daily basis, teach their children hatred for the enemy, the use of weapons, and the value of destroying the enemy. Ethnic identity and survival of the ethnic group are inseparable.

Culture, therefore, can be conceived as a dynamic process that is reconstructed in the very activities whose purposes are to transmit survival skills and the rationale for using such skills. The parameters within which a society exists define the nature of the cultural values transmitted. These parameters are linked to macro-social elements, as well as to a number of micro-interactional factors surrounding survival activities. It is here that values generally shared by the entire society have different significance for different peoples, depending on the social context of their upbringing. Hunting, canoeing and physical endurance skills can be highly functional in a riverine culture of the Piraparana, in Matto Grosso, but not very functional in New York or Chicago. While there is a great deal of individual differentiation in ethnic groups (their notion of living in a family, of attending school, and cooperating in a community), there are also similar responses to the new culture (responses to a market economy, a democratic political system, demands for the use of English as a national language or as language of instruction), responses to demands for conformity in behavior, etc. These similar responses reflect a secondary socialization into a new common culture. It is precisely through this process of transmission of American culture (which for newcomers often occurs in schools) that American culture takes new life and becomes a powerful instrument for social cohesiveness. In this sense, American culture is not an abstract concept of new cognitive codes resulting from assimilation of school values through school activities. What we mean is that the acquisition of American culture by individuals from other cultures in not a cumbersome and somewhat amorphous sum total of the home cultural values and traditions plus those of school. It is the result of a selective process of acceptance of some values, rejection of others, integration of others, and a final commitment to adopt a particular life style.

Thus, what culture becomes, if understood as a dynamic force resulting from actual tangible transactions in given multicultural interactional contexts, is a powerful force that has led many different individuals to the pursuit of same values: values of freedom and competitive search for economic prosperity. Culture is revealed to us in what people do, and it is a concept helpful in understanding why people do whatever they do. Thus, there is an intimate relationship between action and culture, as well as between motivation to act and to hold cultural values (Spindler, G., 1959, 1977; Trueba, Spindler and Spindler, 1989). Much effort in our lives is invested in action, but action that is motivated by the need to pursue and protect certain values. When values change, action changes.

All societies have mechanisms to teach their youngsters how to live in a social group and enhance its survival through the transmission of knowledge accumulated over generations. The teaching of fishing, hunting and agricultural techniques is essential to some pre-literate societies; for modern technological and industrial societies, the teaching of literacy and critical thinking skills is essential to survive. What holds societies together is their members' ability to acquire and transmit knowledge. Without the transmission of the knowledge gained in previous centuries in industrial societies, our cities would be paralyzed and our health would decay rapidly. Hence the importance of education and schooling. Education is a transactional (interactive) process that aims at transferring, sharing from one generation to the next the cultural capital (knowledge, traditions and values) stored and enlarged by the efforts of our ancestors. Education is indeed the instrument that permits modern societies to motivate its youngsters to learn what is collectively indispensable to maintain the quality of life known to members of society. The cultural capital of America is highly diversified and continuously changing with the influx of immigrants. Its unique ways to handle cultural conflict, to respect ethnic identities and the dialectical nature of democratic institutions has a long and strong philosophical tradition that finds its way in our daily way of life and our schools.

American philosophers and historians, such as Crevecoeur, Jefferson, Martineau, Toqueville, von Hubner, and Turner deal, in the interpretation of George and Louise Spindler, with the crux of cultural transmission, conflict and accommodation, religious affiliation and of children's socialization into roles to be played at home in the family, as well as in public life. The Spindlers view American culture as a dialogue (Spindler and Spindler with Trueba and Williams, 1990) between individuals and collectivities, but a dialogue that leads people to rediscover and restructure democratic concepts, behaviors, values and the historical interpretation of such concepts. To recognize that cultural transmission does not occur in a historical vacuum, but that it is continuously shaped by the historical present of Americans as they live their collective conflicts, and find appropriate adaptative strategies that lead them to success, is to recognize the dynamics of American democracy.

If conflict is at the essence of democracy, a successful democracy must include the mechanics for conflict resolution. American cultural values, as opposite and polarized as they may seem in history, must be instrumental to resolve conflict. Cultural transmission must reflect the inherent conflicts of democratic processes, the polarization in movements that mirror antagonism, or advocacy for values that are seemingly opposite: conformity or individualism, cooperation or competition, resistance to law and order or submission to the law, continuity or discontinuity, religiousness or secularism, adherence to strict moral codes or liberal social mores. Americans' ability to respect people with opposed views allows them to reach a critical balance of forces; it permits development of cultural movements and cultural discourse in opposite directions. This is American democracy. In the end, cultural continuity or discontinuity, change or resistance to change, conformity or individualism, high moral standards or liberal attitudes, are all emphasized during the cycles of tolerance and intolerance for diversity; cycles that repeat themselves through history, as newcomers arrive with new contrasting characteristics but a new commitment to define (and redefine) democracy. These cycles affect mainstream people's view of newcomers, ethnic cultures and the role of home languages.

Cultural continuities and discontinuities, which are the result of cultural transmission in given historical contexts, can be best understood in a cross-cultural and long-term perspective, because the cycles of recurring similarities and contrasts are observed best over many years. For example, in the comparative studies presented by George Spindler and his colleagues, we can see a remarkable consistency in cultural values and themes (Spindler, G., Ed., *Educational and Cultural Process: Anthropological Approaches*, 1987a, but especially the chapters by Goldman and McDermott, pp. 282–299; Spindler, G. and Spindler, L. (Eds) *Interpretive Ethnography of Education: At Home and Abroad*, 1987a, especially chapters by the Spindlers, pp. 143–67; by Ogbu, J., 1987, pp. 255–78 and by Gibson, M. 1987, pp. 281–310; see also Spindler and Spindler's 'Schoenhausen', 1988:31–43; Gibson, 1988). Early socialization of the Palau, Ulithi, Hano, and Eskimo led George Spindler to discuss the role of schools in the socialization of Americans (1987:303–334).

The belief by some optimists that American society has overcome its racist biases was shattered by the video of LA policemen brutally beating Rodney King, an African American already apprehended and surrounded by fifteen policemen.[1] The comments of some of the policemen in front of nurses, and their reference to the beating as a game, accompanied by an implied satisfaction of having inflicted such serious physical punishment on an African American, brings home the reality of prejudice. African Americans are not seen possessing the human dignity bestowed upon their white counterparts. Yes, American society has moved along with the passing of Civil Rights legislation and the increase of African Americans in professions and careers reserved for whites in previous years. Today's problems in Los Angeles are not different from the problems observed by George and Louise Spindler in their study of 'model teachers', such as 'Roger Harker' (1988:25–31) and by Hanna's 'Public Social Policy and the Children's World' (Hanna, 1988:316–165). Racism is not a simple attitudinal problem, it is an integral part of some segregated European cultures and some American quasi-apartheid practical living arrangements. Attempts at integration show the far-reaching structural changes needed in all our social and cultural institutions.

Cultural pluralism, with its inherent conflict of shock, dissonance, or incongruence as experienced by the various ethnic groups, and with a successful cultural adjustment, congruence, harmony and balance, as experienced by others, lead us to recognize the complexity of American democracy. American democracy, which is cemented in cultural diversity, requires continuity and change. To explain the flexibility of American culture that accommodates continuity and change, George Spindler had discussed two important concepts that will later be used to help analyze the events in Woodland: the concept of the *enduring self* (the consistent self-perception as being culturally attached to a given cultural setting) and of the *situated self* (the part of ourselves adapting continuously to new settings). The world moves too fast and does not permit us to anchor ourselves and our families in any value system. Long-term ethnographic studies have capitalized on the contributions of the Spindlers and produced important theoretical developments. The cycles of 'compression and decompression' or the variations in emotional intensity experienced by humans in their transition from one status to another, were used by Borish to describe the transitions from childhood to adulthood, from peaceful schooling to training for war activities, and from oppression to emancipation among the Kibbutz (Borish, 1988:181–199). Other researchers, also capitalizing on the work by the Spindlers, have established cross-cultural comparisons to examine cultural characteristics and values. Fujita and Sano (1988:73–97) for example, using the Spindlers' *Reflective Cross-cultural Interviewing* technique, compare and contrast how children were treated in American and Japanese daycare centers, and the basic cultural assumptions of the teachers in these centers; Macias working with the Papago Indian children (1987:363–380) and Anderson-Levitt working with French children (1987:171–92) use cross-cultural approaches pioneered by the Spindlers many years before.

The Essence of American Culture

The authors' view is that ethnographic research is a very useful instrument to study democratic processes in action. The very nature of ethnographic research as a scientific inquiry (Spindler discusses the main requirements and characteristics 1987:17–23), through the use of field-based methods such as participant observation and interactional analysis, must be clearly connected to the context in which behavior occurs. This context is not static, it is socio-historically dynamic, moving with time and explaining changes through time. Social, political, historical, economic and cultural context form part of individual behavioral phenomena ethnographically recorded in the form of interactional patterns, participant structures and sociolinguistic usages of a single event. Ethnographic approaches have been highly instrumental in the study of immigrant families who bring their language and culture to America. These families are deeply committed to endure hardships in pursuit of their dreams. They clearly buy into American ideals of mass education, political participation and economic opportunity for all. They know that the very foundations of democratic institutions are linked to peaceful and productive working relationships in a culturally diverse society. They see America's cultural and linguistic diversity as the cornerstone of American democracy and the source of its continued strength over the last two hundred years (Spindler, 1977; Spindler and Spindler, 1983, 1987b).

Perhaps no other area has shown any greater debate than the very conception of American society, its nature, its essence, its values. Why are there major disagreements? Historically the interpretation of democracy in the US has generated a profound conflict and controversy over the limits of individual freedom or those of social institutions over the individual. Hence the cycles of racism and intolerance of diversity, and even violence against ethnic and other disenfranchised groups (women, gay, homeless, senior citizens, people of color, the poor, the sick, and the handicapped).

Anthropologists have dedicated considerable time and effort to the study of most cultures of the world, and also to American culture in its broad cross-cultural context. In 1983, George and Louise Spindler, using 161 selected studies published until that year, discussed what American anthropologists have written about American culture, and conclude with the following statement:

> Within the USA the diversification is particularly impressive. All of the skills and insights gained by anthropologists in cultures away from home can be used to good advantage at home. Anthropologists attend to symbols, ceremonies, rituals, communities, language and thought, beliefs, dialects, sex roles and sexuality, subsistence and ecology, kinship, and a multitude of other topics in ways that historians, sociologists, political scientists, and psychologists will not, because of the heritage of experience with 'other' cultures from primitive to peasant to urban away from home (Spindler and Spindler, 1983:73).

The enormous diversity of Americans as well as their commitment to participate fully in the life of society, is remarkable. The classic work by Boas on 'modern life' (1928) and by Gillin on American traditions and values (1955), has been contrasted and complemented by the Case Studies in Cultural Anthropology edited by George and Louise Spindler, covering Africa, Asia and Southeast Asia, Europe and the Middle East, Pacific Oceania, Central and South America, North America and American Indian groups. They have conducted studies on many areas of the country, for example, on midwestern towns and schools (Peshkin, 1978, 1988), African American city gang groups, Mexican Americans and undocumented immigrants from Mexico (Chavez, 1992), Mexicans and African Americans from Stockton (Ogbu, 1978), Mexican families in California (Delgado-Gaitan, 1990), Mexican immigrants from Baja California (Alvarez, 1988), Central Americans in Northern California (Suarez-Orozco, 1989), and many others.

There is no clear and simple way to classify all Americans. In a historical perspective we all are ethnics. But some of us look more 'ethnic than others', or sound more ethnic than others. While we cannot divide Americans into ethnic and non-ethnic, or into mainstream and marginal, because these are fluid and changing categories, there are clues that help us identify members of the various social classes and groups. If America was divided into the first two major categories, ethnic and non-ethnic, would there be a consensus as to who qualifies as ethnic and who does not? Along the spectrum of possible ethnics in current folk taxonomies we could find people who have been in this country for generations, who may have lost their parents' language and culture, and who may have moved away from their ethnic community, but despite all, who still insist in calling themselves Italian, or German, or Scottish, or Hispanic . . . The non-ethnic category also has serious problems. It seems to be a category frequently chosen and applied by other individuals and imposed on Americans on the basis of physical appearance, speech patterns, and behavioral characteristics. It is quite possible, however, that many people looking non-ethnic see themselves as mainstream Americans from an ethnic extraction, but not totally uprooted from their parents' ethnic culture. Therefore, we all are and feel American, because we are willing and able to participate fully in the social, cultural and educational institutions of this country, regardless of our own personal ethnic identity. An Anglo-Saxon,

17

fourth generation American, who may have lost memory of his ethnic affiliation, will function next to Americans of color, recent immigrants and refugees (including those who just become naturalized citizens) in our public institutions, regardless of family values. Ethnic prejudice, preference for certain values, lack of tolerance for the use of other languages, life styles and cultural traditions, may show up in public institutions, but they are socially sanctioned and not compatible with American democratic principles. At times, prejudice may take the form of cohesive political group pressures. These groups advocate national policies curtailing the use of languages other than English and clearly oppose individuals from certain ethnic and minority groups — as it happened, for example, with the Japanese in the 1930s, and is now happening with some Hispanics and Indochinese. Again, the discourse and action to protect democratic principles are defended and protected in order to keep the democratic experiment in action.

There are differences in opinion and differential views of what America is all about. Some Anglo-Saxon Americans would tend to see America as the country associated with the good things of life resulting from the efforts, merits, power, connections and accomplishments of the upper socioeconomic classes, and they may stereotype people of color as those involved with crime, welfare and drugs. By the same token, African Americans and other people of color may tend to see whites as Oppressor. Kozol records the comments by a psychiatrist commenting on the violence and crime in Roxbury and Dorchester, Boston, where most nonwhite people live:

> When they [white people] hear of all these murders, all these men in prison, all these women pregnant with no husbands, they don't buy the explanation that it's poverty, or public schools, or racial segregation. They say, "We didn't have much money when we started out, but we led clean and decent lives. We did it. Why can't they?" . . . "They don't have it." What they mean is lack of brains, or lack of drive, or lack of willing-ness to work. "This is what they have become, for lots of complicated reasons. Slavery, injustice or whatever." . . . And they don't believe that better schools or social changes will affect it very much. So it comes down to an explanation that is so intrinsic, so immutable, that it might as well be called genetic (Kozol, 1991:192).

But for the recent immigrants and refugees, who left everything behind, and whose wounds and traumas associated with their journey to this country are still fresh, America is truly the land of hope and opportunity. Most of all, for them America is the land of ethnic and cultural diversity where democracy is color blind and classless. America is the country where freedom and fair treatment are the right of all peoples, regardless of religious, economic, ethnic, racial and social background. However, it is not easy for youthful immigrants and refugees to believe that if one is willing to take the responsibility for participating in public institutions (notably political and economic), one can become a mainstream American. Rampant abuse by public officers, and unpunished discrimination against them often shatters their hopes to achieve the American dream. The comments about many of these new minorities are often self-fulfilling prophecy: 'They don't have it.' Mexican-American youth are overrepresented in most Southwest peni-tentiaries and correctional institutions. How much of the current fate of youth offenders is to be blamed on society?

Kozol narrates an interview with a woman who knew of a boy who eventually became disenfranchised and a destructive member of our society:

> An eight-year-old, a little boy who is an orphan, goes to the school to which I've been assigned. He talks to himself and mumbles during class, but he is never offered psychiatric care or counseling. When he annoys his teacher, he is taken to the basement to be whipped. He isn't the only child in the class who seems to understand that he is being ruined, but he is the child who first captures my attention. His life is so hard and he is so small; and he is shy and still quite gentle. He has one gift: He draws delightful childish pictures, but the art instructor says he "muddies his paints". She shreds his work in front of the class. Watching this, he stabs a pencil point into his hand.

A few years later he is out in the streets, becomes an alcoholic, has a child he abandons, and is seen in front of the rich stores with a long leather coat and hat as 'the embodiment of evil'. Kozol continues:

> He laughs at people as they come out of the store; his laugh is like a pornographic sneer. Three years later I visit him in jail. His face is scarred and ugly. His skull is mapped with jagged lines where it was stitched together poorly after being shattered with a baseball bat. He does not at all resemble the shy child that I knew ten years before. He is regarded as a kind of monster now. He was jailed for murdering a white man in a wheelchair (Kozol, 1991:194–195).

When large portions of the population of a democratic nation seem to fail to belong, and become marginal for reasons to a great extent beyond their control, then this nation needs to review its chart and redefine its principles, policies and practices. Poverty and isolation of the many continue to be the focus of ongoing debate. The larger portion of the population, particularly those from North European, Anglo-Saxon Protestant backgrounds, see their cultural values, behaviors, work ethic, aspirations, beliefs and goals as the very foundation of this country. In their minds, the contributions of other groups are insignificant. Ethnic and racial minorities, however, do not have a monopoly on social problems. There is an increasing number of White, Anglo-Saxon marginal groups which has emerged during the recent economic crises in America, such as the homeless, the hippies, the low-income urban folk, the drug-addicts, the run-away youth, mental patients put out in the streets, and other semi-permanent segments of our society displaced by cut-throat economic policies of the last three presidential periods. Indeed, these 'new minorities' understand well the experience of disempowerment, without having ever been members of ethnic or racial minorities.

The American Dream and Schools

Our view of American education, and of educational institutions in general, is not neutral. The authors present, in this volume, information and ideas that confirm their fundamental agreement with the eloquent statement made by Michael Apple:

... [M]y position has embodied a political commitment. Implicit in my exploration of some aspects of the ways schools and intellectuals function in the cultural and economic reproduction of class relations is a claim that it is very difficult for educational and social theory to be neutral. Thus, ... curricular and more general educational research needs to have its roots in a theory of economic and social justice, one which has as its prime focus increasing the advantage and power of the least advantaged (Apple, 1990:158).

In other words, the authors see the process of democratization as one of continuous change permitting those at the bottom of society to share in the benefits often given only to mainstream Americans. Mainstream Americans, if we accept the pluralistic and multicultural fabric of the United States, are those who, regardless of color, race, religion, ancestral background, political credo, and social class, succeed in establishing an economic base, a permanent residence in this country and become competent and active participants in the public educational, social, economic, and political institutions — banks, political parties, military organizations, public health systems, schools, businesses, industries, and voluntary organizations. In other words, mainstream Americans are those who can play a role in the acquisition and transmission of cultural values. Consequently, mainstream persons must be empowered to reinterpret and transmit American cultural values through national traditions and day-to-day dealings, such as the celebration of national holidays, folk art festivities, musical events, folk dancing and theater activities, parades, symbolic events to honor the American flag, American heroes, war veterans and persons of authority.

All of the above can be done by ethnic minorities, refugees and immigrants, without betraying their ethnic identity, religious traditions and family values. In their minds, they can become mainstream members of society if they learn to participate actively in cultural activities and social institutions, without necessarily sacrificing their ethnic identity. At least, many of them think this way. Indeed, many immigrants have found a way of integrating their own ethnic festivities in the national calendar (St. Patrick's Day, Cinco de Mayo, La Bastille, and others). In the final analysis, all of us, old and new immigrants, refugees and ethnic groups, manage to establish legitimate grounds for claiming the right to belong in America and to authoritatively interpret, define and promote the American way of life. Consequently, in the end, through daily debate and open discourse, we come to agree on a set of core fundamental values shared by Americans regarding the supremacy of individual rights, freedom of speech, self-government, respect for cultural and religious differences, and support for an open and competitive economic system. These values are readily embraced by most of the national origin groups and the near 40 million Americans whose mother tongue is other than American English, especially by the four major ethnic groups into which the national origin groups divide: Hispanics, European (French, British, German and Italian), Asian (Chinese, Japanese and Pacific Islanders) and Indochinese. It seems that in order to share in the American dream we all have to buy into these values.

Regardless of cultural, linguistic, economic and social differences, what immigrants, refugees and other minorities share in common is not just hope to survive, but the will and commitment to reach the American dream, to succeed and to progress economically without sacrificing personal freedom. For this reason precisely, immigrants and refugees often become the custodians of American cultural values as they discover for themselves the true meaning of freedom and democracy. Immigrants and refugees also discover soon that schooling is essential to succeed in American society. They learn that persistent low literacy levels in English prevent them from obtaining high paying jobs and from participating in social institutions. Overall participation of immigrants and refugees in social institutions, however, particularly in the schools, seems to require social support and assistance from mainstream members. There are structural factors (residential segregation, prejudice, language barrier, cultural — especially religious — differences, and others) beyond the control of newcomers that may isolate them and prevent them from entering the community and school. These factors, if neglected, would result in a quasi-permanent position of disadvantage, alienation and social distance between newcomers and mainstream persons.

We do not know enough about the process of marginalization and the 'castification' or disempowerment of newcomers. We know it can happen in America. Indeed, the alienation of African American low income populations is a case in point. What is the nature of American society and American institutions that, in spite of its democratic principles, allows some groups to become and feel alienated? Is there a structural rejection of certain populations? Is failure part of the general plan? Is the success of some built upon the failure of others? Is education systematically failing some members of society? Is academic underachievement part of this systematic failure? In the case of newcomers, children of immigrant and refugee families, what is the role of schools in preparing them to participate fully in American democratic institutions? How successful are schools in teaching English literacy to them and in preparing them for academic careers? Obviously we cannot answer all of these questions here, but, as we unfold the story of Woodland immigrants, we will keep these questions in mind. Indeed, most of the minority persons in Woodland become active participants in social institutions and functional members of American society. Indeed, many ethnic minority children become models of academic achievement without sacrificing their home language and ethnic identity.

One of the reasons we selected ethnographic research methods for this study is that, in order to answer the above questions we needed to make serious inquiries and explore systematically, over a period of time, the complex issues of adaptive strategies of ethnic minorities (Hispanics primarily) in Woodland. School administrators, teachers, and researchers soon realized that parents and students from ethnic backgrounds pursued literacy — in the home language and in English — as a crucial component of the process of adaptation to the new life in America, as an instrument of empowerment, and ultimately as a necessary condition for reaching the American dream. Their insights are congruent with much of the research in educational anthropology (Spindler, 1974, 1982; Spindler and Spindler, 1983, 1987a, 1987b; Giroux and McLaren, 1986; Shulman, 1987; and Sockett, 1987; Delgado-Gaitan, 1990; Delgado-Gaitan and Trueba, 1991).

An ethnography and ethnohistory of empowerment, as used in the present study of immigrant and refugee children, is in the interest of the authors and of the public in general. The reason is that the maintenance of democracy depends on a deeper understanding of the process of empowerment in American democracy, that is, the process alluded to earlier by Apple as 'increasing the advantage and power of the least advantaged' (Apple, 1990:158). Beyond considerations of cultural understanding, compassion, and sound pedagogy, we need to reflect seriously on the survival of American democracy and its quintessential infrastructure built by the knowledge and core values inculcated in school. We can safely assume that the American dream is intimately related to the strategic position of America in the world's hierarchy of economic, military and technological superpowers. We can also assume that the children, on whose shoulders will be the awesome responsibility of keeping America in that hierarchy, have already been born and many of them are children of immigrant and refugee families. Schools must find ways of assisting these families to facilitate their acculturation and active participation in American institutions. In other words, the future of American society is, to a large extent, in the hands of children whose talents will develop through both their mother tongues and home cultures, as well as in English; consequently, we cannot afford to neglect these children; we must invest in them and help them become productive members of our society.

In the final chapters we will discuss issues related to acculturation and various adaptive strategies of immigrant, refugees and ethnic minority persons in the context of cultural therapy. Some research would suggest that the process of integration contrasting or conflicting cultural values is slowed down or regressed by the exacerbation of conflict, degradation incidents and neglect of refugee and immigrant children. The excessive stress associated with traumatic change and the loss of familiar environments which occurs with sudden uprooting of young children seems to affect the selection of appropriate mechanisms of adaptation and the ultimate success in becoming a functional member of a new social group without losing one's own ethnic identity. The pace of adaptation is affected by the trauma associated with new cultural encounters. Often recently-arrived children are observed as being in total shock, unable to respond to the most simple requests and kinetic suggestions (Trueba, 1991:137–158). Efforts to treat the trauma of newcomers and counteract the degradation incidents to which immigrant families and school children are exposed will receive more detailed discussion in the latter part of this book. At this point, however, it is important to point to the need to go beyond simple attempts to modify behavior. Cultural anthropology has emphasized the need to understand the fundamental difference between behavioristic and cognitive paradigms:

> The major difference between the behavioristic and cognitive paradigms concerns the role of internal representations. In the behaviorist tradition, what a creature does is controlled, in large part, by various external conditions, such as the presence of conditioned and unconditioned stimuli and the number of hours of deprivation. In the cognitive paradigm, what a creature does is, in large part, a function of the creature's internal representation of its environment. For many anthropologists, the emphasis of the cognitive paradigm on internal representations had a better fit to their intuitions about the nature of culture than did the behaviorist notions of stimulus control (D'Andrade, 1984:88).

Often older immigrant and refugee children are burdened with adult responsibilities, such as taking charge of the family business, looking after younger siblings, and dealing with outside agencies (hospitals, banks, shops, etc.) on matters affecting the entire family (Delgado-Gaitan, 1990; Trueba, Jacobs and Kirton, 1990; Delgado-Gaitan and Trueba, 1991). The mental health of many immigrant families, and the vicarious sufferings of their children require attention and warrant the overall concern of the authors in healing American society and schools. Apple's concern with the genuine nature of the healing efforts is here relevant:

> Educators talk of giving certain specifiable 'treatments' to bring about certain special 'results' or outcomes. Discounting the fact that the supposed cause and effect relationships between treatment and outcome are rather psychologically and logically difficult to establish, there are ethical and especially legal implications concerning the perspectives out of which clinical and therapeutic categories, labels, and procedures arise that must be brought to the fore and that can provide tactical means for challenging many of the common practices within educational institutions (Apple, 1990:164).

Teachers have distinguished themselves in advocating for immigrant and refugee children in historical periods. In the Sierra of Zacapoaxtla, Mexico, teachers who were native speakers of Otomi and Nahuat, maintained the schools open during the persecution years of the 1930s when teachers were accused of being *comunistas*. Many of them lost an ear, nose, limbs, mental health, and even their lives to keep the Indian rural schools open for children. They knew that the future of these children as first-class Mexican citizens was dependent upon their ability to learn Spanish and mathematics, and to function effectively in the Mexican national economy. Indeed, second and third generation Indian children have become doctors, lawyers and teachers. Also in the United States, the active involvement and innumerable sacrifices of teachers kept the schools open and well supplied during the tough post-depression years. Likewise, exemplary teachers are now exploring new ways of dealing with large numbers of immigrant children whose language and culture are unknown to most Americans. Many Indochinese, Hispanic and African American children who go to schools in economically depressed areas have survived thanks to their teachers. American teachers have yet to receive the recognition and rewards they deserve. The American public has yet to appreciate the role of schools in maintaining the quality of life and the integrity of democratic structures. We have become insensitive to teachers' low prestige, low salaries and inadequate benefits. Many schools in the United States are unhealthy, in disrepair and dysfunctional for teaching and learning activities. But this has not discouraged American teachers. How many secret heroes we must have in urban schools? The role of teachers is essential for the future of American democracy, because teachers are ultimately responsible for the transmission of cultural values.

Education in its broader sense is seen by the Spindlers and their associates as 'cultural transmission' (Spindler, G., 1955, 1987b; Philips, 1982; Fujita and Sano, 1988). The central question is 'how neonates become talking, thinking feeling, moral, believing, valuing human beings — members of groups, participants in cultural system' (Spindler, G., 1987b:303). More specifically, the question Spindler asks is 'how young humans come to want to act as they must act if the cultural system is to be maintained?' (Ibid.). Because education is a cultural phenomenon that takes places in specific social contexts, a cross-cultural perspective is most desirable:

> Without attention to cultural differences, and the way education serves those differences, we have no way of achieving perspective on our own

culture and picture of education as affected by culture (Spindler, G., 1987b:302).

Cultural transmission viewed from a cross-cultural perspective, presents different cases. For example, for some of the American Indian groups (the Tiwi, Tewa and Hopi) cultural transmission produces continuity in the entire cultural system. That is, the rites of passage which produce an abrupt change in the roles of adolescents (or 'sudden compression of cultural requirements', to use George Spindler's words — 1987b:326) dramatize the need for the individual to make a profound commitment to the system. The symbols and meanings of rituals encapsulate the quintessence of cultural values which are ritually validated in the presence of the adults.

In other societies, the new schools bring cultural discontinuity and a denial of traditional culture (for example, among the Sisala of Northern Ghana — Spindler, G., 1987b:329). People make explicit their hostility towards schools and school personnel. The natives interpreted teachers' activities as making children disrespectful of their elders. The conflicts created between the junior and senior generations as a result of schooling are not unique to the Sisala, but well known among other groups:

> Because the curricular content is alien to the existing culture there is little
> or no reenforcement in the home and family, or in the community as a
> whole, for what happens in the school. The school is isolated from the
> cultural system it is intended to serve (Spindler, G., 1987b:329).

While schooling can cause, in some instances — especially during the periods of cultural compression — cultural discontinuities, many cultural systems can manage the period of discontinuities with resulting reaffirmation of cultural commitments. It is possible that, in the case of industrial societies, such as America, there is no way to avoid the cultural discontinuities caused by instruction of those children who come from drastically different cultural systems. The question is how to assist children to adjust to the new cultural system inculcated by school.

While most of the Hispanic population is currently urban, there is considerably less prejudice against Mexican immigrants in rural areas where they are known for their work ethic and family cohesiveness. The positive experience of employers and other rural Anglo-Americans working with Mexicans has led them to recognize them as humble, hardworking, responsible, grateful and loyal. During the 1987 and 1988 periods of grace to legalize undocumented workers, many Anglo-American employers in central California paid from their own pockets the cost of legalizing their Mexican employees and spent a great deal of time helping them through the entire process.

In the urban areas, the preference given to Hispanics (particularly undocumented Mexican people who earned lower salaries than other workers) in the Los Angeles textile companies was seriously challenged by the 1987 and 1988 raids conducted under the new laws of the Immigration and Naturalization Office. Some of the companies were almost destroyed, and many families of undocumented immigrants were penalized. All these workers wanted was a chance to work hard and offer their children a better life. Many of those undocumented workers were forced to leave their children in this country, in the hope of returning to join them in the future. The hotels and other buildings that housed 'abandoned' alien children in Texas and California remind us of the inhumane massive relocation of ethnic and low-income children 'abandoned' in New York, Chicago and other industrial cities during the last two decades of last century. Except last century's children had some hope, as they were being placed with midwestern families. The only hope of today's alien children are the liberal lawyers working for the Mexican American Legal Defense Educational Fund (MALDEF).

The contributions of many refugees and immigrants are now being studied and will surface in the historical reconstruction of modern America. Companies producing electronic equipment in the San Jose and Palo Alto areas of California, for example, clearly increased their productivity and the quality of their instruments after they hired Vietnamese, Cambodian and other Indochinese workers. The entire agricultural power of the central valley in California (from Bakersfield to Davis) is operated with Mexican Labor. Yet, Mexican immigrants continue to be seen as a liability. The increase in vigilantism on the border and the legitimate attempts to control the influx of immigrants has translated into an opportunity to express racism and hatred, a true characteristic of a society undergoing cultural conflict and xenophobia.

Notes

1 The riots started on Wednesday April 29 in Los Angeles. The March 3, 1991 beating of Rodney King, an African American, has been displayed many times on the screen during the past year. He had led the police on a high-speed chase that reached 115 miles per hour on the freeway, and then had laughed at the officers that surrounded him with guns. King had received 56 brutal blows in 81 seconds. A year later, an obviously biased verdict caused 72 hours of riot from the night of Wednesday, April 29, to Saturday night, May 2, 1992. Rodney King himself on May 1 pleaded for peace and order. The verdict that was seen as a miscarriage of justice had left some 50 persons dead, over 2000 bleeding and part of the city charred and in debt for $1 billion. President Bush finally sent a team of Justice Department prosecutors to investigate violation of civil rights charges and soon after sent 5000 troops from the National Guard. During the looting and violence, the LA police were charged with disorganization and neglect, especially at the beginning of the disorders. These were the worst riots in 25 years. The anger and senseless violence was captured by casual video owners. The impact of the riots in America and the world made them one of the most tragic in the history of the United States. This map of Los Angeles, published in *Newsweek*, May 11, 1992, shows the locations surrounding the trial of Rodney King and the subsequent riots in April, 1992.

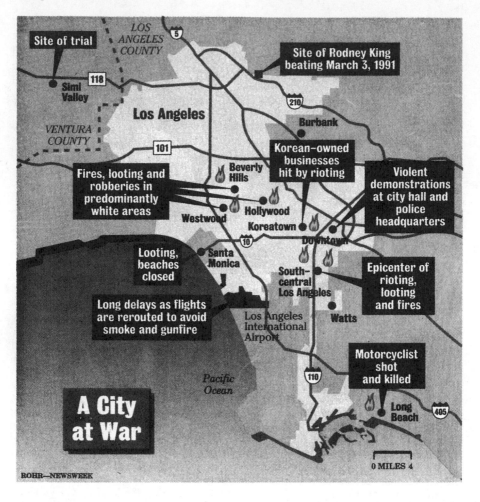

Site of trial

LOS ANGELES COUNTY

Simi Valley

VENTURA COUNTY

Los Angeles

Site of Rodney King beating March 3, 1991

Burbank

Korean-owned businesses hit by rioting

Violent demonstrations at city hall and police headquarters

Fires, looting and robberies in predominantly white areas

Beverly Hills

Westwood

Hollywood

Koreatown

Downtown

Looting, beaches closed

Santa Monica

South-central Los Angeles

Epicenter of rioting, looting and fires

Long delays as flights are rerouted to avoid smoke and gunfire

Los Angeles International Airport

Watts

Pacific Ocean

Motorcyclist shot and killed

A City at War

Long Beach

0 MILES 4

ROHR—NEWSWEEK

NEWSWEEK/MAY 11, 1992

References

ALVAREZ, R. (1988) 'National politics and local responses: The nation's first successful school desegregation court case', in TRUEBA, H. and DELGADO-GAITAN, C. (Eds). *School and Society: Learning Content Through Culture*, Praeger Publishers, pp. 37–52.

ANDERSON-LEVITT, K.M. (1987) 'Cultural knowledge for teaching first grade: An example from France', in SPINDLER, G. and SPINDLER, L. (Eds) *Interpretive Ethnography of Education: At Home and Abroad* (1987) Hillsdale, NJ: Laurence Erlbaum Associates, Publishers, pp. 171–92.

APPLE, M. (1990) *Ideology and Curriculum*, New York, NY: Routledge.

BOAS, F. (1928) *Anthropology and Modern life*, New York, NY: Morton.

BORISH, S. (1988) 'The winter of their discontent: Cultural compression and decompression in the life cycle of the Kibbutz adolescent', in TRUEBA, H. and DELGADO-GAITAN, C. (Eds) *School and Society: Teaching Content Through Culture*, New York, NY: Praeger, pp. 181–99.

Chavez, L.R. (1992) 'Shadowed lives: Undocumented immigrants in American Society', in SPINDLER, G. and SPINDLER, L. (Eds), *Case Studies in Cultural Anthropology*, New York, NY: Harcourt Brace Jovanovich College Publishers.

D'ANDRADE, R. (1984) 'Cultural meaning systems', in SHWEDER, R.A. and LEVINE, R.A. (Eds), *Culture Theory*, Cambridge, MA: Cambridge University Press, pp. 88–119.

DELGADO-GAITAN, C. (1990) *Literacy for Empowerment: The Role of Parents in Children's Education*, London, England: Falmer Press.

DELGADO-GAITAN, C. and TRUEBA, H. (1991) *Crossing Cultural Borders: Education for Immigrant Families in America*, London, England: Falmer Press.

FRAKE, C. (1964) 'Notes on queries in ethnography', *American Anthropologist*, **66**(3), pp. 132–45.

FUJITA, M. and SANO, T. (1988) 'Children in American and Japanese day-care centers: Ethnography and reflective cross-cultural interviewing', in TRUEBA, H. and DELGADO-GAITAN, C. (Eds) *School & Society: Teaching Content Through Culture* New York, NY: Praeger, pp. 73–97.

GIBSON, M. (1987) 'Punjabi immigrants in an American High School', in SPINDLER, G. and SPINDLER, L. (Eds) *Interpretive Ethnography of Education: At Home and Abroad*, Hillsdale, NJ: Lawrence Erlbaum Assoc., (pp. 281–310).

GIBSON, M. (1988) *Accommodation Without Assimilation: Sikh Immigrants in an American High School*, Ithaca, NY: Cornell University Press.

GILLIN, J. (1955) 'National and regional cultural values in the United States', *Social Forces*, **34**, pp. 107–13.

GIROUX, H. and McLAREN, P. (1986) 'Teacher education and the politics of engagement: The case for democratic schooling', *Harvard Educational Review*, **26**(3), pp. 213–38.

GOLDMAN, S. and McDERMOTT, R. (1987) 'The culture of competition in American schools', *Education and Cultural Process: Anthropological Approaches*, Second Edition, Prospect Heights, IL: Waveland Press, Inc, pp. 282–89.

GOODENOUGH, W. (1976) 'Multiculturalism as the normal human experience', *Anthropology and Education Quarterly*, **7**(4), pp. 4–7.

HANNA, J.L. (1988) 'Public social policy and the children's world: Implications of ethnographic research for desegregated schooling', in SPINDLER, G. (Ed.) (1988) *Doing the Ethnography of Schooling: Educational Anthropology in Action* Prospect Heights, IL: Waveland Press, Inc., pp. 310–55.

KOZOL, J. (1991) *Savage Inequalities: Children in America's Schools*, New York, NY: Crown Publishers, Inc.

MACIAS, J. (1987) 'The hidden curriculum of Papago teachers: American Indian strategies for mitigating cultural discontinuity in early schooling', in SPINDLER, G. and L., (Eds) *Interpretive ethnography of education: At Home and Abroad*, Hillsdale, NJ: Lawrence Erlbaum Assoc., pp. 363–80.

OGBU, J. (1978) *Minority Education and Caste: The American System in Cross-cultural Perspective*, New York, NY: Academic Press.

OGBU, J. (1987) 'Variability in minority school performance: A problem in search of an explanation', *Anthropology and Education Quarterly*, **18**(4), pp. 312–34.

PESHKIN, A. (1978) *Growing up American: Schooling and the Survival of Community*, Chicago, IL: Chicago University Press.

PESHKIN, A. (1988) 'The researcher and subjectivity: Reflections on an ethnography of school and community', in SPINDLER, G. (Ed.) (1988) *Doing the Ethnography of Schooling: Educational Anthropology in Action*, Prospect Heights, IL.: Waveland Press, Inc., pp. 20–46.

PHILIPS, S. (1982) *The Invisible Culture: Communication in Classroom and Community on the Warm Springs Indian Reservation*, New York, NY: Longman.

SHULMAN, L. (1987) 'Knowledge and teaching: Foundations of the new reform', *Harvard Educational Review*, **57**(1), pp. 1–22.

SOCKETT, H. (1987) 'Has Shulman got the strategy right?', *Harvard Educational Review*, **57**(2), pp. 208–19.

SPINDLER, G. (Ed.) (1955) *Anthropology and Education*, Stanford, CA: Stanford University Press.

SPINDLER, G. (1959) *Transmission of American Culture*, The Third Burton Lecture, Cambridge, MA: Harvard University Press.

SPINDLER, G. (1974) 'The transmission of American culture', in SPINDLER, G. (Ed.) *Education and Culture: Anthropological Approaches*, New York, NY: Holt, Rinehart & Winston, pp. 279–310.

SPINDLER, G. (1977) 'Change and continuity in American core cultural values: An anthropological perspective', in DeRENZO, G.D. (Ed.) We the People: *American Character and Social Change*, Westport CT: Greenwood, pp. 20–40.

SPINDLER, G. (Ed.) (1987a) *Education and Cultural Process: Anthropological Approaches*, Second Edition, Prospect Heights, IL: Waveland Press, Inc.

SPINDLER, G. (1987b) 'The transmission of culture', in SPINDLER, G. (Ed.) *Education and Cultural Process: Anthropological Approaches*, Second Edition, Prospect Heights, IL: Waveland Press, Inc., pp. 303–34.

SPINDLER, G. (Ed.) (1988) (second edition) *Doing the Ethnography of Schooling: Educational Anthropology in Action*, Prospect Heights, IL: Waveland Press, Inc.

SPINDLER, G. and SPINDLER, L. (1983) 'Anthropologists view American culture', *Annual Review of Anthropology*, **12**, pp. 49–78.

SPINDLER, G. and SPINDLER, L. (Eds) (1987a) *The Interpretive Ethnography of Education: At Home and Abroad*, Hillsdale, NJ: Lawrence Erlbaum Assoc.

SPINDLER, G. and SPINDLER, L. (1987b) 'Cultural dialogue and schooling in Schoenhausen and Roseville: A comparative analysis', *Anthropology and Education Quarterly*, **18**(1), pp. 3–16.

SPINDLER, G. and SPINDLER, L., with TRUEBA, H., and WILLIAMS, M. (1990) *The American Cultural Dialogue and its Transmission*, London, England: Falmer Press.

SUAREZ-OROZCO, M.M. (1989) *Central American Refugees and US High Schools: A Psychosocial Study of Motivation and Achievement*, Stanford, CA: Stanford University Press.

TRUEBA, H.T. (1991) 'Learning needs of minority children: Contributions of ethnography to educational research' in MALAVE, L.M. and DUQUETTE, G. (Eds), *Language, Culture and Cognition*, Philadelphia, PA: Multilingual Matters Ltd.

TRUEBA, H.T., CHENG, L. and IMA, K. (1993) *Myth or Reality: Adaptive Strategies of Asian Americans in California*, London, England: Falmer Press.

TRUEBA, H.T., JACOBS, L. and KIRTON, E. (1990) *Cultural Conflict and Adaptation: The Case of the Hmong children in American Society*, London, England: Falmer Press.

TRUEBA, H.T., SPINDLER, G. and SPINDLER, L. (Eds) (1989) *What do Anthropologists Have to Say about Dropouts?*, London, England: Falmer Press.

Chapter 2

Castification in Multicultural America

Henry T. Trueba

Why have some of the groups in American society failed (or more to the point, been failed) in their pursuit of the American dream? Why instead of becoming acting members of a democratic nation have they become castelike, disempowered, disenfranchised, and completely unable to pull themselves out of their misery? Why cannot schools do anything to help some children move away from their underclass status? More importantly, why do some immigrants, refugees, or other minority groups become caste-like and others do not?

The central theme of this book is a success story of how a group of Mexican Americans in a small rural city moved out of their castelike status to that of full members of a community and into the role of community leaders, yet continue to retain their culture. Our analysis in the final chapters will essentially spell out the conditions under which castified communities can move out of their underclass status and buy into a democratic system by using democratic institutions and principles. In this chapter, however, it is important to discuss the process of castification to which ethnic groups are subjected in many parts of the world. The nature of this process and its contrast with the events which occurred in Woodland are of pivotal importance to the central theme of the book.

The process of castification (or disempowerment) as well as the subsequent process of empowerment consisting of one's own removal from the castelike status, involve radical social epistemological changes — changes in knowledge that have social consequences for the reorganization of power relationships. As understood by Popkewitz:

> *Epistemology* provides a context in which to consider the rules and standards by which knowledge about the world is formed, the distinctions and categorizations that organize perceptions, ways of responding to the world, and the conception of "self". Concurrently, *social* epistemology takes the objects constituted as the knowledge of schooling and defines them as elements of institutional practice, historically formed patterns of power relations that provide structure and coherence to the vagaries of everyday life . . . I use the phrase *social epistemology* as a means of making the knowledge of schooling as a social practice accessible to sociological inquiry; it is intended to emphasize the relational and social

embeddedness of knowledge in practices and issues of power (Popkewitz, 1991:15).

The kinds of changes in the social, cultural and political life of ethnic minorities in Woodland goes beyond a simple change in behavioral patterns of both minorities and mainstream persons, and beyond their cultural understanding and sensitivity. These changes have altered the economic infrastructure and the network of relationships that form the political machinery of the city. These changes are rooted in the knowledge of the political system acquired by immigrants, and their ability to use this knowledge for altering the culture of Woodland. In other words, these changes in culture have restructured the ecology of power, the *modus operandi* of school district personnel, and consequently they have changed the 'structural relations [that] provide the patterned relations and symbolic systems of classification and categorization' alluded by Popkewitz (1991:26).

Ethnic Conflict and Castification

Castification is fundamentally an institutionalized way of exploiting one social group (ethnic, racial, low-income, or other minority group), thus reducing this group to the status of a lower caste that cannot enjoy the same rights and obligations possessed by the other groups. The most effective way of disempowering and disenfranchising a social group is castification. While in theory castification should be diametrically opposed to a democratic form of government (one in which all people have the same status, rights and obligations), castification has co-existed with the European post-colonial democratic systems, indeed it has become perpetuated by such systems. European, and to a large extent, American societies, have retained organizational structures that seem to be anachronic and dysfunctional in modern democratic times. They have imported or encouraged cheap labor and immigration from third world countries in order to retain economic competitiveness, and have denied rights to fair pay, medical care, safety and education to workers and their families. The acceptance or tolerance of a castelike status in immigrant or refugee groups seems to affect differentially ethnic groups. The continuing economic pressures, human rights violations and ethnic conflicts around the world have motivated many communities to seek asylum elsewhere. Thus, castelike status becomes a lesser evil for many uprooted families. Under what conditions can these families and communities overcome the degradation and oppression of being treated as castelike and become part of a democratic nation? This is what we want to explore in the present volume. At this point, however, we need to discuss ethnicity, and the relation between ethnic conflict and castification.

Ethnic hostility all over the world is frequent and violent. We have many examples: Northern Ireland, Chad, Lebanon; warfare in Burma, Bangladesh, the Sudan, Nigeria, Iraq, and the Philippines; the Somali invasion of Ethiopia; the Turkish invasion of Cypress; killings in Uganda, Syria; India-Pakistan; Burundi, and Indonesia; Sikh, Basque, Corsican, and Palestinian terrorism; expulsion of Chinese from Vietnam, of Asian from Uganda; separation of Walloons and Flemish in Belgium (Horowitz, 1985:3). Ethnic conflict can be disguised by wartime alliances, and it can be justified on the basis of national security, determination and future glory. While colonization created castelike status in many oppressed ethnic groups, by forcing them to submission, it kept some peace. In turn, decolonization set in motion a chain reaction that resulted in movements of independence and ethnic separatism. What we have seen recently in the Soviet Union and Eastern Europe is not a new phenomenon. If ethnic conflicts have been repressed by strong political and military oppression, as soon as the oppression ends, internal ethnic struggles reappear and replace the fight against the outside oppressor. Horowitz documents several historical cases:

> The grant of sovereignty to the former Belgian territories in Africa (Zaire, Rwanda, and Burundi) helped stimulate ethnic claims among Flemings in Belgium itself. If, they said, tiny Burundi can have an autonomous political life, why should the more numerous Flemish population be deprived of the same privilege? (Horowitz, 1985:5)

The emancipation of Africa also had an impact on African Americans. Ethnic conflicts that have resulted in the oppression of peoples of color all over the world are naturally of universal interest to American democratic society in which African Americans have committed their lives to emancipate themselves from white oppressors. The element of universality of ethnic conflicts is now, more than ever, present in democratic societies. American foreign policy reflects the concerns of Americans over racial polices and human rights violations in other parts of the world, especially in places where ethnic conflict is profoundly embedded in racial prejudice (in South Africa, for example). According to Horowitz, at the basis of interethnic conflict is the human need for a strongly felt ethnic identity and the resulting hostility towards other groups in stratified societies:

> The salience of ethnicity is reflected, too, in the segmented organizational structure of ethnically divided societies. This applies to the structure of economic organization, as it does to political organization. . . . In Fiji, the mineworkers' union is mainly Fijian; the canegrowers' federation, mainly Indian; and there are two teachers' unions, one for each group (Horowitz, 1985:8–9).

There is an inherent inter-ethnic conflict in multicultural societies, a conflict resulting from competitive bidding for scarce resources, political and economic power. In non-democratic societies there is also a socially-accepted hierarchy that bestows differential rights to various ethnic groups. Organized ethnic pluralism can be reflected in party systems. Ethnically-based parties have grown to become adversaries.

Ethnic hostility can be repressed for years and then unexpectedly explode. The feelings of African Americans against successful Korean entrepreneurs are well known in New York, Los Angeles and other metropolitan areas. In the most recent Los Angeles riots, the frustration of thousands of unemployed African Americans in the face of the unexpected Rodney King verdict (April 29, 1992, that followed the incident that took place over a year earlier) motivated youth to scapegoat hated Korean businesses in the areas that the police chose to ignore or were unabled to protect. Recently a Korean grocery store owner had killed an African American youth for stealing merchandise, and had received no jail sentence. Recent Asian immigrant families are seen in the ghetto to prosper quickly.

African Americans, in contrast, feel not only victims of a system that prevents them from obtaining loans and becoming entrepreneurs, but also feel mistreated by the new immigrants.

Nigeria had, at the time of its independence, three parties each dominated by a different group: one by the Ibo, another by the Yoruba, and another by the Hausa. In the Sudan, the Communist Party was controlled by the Ansaris, in Sri Lanka by Sinhalese, in Indonesia by the Javanese, etc. Ethnic identity and affiliation can become such a basis for social organization in societies that competition for power is of great significance. Ethnic hatred can also affect party policies (Horowitz, 1985:9–10) in the absence of democratic checks and balances. In societies in which ethnic conflicts are violent, political activities have repercussions for ethnic groups which are less powerful. In these societies ethnic conflict is at the center of politics. Ethnic hatred that has been repressed places societies in a state of disequilibrium and becomes highly volatile with any political and military changes. The most recent cases of Yugoslavia and Afghanistan illustrate how deep-seated ethnic hatred becomes a motivation for violent abuses, in a short time and with any excuse, if military power shifts and thus restricts the penalties for overt manifestations of ethnic hatred.

A recurring bias of social scientists, according to Horowitz (1985), is that they conceive of ethnic relations as necessarily between superiors and subordinates, between dominant groups and the victims they oppress or exploit. This bias obscures the fact that ethnic conflict is often the result of rational calculations of profit.

> The dogma of the inevitability of ethnic subordination has clouded out a significant set of relationships. . . . The comparable dogma of the supremacy of social class asserts that common class interests will (or, at any rate, should) overtake ethnic interests. On the other hand, it is asserted that the competition for scarce values and material goods is exactly what propels people to see themselves as members of distinct ethnic groups, whose interests conflict with those of other ethnic groups. . . . Theories of ethnic conflict need to specify what the groups are fighting over — which is not as obvious as it seems — and why ethnic lines of conflict are so important. It is also argued that one or another factor is the key element in ethnic conflict — that a common religion or a common language is what 'knits people together' and that its absence is what pulls them apart. This, despite the presence of ethnic conflict in countries where there is a common language or religion (Horowitz, 1985:15).

To deal with the nature of ethnic conflict and the resulting castification it is important to clarify the concept of ethnicity. The use of the term ethnicity has regained currency and significance in social science research, in the context of the real or perceived threats that ethnic minorities in Europe and in America represent for the mainstream populations. The visibility of the ever-increasing numbers of Turks, Moroccans, Italians, Spaniards and other immigrants in France, Belgium, Germany, Sweden and other European countries, has motivated private and public organizations to sponsor studies intended to increase governmental control of immigrants in order to reduce the flow of immigrants and expedite assimilation of those already settled. To be sure, it is not the Spaniards or Italians that worry those countries; European immigrants are welcome and valued because they provide cheap labor in areas where European workers are less interested in working, or would be too costly. Besides these immigrants belong in Europe, they are white, share cultural and religious values with other Europeans, and are viewed as law-abiding citizens. What worries policy-makers and government officials in countries such as France, Belgium, Germany and Sweden is the coming of Moslem people of color, especially as such immigrants are seen as 'fanatic Islam fundamentalists'. There is a xenophobic spectrum in which immigrants and refugees are placed. In the least threatening end of the spectrum European immigrants who speak the dominant language (for example, Italians or Spaniards who speak French in Brussels or German in Munich) are placed. At the other end of the spectrum are placed dark North Africans who are Moslem and do not speak the dominant language. In between you may find Chinese, Japanese, Latin Americans, and others.

Xenophobia in the American Continent

In the United States, xenophobia has many expressions and a measure of profound racism. The fear of ethnics has motivated Neo-Nazis to organize vigilante raids, conservatives to advocate for monolingualism and monocultural policies (through the English Only Movement), the Ku Klux Klan members to infiltrate political parties which exclude certain individuals on the basis of color or race, the members of the Moral Majority to impose moral codes and protect them through political organizations, and other radical movements of the right to restrict speech and freedom of expression viewed as offensive to some, and to sponsor a highly militant organized membership to restrict public services to ethnics on the grounds that ethnic groups do not contribute their fair share to the cost of such services. In their view, the funding of education in the home languages of ethnic groups who do not speak English is unjustified. Also, in the view of right radicals (conservatives), the use of affirmative action criteria to implement fair employment policies (policies that reflect the ethnic composition of the labor force), or to provide remedial mechanism for ethnic students, is equally unacceptable. There are many other instances of ethnic (often racially motivated) hatred. For example, the concerted efforts of private individuals to supervise the southern borders in order to stop undocumented aliens, or to prevent them from using public services (legal and medical). Many Americans see nothing wrong with the demonstration of ethnic hatred if there is a justification for it in terms of the 'national good'. This is sad, but still more distressing is the fact that members of ethnic groups who want to be accepted by mainstream Americans display conspicuous support to policies and activities against members of ethnic groups who have arrived recently. The Mexican American policemen in MacAllen, Texas were shown brutally beating Mexican illegal aliens (women included) in the police headquarters. It is not uncommon in the Theater of Liberation genre (for example, as reflected in the plays presented by the Teatro Campesino in California) to denounce the *vendido* sold Mexican who has betrayed his own *Raza* and has become the oppressor of his own ethnic group.

Ethnic conflict and ethnic issues in the Americas have a long history that has been explored by social scientists. The Center for Latin American Studies at the

University of Uppsala, Sweden, has published a Special Issue on *Ethnicity in Latin America* (see Alvarsson and Horna, 1990) that gathers a series of important articles discussing this concept of ethnicity and social structures that facilitated the castification of colonized people in the Americas. European sociologists provide a base for our current understanding of the terminology and theoretical developments related to ongoing research on ethnic groups around the world; they also emphasize the need to examine ethnic issues in a historical perspective. For Azril Bacal ethnic are 'autochthonous, indigenous people' who are 'marginalized, in the territorial fringes and socio-economic bottom of the world-system' (Bacal, 1990:15). According to Bacal, there are some 5000 ethnic groups in the world who fit such a category. The United Nations Sub-Commission on Prevention of Discrimination and Protection of Minorities describes Minority communities or nations as those that maintain a continued history of ethnic identity in pre-invasion or precolonial times, and that are determined to maintain and transfer to the future generations their ethnic identity. The implication is that all peoples have the right to self-determination, and that the language, culture, religion and other components of their ethnic identity play a key role in the exercise of this right (Bacal, 1990:16). More specifically, ethnicity can be described as follows:

> Ethnicity is a complex, comprehensive concept, related to issues of ethnic classification or affiliation. It is contextual, appearing only in contacts between peoples in some type of opposition. It involves psychological, cultural, socio-economic and political factors. It emphasizes contrast and expresses the differences between "us" and "them" in terms of culture, kinship, language, race, religion or societal organization (Alvarsson, 1990:12).

Beyond the concept of being an indigenous people determined to keep their own cultural and political identity, ethnicity, in Alvarsson's mind requires that such a group maintains a social setting in which the contrast between groups is socially relevant and contextually defined (the us versus them). Along the same lines, Morner, based on the seminal work of Max Weber presents a notion of ethnic groups as those that maintain a conscious belief in a common origin, common characteristics, traditions and activities, and a common oral history. What is significant in this notion is not so much that this belief has been accepted on the basis of substantive empirical evidence, as much as our shared human sense of its symbolic power keeps a social group cohesive and functional. Another significant feature of this notion is that in order to maintain ethnic identity over a period of time, there must be an active process of socialization of the members of the group, even if there are no strong blood relationships among the members of such group (Morner, 1990:30–31). The essential element is the symbolic expressions of common desent. Clearly a less important factor is the actual reality of blood relationships and genuine common descent. This is particularly true in the case of multiple migrations of people who have left their country of origin for a long time and who are bound to engage in exogamous marriages with groups of people who become members of the ethnic group by affiliation, not by birth. A case that comes to mind is that of the Indochinese refugees who live now in the United States, especially the Hmong (Trueba, Jacobs and Kirton, 1990).

In the United States ethnic affiliation is complex because this country has a large portion of immigrants whose blood or affinal relationships in pre-arrival times are replaced upon arrival with fictitious kinship relationships. These relationships become integral to the formation of cohesive ethnic enclaves through symbolic expressions of solidarity in social institutions that tend to replace the home country institutions. Also, in the case of individuals who lived in America prior to the arrival of the Europeans, such as the North American Indians and some Mexicans in the Southwest (Mexican territory prior to 1848) and who felt displaced and destroyed by European colonization, intertribal organizations adopt religious rituals familiar only to members of certain tribes, but rituals that acquire a new symbolic meaning of common opposition to the dominant society.

By the same token, *Latinos* or Hispanics from various backgrounds (including Latin Americans and Spaniards residing only temporarily in the United States) join together with *Mexicanos* (recent Mexican arrivals) and Chicanos to celebrate the *Cinco de Mayo*, or *Dia de los Muertos*, or Christmas, and symbolically reaffirm their Latin identity through the use of the Spanish language.

Ethnic minorities, understood as minorities not in the numerical sense, but ethnic groups controlled by the ruling dominant society, suffer 'social closure' or the exclusion from resources and opportunities offered to other citizens (Morner, 1990). This closure is rationalized on the grounds that ethnics are incompetent or unreliable; for example, Indians were called *gente sin razon* (people without reasoning ability) by the Europeans in Latin America, meaning, people not having level of intelligence to perform difficult tasks; and African Americans were labeled *lujuriosos descontrolados* (uncontrolled lascivious people), and consequently individuals who should not be trusted to execute tasks requiring moral integrity. According to Morner, oppressed minorities respond to this social closure with 'usurpation closures' or common strategies to obtain through alternative means the resources and opportunities denied because of prejudice.

Ethnicity in Multicultural Societies

Because ethnicity is contextually defined in opposition to other groups (especially to the dominant ruling group), ethnic members often develop, in addition to the usurpation closure, a 'dual closure', which consists of strategies to gain access to denied resources and strategies to prevent other groups from getting access to such resources. This phenomenon replicates segmentary opposition and internal factionalism. In some instances, oppressed groups see each other as enemies, and in others, they create alliances to protect themselves from a common oppressor. This social mechanism may have some applicability to the United States, particularly with respect to minority groups with high intra-group diversity, as in the case of the Hispanics. There are significant differences between Mexicans, Puerto Ricans, Cubans, Central Americans, South Americans, Spaniards; and there are important differences in life-style and cultural values among rural, low-income and an upper-income person within the same subgroup. Under what conditions and in what contexts would all Hispanics join forces against another ethnic group? In what contexts would all minorities (via a type of 'rainbow coalition') join forces to protect their rights and gain support from mainstream whites? Income, social class, education, language variety, cultural values (such as work ethics), race, religious and political philosophies, and many other factors tend to segment ethnic groups. Newspapers often talk about ethnic diversity as a 'slick issue', that has upset the white middle-class. The influx of 'ethnics' has sparked conflicts between Hasidic Jews and blacks ending in riots in Brooklyn (New York); it has motivated active Ku Klux Klan organization resulting in cross-burnings in Dubuque (Iowa), concerns over ethnic conflicts in New Orleans (Louisiana) and Portland (Oregon), and alarm in even the most affluent school districts of America, including Madison, Wisconsin. The politics of ethnicity in times of inter-ethnic conflict has paradoxically pitted against each other two of the most oppressed groups in New York and in the world: Jews and persons of African descent. In turn, what has created a strong cohesive political conservative group of whites has been the fear of African Americans people and Jews. While abuses from mainstream white people is often tolerated by oppressed ethnic groups, any semblance of abuse from another ethnic group becomes a serious breach of the principle of solidarity of the oppressed. The destructive impact of oppression on inter-ethnic harmony shows clearly that collective psychological price that racism has extracted from American society. The explosiveness of low-income ethnic areas, controlled by gangs, can be shown not only during events such as the Los Angeles riots, but even during sports victory celebrations that end in looting. For example, the victory of the Chicago Bulls, who won the national championship of the National Basketball Association on June 14, 1992, resulted in massive looting of one of the rich commercial areas of the city, and hundreds of arrests.

The multicultural character of American society has finally faced communities that had been untouched and had remained entirely white. The anxiety over the discovery of minorities is parallel to the reaction Europeans are facing today. The Council of Europe, in their final report (Council of Europe, 1986, Strasbourg) on Project No. 7 entitled *L'education et le developpement culturel des migrants* states the following:

> Supposer que le caractere multiculturel des sociétés europeennes est certainement une question de pluralism du à la présence de population immigrees, serait réduire ce phenomene a une seule de ses dimensions. Ce serait aussi succomber a l'illusion qu'il s'agit d'un tendance cyclique qui peut etre arrêtee, voire inversee. Ce pluralism, toutefois, est incontestablement le lot de nos sociétés d'aujourd'hui, prises de plus en plus dans un procèssus d'envergure mondiale, qui obligé a reconnaître le caractères particuliers des individus et des groups si l'on veut préserver et promouvoir la démocratie culturelle (Council of Europe, 1986:27).

> To assume that the multicultural character of European societies is, to be sure, a question of pluralism due to the presence of immigrant populations, would be to reduce these phenomena to only one of their dimensions. This would also be to succomb to the illusion that one is dealing with a cyclical tendency that can be stopped or even reversed. This pluralism, indeed, is the undeniable mark of our modern societies, caught more and more in a process of global importance, a process that requires the recognition of the particular characteristics of individuals and groups, if one wants to preserve and promote cultural democracy (Council of Europe, 1986:27) (Our translation).

Ethnic pluralism is indeed multicultural in essence, and it goes beyond the presence of a mosaic of ethnic and linguistic groups; it redefines the relationships of these groups to each other as well as their collective relationship to the mainstream society. When the collective presence of ethnic groups is insignificant in numbers and importance, and when political control is relatively uncomplicated, ethnic pluralism may be tolerated. It is now becoming an international phenomenon of unique complexity, such that is forcing the serious consideration of structural, institutional repressive mechanisms to regain control, to manipulate access to resources, status and political power in such a way that these ethnic minorities do not take over. At least, this is the fear of members of mainstream society. Therefore, the study of ethnic pluralism has become the study of cultural conflicts and political struggle in a global context of social, economic, cultural and legal relationships. Hence, its significance and the increasing attention given to it by governments around the world.

The implications for education are incalculable. Suarez-Orozco summarizes the issues as follows:

> How are the children of European Community (EC) and non-European Community immigrants adapting to schooling in the new setting? Are there important differences in adaptation patterns between non-EC immigrants such as Moroccans, Tunisians, and Turks and EC immigrants such as Spaniards and Southern Italians? What are the differences facing the foreign-born generation and the so-called 'second generation' immigrants? . . . What is the meaning of education in a host society among those immigrants who hope to return 'home' in the future? (Suarez-Orozco, 1991:99).

Marie-Claire Foblets, from the *Centrum voor Sociale en Culturele Antropologie* at the Katholieke Universiteit te Leuven has studied the legal consequences of ethnic pluralism in Belgium, and she analyzes the report of the Council of Europe on cultural pluralism or multiculturalism as a potential asset if indeed the ethnic identity of the various groups is respected (Foblets, 1988). It is indeed a challenge because it forces European societies to share their lives with people with different life styles, cultural values, languages, religions and physical appearance. She discusses the complex and serious consequences of ethnic pluralism with respect to the treatment of children from mixed marriages, as in the case of Moroccan and Belgium parents. The rights of women are entirely different in each of these two legal systems. Cammaert (1986) studies Moroccan women immigrating in Brussels from Nador. She states:

> The woman who has just immigrated and who may not or has not yet left her home alone sees the permission to cross the boundaries of the apartment to be an essential form of freedom. The second level concerns a relative openness to the outer world. The Berber woman seeks, consciously or not, a further expansion of her own territory within the world of the host country (Cammaert, 1986:643).

Belgium, a country of 10 million people has a very large population of immigrants (20 per cent) who were recruited to work in the mines and other jobs that the Belgians did not want to do. The latest available figures (1984 census, cited in Roosens, 1989:127–128) indicate that there are 270,521 Italians, 119,083

Moroccans, 70,033 Turks, and 55,952 Spaniards. In a relatively small territory, where the historical division between the Wallons and the Flemish has been reflected in the legislated use of French in some areas and of Dutch in others, the use of other languages either for public instruction or for services can create serious political problems.

Racial problems and debates in Europe seem to repeat history. The attributed lower intellectual capacity to some races still persists in England (Tomlinson, 1989), and the idea that some groups are 'unassimilable' (as the mainstream Americans thought of some ethnic groups at the turn of the century) is now appearing in Belgium (Suarez-Orozco, 1991:102–103).

Roosens describes the historical process of language differentiation and use as follows:

> When Belgium was founded in 1830, the everyday language of the educated class was French, even in Flanders, where the language of the masses was Flemish, a variant of Dutch. The enmity of both the North and the South was at that time directed against a common oppressor, King William I of the Netherlands. The present-day opposition between Flemings and Walloons has developed gradually since then. Early in the nation's history, a small group of Flemings argued that an injustice was being committed against the people by the imposition of French in the political, judicial, military, cultural, and administrative sectors. By sheer demographic expansion and institutional democratization, the Flemings gradually succeeded in getting Flemish recognized as a national language and in having language use specified geographically in the country (Roosens, 1989:128).

While Walloon nationalism is seen as a more recent phenomenon (Wallonia was inclined to the culture of France), Flemings were able to generate a genuine national consciousness through the use of Flemish as a national language and by stressing Flemish cultural traditions and ethnic identity. Belgians recognize the reality that Belgium is composed of three groups: the Walloons, the Flemish and a few German speaking citizens. Other people are aliens:

> Belgians widely recognize that being alien entitles people to a number of rights and creates for them certain duties under a kind of natural law. But few Belgians are prepared to see Belgium as a country where, together with the Flemings, the Walloons, and a small German-speaking community, other groups of people with their own cultural traditions can settle and remain settled (Rossens, 1989:129).

Belgium is certainly not alone in taking this position. Other European countries are highly nationalistic and separate clearly the outsiders from themselves. But there are different types of outsiders. Non-Europeans, especially people of color, are the farthest removed. Other Europeans are outsiders, but recognized as member of the European community. The European Community (EC), while much talked about, has its limitations. Immigrants from European countries are either welcome or at least accepted as a necessity (temporarily). The cultural, racial and religious backgrounds of Italians and Spaniards are similar and pose no threat to Belgian ethnic identity. Not so in the case of Turks and Moroccans. Muslim groups, with a life-style unfamiliar to Europeans, are perceived as a clear threat to the very character of the country, its values and traditions.

Guest-workers have become essential to the Belgian economy in order to compete with the Japanese and the Americans. The underclass created by the cheap labor hired from Europe, Africa, and Turkey was permitted with the understanding that Belgians would not lose any jobs they wanted for themselves. This is changing rapidly. Second generation children feel they belong in Belgium, and they look much like the native youth of the country (Roosens, 1989:137). The children of immigrants go through the Belgian school system and speak and write French and/or Dutch, although they also study their own language. These children, however, 'fall significantly behind in their curriculum because of inappropriate teaching' (Roosens, 1989:138). There is certain cultural conflict for the children of immigrants:

> Several detailed anthropological studies have shown that many migrant children, under the influence of the school and their peers, come to see the life-style and values of their parents as dated and backward. This does not necessarily mean that the immigrant children openly break with their parents or are in conflict with them more than native children are in conflict with their parents, but the stresses are real enough (Roosens, 1989:138).

Along with the cultural conflict at home, children of immigrants face an isolation and shock that often disenfranchises them from mainstream society. Their peers reject them outright, employment opportunities are scarce. As Roosens eloquently states:

> They belong overwhelmingly to a category of people of which the present economy has no need. . . . Among many second-generation immigrants, there is a return to ethnic roots. . . . Young adults who have resolutely grown away from the cultural environment of their early youth can simulate their traditional culture, but they are never completely at home again in what they have left. If the first migration was a transition from a rural culture, with little education, to an urban civilization based on universal public and secular education, there is no real turning back for the second generation, no matter how dejected they may feel about their social and economic isolation in the dominant society (1989:138–139).

The marginalization of children of immigrants is clearly related to their isolation and the rejection they feel on the part of the mainstream society. Yet this marginalization is interpreted by mainstream people as an inability or unwillingness to assimilate, to participate in mainstream social institutions and become genuine Belgians. There is a clear social ambiguity: on the one hand, Belgians see these children of immigrant as aliens and want them to remain as outsiders or to go back home (meaning the country of their parents); on the other hand, Belgians blame children of immigrants for not assimilating, for not belonging to the culture, for attempting to maintain their ethnic identity, which is what would logically follow if children of immigrants born in Belgium are not accepted as Belgians.

The Alienation of the Children of Immigrants

First-generation immigrants are seen as individuals who would eventually leave, as temporary outsiders, and as a problem that time will resolve. All over Europe second-generation immigrants who do not conform with cultural norms are seen as a serious menace and evoke private and public xenophobic reactions, especially as their numbers increase proportionately with the local populations of natives. Often, as in the case of Turks and Moroccans, individuals cannot go unnoticed because of their phenotypic characteristics, even if they attempt to assimilate, in contrast with Italians or Spaniards who disappear in the masses of Belgians. There are interesting exceptions:

> Young people of Sicilian origin, for example, will cite as belonging to their own past or culture, the political success of Roman antiquity or the current achievements of great Italian authors or movie directors. At the same time they may form an association to purchase land in Sicily and thus create a highly emotional symbol as a group possession. . . . Nevertheless, it is understandable why members of the second generation now think they have been robbed of a part of their culture by the dominant school system and why they believe that things would have been different if the 'cultural uniqueness' of migrant children had been respected. This feeling that the dominant society has taken something away that can never be recovered is, of itself, significant (Roosens, 1989:141).

There is no simple solution in Belgium or any other country. A language policy carefully balanced as a political compromise between Walloons and Flemish does not allow for the tipping of such balance by allowing the use of other languages in schools, or by granting children of immigrants rights and privileges comparable to those of the natives. The fear that many immigrants (who work in the French-speaking area) would side with the Walloons is a clear deterrent. Another deterrent is the sheer demographic trends of ever increasing numbers of Moroccans and Turks whose values and life-style are perceived as the single most serious threat to Belgian society and culture.

The social and educational problems facing ethnic, refugee and immigrant minorities in the United States are comparable to those faced by similar groups in Europe:

> Lack of equal opportunity resulting in higher unemployment and under-employment rates (particularly among youths) . . . conditions of domestic poverty, disparagement from the majority population, generational conflict, the emergence of peer reference groups fostering a counter-cultural identity among youths, high minority dropout rates from school, high grade 'retention' rates . . . and delinquency rates (Suarex-Orozco, 1991:103).

As in the United States, Great Britain exhibits considerable achievement differences among its various ethnic minority groups; East African and Indian students do better than Turkish Cypriot, Afro-Caribbean, Bangladeshi, and Vietnamese students. As Suarez-Orozco states it, Americans are facing serious theoretical challenges as we compare and contrast the situation in Europe with that of the United States:

Is De Vos' model of ethnic identity, 'minority selective permeability' and non-learning (De Vos and Suarez-Orozco, 1990), at all suitable to explain the excessively high dropout patterns and grade-retention rates among Moroccan youths in Brussels? Is Gumperz' sociolinguistic model of language discontinuities, miscommunication, and the reproduction of inequality suitable to explain language learning problems among Turks? (Gumperz and Hymes, 1972; Gumperz, 1981). Is Ogbu's cultural ecological model at all applicable to the Turkish experience? Should these groups be heuristically conceived as immigrant minorities? Or, is the 'castelike minority' (also referred to as 'involuntary minority') model developed by Ogbu (1974, 1978) to understand the African American experience in the United States a better bet to approach some of the serious problems now facing the second generation non-EC immigrants in Northern Europe . . .? (Suarez-Orozco, 1991:106).

The problem of ethnic minority education in Europe is intimately linked to European economic and political history, its nationalist policies excluding foreign-born, non-EC persons from ever belonging in Europe, while at the same time inviting those outsiders to come and work for lesser wages. The left hand of European economic use (or exploitation) of cheap immigrant labor does not want to know what the right hand is confronting in the form of social consequences for the children of immigrants who are born in the host country and who no longer belong in their parents' country. In contrast, however, second-generation immigrant children in America are linked not only to the right of working and belonging in the country, but to the expectation that, if taught appropriately and given an opportunity, these children should reach acceptable levels of performance in school and society.

In contrast with Europe and the United States, ethnic pluralism in Latin America took a different turn. Its historical dependence on the caste structure brought to Latin America from Europe was eventually destroyed by rapid miscegenation between Europeans and American Indians. The hierarchy of political power originally linked to the caste system lost its functional value and gave room to an integrated colonial multicultural society which eventually was taken away from the political and economic control of the Europeans. Morner suggests that:

> The exclusion strategies are historically the most important in the Latin American context, whatever the degree or subtlety of discrimination may be. . . . I believe that still in 1967, to some extent at least, the caste society in Hispanic America constituted a variation of the European model. That is how through legislation the state developed a gradual official "closure of exclusion" strategy, that was more tolerant with mestizos and more rigid with Africans and their descendants stigmatized by slavery. But the most important was the proper strategy developed by the white colonial group, a majority group in sociological terms. For this group, the Indian masses could be spared more easily than the relatively expensive African slaves, who, additionally, would become culturally closer than the Indians once they learned Spanish and the new costumes. Therefore the Indian masses were at the bottom of the social scale (Morner, 1990:32). (Translation from Spanish by the authors)

Because the new world emphasized principles of cultural democracy (in conflict with the intent of economic and political control sought by white European colonial groups), the channels for upward social mobility became entangled in efforts to identify relative distance of Mestizo or mixed-blood persons to European classes. Indeed, with the conversion to Catholicism and the acceptance of European legislation, natives of the Americas were subject to a classificatory system designed by the colonizers in order to assess rank and place of all individuals, especially when there was a conflict between phenotypic characteristics and presumed genetic background. This hierarchy went from *criollos* who were genetically Europeans but born and raised in Hispanic America, through various degrees or combinations of European and American Indian, European and African, or African and American Indian blood. The Creole elites would find ways to segregate rich *pardos* (brown or mestizos from European and native ancestries) or *mulattos* (combination of European and African ancestries) in Venezuela, Cuba and Mexico during the nineteenth century (Morner, 1990:29–35).

The social structure of Latin American countries is loaded with contradictions between the cast structures *de jure*, and their *de facto* application. Many times rich Indians married Spaniards and developed a group of social leaders. Indians tended to see the European as superior and the Indian as inferior, thus reinforcing the European caste system. The relative absence of European women (questioned by some) tends to be accepted as the main reason for the rapid miscegenation in Hispanic America. According to Morner, in 1539 only 6 per cent of all European immigrants to Hispanic America were women; by the 1600 at least one third were women. Yet, miscegenation was also the result of clandestine sexual relationships between European and the low castes (Morner, 1990:34). In general, the ethnic labels that form part of the European classificatory system of castes, became obsolete and inaccurate due to the enormous variety of phenotypic characteristics and the difficulty in documenting descent, especially in cases of illegitimate children. Morner has pointed out that at the turn of the eighteenth century, the census data suggest a change between 30 and 60 per cent in ethnic affiliation of residents in Valparaiso, for example. He also suggests that the illegitimacy decreased in many places during the eighteenth century. For example, in Guatemala, between 1650 and 1750 it decreased from 40 per cent to 26 per cent of the total population of the City of Guatemala. This is also debated; another author cited by Morner, Inge Langenberg, who studied in detail the census data of that city from 1773 to 1820, suggests that 49 per cent of the baptized children were illegitimate, and that there were additional illegitimate births of children not baptized (Morner, 1990:34).

The case of Mexico is unique in some respects. The wars of independence were led by Creole or mestizo individuals such as Miguel Hidalgo, Jose Antonio Paez and Jose Maria Morelos. While most historians feel that the European caste system transferred from the colonial to the independence periods with minor changes, other recent historians feel that the challenges faced by the colonial system around 1810 guaranteed that the actual independence occurred during the period of social changes following after 1810 (Morner, 1990:37).

Cultural Pluralism in the United States

In what ways was the ethnic pluralism developed in the United States different from that in Europe and Hispanic America? Were there similar processes of castification and disempowerment of the ethnic groups controlled by Europeans? Was the relative low incidence of miscegenation (mestizaje) with people of color and American Indians a distinctive factor perpetuating racial prejudice and determining the organization of exclusion structures for ethnic groups in the United States? What were the roles of Asian and Latin American subsequent waves of immigration in determining exclusion structures and oppressive working conditions for guest workers? How did the forced annexation of the Mexican territories in 1848, and the attempts to assimilate their Hispanic and Indian populations affect the castification of these groups?

The United States of America represents a unique and complex experiment in democracy in which a cycle of immigration waves was patterned after a peculiar democratic philosophy that guaranteed (in principle) all new arrivals the rights of free speech and equal social, economic and educational opportunities. American culture imprinted its own character in immigration policies, political debates and its competitive open economy. Yet, during the last three hundred years of American history, the treatment of immigrants, refugees and hired hands has been selectively discriminatory, and unequally tolerant of linguistic and cultural differences. There has been more tolerance of immigrants from Europe, (especially those affiliated with Protestant churches). The tolerance for ethnic diversity may have been more a function of perceived economic and political gains than of humanitarian principles. Attitudes towards ethnic pluralism have changed over the years in response to the types of immigrants (Hispanic, Asian, Caribbean), the relative flow of immigrants, and the speed with which immigrants are assimilated. In times of economic prosperity, when there is a need for cheap hand labor to expand businesses, we tend to minimize the 'dangers of unassimilable' immigrants, and tolerate increased immigration quotas, and adopt more liberal policies related to illegal aliens; we even stop enforcing laws that penalize employers of illegal aliens.

Do Americans see a conflict between the retention of ethnic ties and the adoption of American citizenship? If we see the essence of ethnicity as a set of unique cultural values shared by a group who may also share other values with the larger multicultural society, then there is no less cultural opposition or conflict. But if we define the essence of an ethnic group as contrasting or contradicting the dominant mainstream culture, then a person cannot remain affiliated to his/her ethnic group and become a full American citizen. In some sense, ethnic identity further defines an individual's affiliation beyond its role as member and active participant in mainstream American society. There are many types of ethnic groups and many ways to belong in America. On one extreme we may have a totally independent, autonomous and isolated ethnic group characterized by different language, culture, life-style, political system, religious organization and economic self-sufficiency. On the other extreme, we may have an ethnic group assimilated to mainstream society, retaining certain symbols, rituals and memories of previous affiliation to other cultural traditions and ancestry. While in Europe many immigrants retain their home languages and use them at home with their children, immigrants in America tend to lose their home languages under strong social pressure to become Americans. Why does one have to become monolingual in English in order to become American? In Europe, there are important reasons why languages are maintained both as 'ethnic markers' (part of the identity-kit of immigrants) and in order to permit communication across ethnic boundaries in many European nations. In the United States, relatively few members of minority language groups retain fluency in their home languages because the incentives are few. The loss of home languages is also complicated in the historical insistence of

United States' unwritten public policy of attaching social stigma (often it is seen as unpatriotic or un-American to speak other languages in public). Indeed, national policies in the last century and up to the late 1920s penalized individuals who used languages other than English in public. The modern movements (such as the English Only Movement) are equally active in building support for a rapid assimilation through the use of English in lieu of the home languages brought by immigrants and refugees.

It is perhaps important to distinguish ethnic pluralism (which has clear elements of multiple cultures) from multiculturalism in the strict sense of the word. Ethnic pluralism denotes the peaceful and integrated coexistence of diverse ethnic groups under a single socio-economic and political system. Given the diversity of the ethnic groups and cultures represented in the United States, most Americans would require that ethnic groups also share a *lingua franca* (English) and a democratic philosophy of equal opportunity for all. Multiculturalism, however, if taken literally, would require that most members of society could effectively function in many cultures and through many languages; in its less strict form, it would require some knowledge about those cultures and the ability to understand those groups. The multiculturalism as it exists in Europe includes the ability of many individuals to communicate well with other Europeans of different language groups; this does not exist in the United States. However, in Europe, this multiculturalism coexists with a strong nationalism (often defined in a narrow sense — for example, being a Walloon, or a Flemish, rather than being a Belgian or a European) and a knowledge of common European history, languages and traditions. A Flemish can also speak English, French, German, and even other languages like Italian, Spanish, and Berber, without losing his/her nationalism.

The functional distribution of languages and cultures in Europe, and the rewards attached to the ability to communicate with other language groups in Europe are incentives enough to allow the development of a higher level of multiculturalism. Unfortunately, in America these incentives and opportunities do not exist. Native speakers of Spanish or of other non-prestigious languages tend to feel forced to lose their home languages within one or two generations. Certainly, the World War II language policies did enough to discourage German and Japanese citizens from using their native languages. Current discriminatory policies against speakers of Chinese or Spanish have also discouraged the use of these languages in public, in spite of the fact that federal funding was made available for selective use of home languages in public schools.

Cultures as they exist in modern societies become more complex and more difficult to study, because they include structural elements (social class, ethnic diversity, etc.) of the larger society along with the unique ethnic traits characteristic of regions (Chinese and Mexican cultures in the Southwest, Scandinavian and Native American cultures in the Midwest, Puerto Rican and Jewish cultures in the East). When different groups coexist in the same society, under the same socio-political and economic system, these groups affect each other's existence and enrich each other's ethnic cultures. Newcomers learn to select adaptive strategies in function of their coexistence with other groups (African American, Puerto Rican and Jewish school friends learn a great deal about each other's groups). The study of adaptive strategies of immigrant groups can only be understood in the multicultural context of their environment. Many of the original inhabitants of the United States and Canada are still attempting to adjust to the demands of European

American values, and some have sought isolation and autonomy; on the other hand, they also seek economic support and compensation for the losses caused by the European invasion and expropriation of their lands. The overall result of these adaptive strategies has been most dysfunctional and destructive. The isolation of American Indians has permitted some of them to retain their language and culture, as well as their legal system, but it has effectively deprived them from obtaining justice in the highly competitive American system. Some American Indian groups have done fairly well economically and retained much of their Indian identity (the Navajos, for example). Among the others, the rate of suicide and alcoholism is among the highest in the country. Conflicts with the law have often become a symbolic gesture to register their discontent and lack of effective mechanism to retain their self-identity.

In contrast with the American Indians, until the turn of the century, the majority of immigrants came from Europe and founded American ethnic communities that assisted them in getting settled, finding jobs and learning English. The fairly rapid assimilation of these immigrants to American society was a function of the cultural affinity and their physical similarity to other Americans of European ancestry. There was indeed prejudice against them and considerable economic exploitation, but normally, by the second or third generation, families became recognized as being fully American. There were also some disputes and controversies about the use of their home languages. German in the Midwest, French in the South and Spanish in the Southwest were frequently used. Attempts to curtail the use of these languages in school found serious resistance on the part of ethnic communities.

Immigration trends during the twentieth century changed drastically. Immigrants from Mexico were escaping the Revolutions following the exile of the Dictator Porfirio Diaz in 1910. The United States, having faced World War I and confronted terrible economic problems, curtailed immigration in the mid 1920s, created gates at its southern borders, and sent back to Mexico many of its emigrants. Immigration increased again immediately after the period of high visibility for the Communist movement, when President Lazaro Cardenas expropriated the oil companies from the hands of European and American investors. Perhaps as a reaction to repatriation of thousand of Mexicans during the Depression years, the period following World War II was of economic expansion and liberal immigration policies. While many jobs were open to Hispanic immigrants, there were still stringent and prejudicial language policies against Germans, Japanese and Mexicans, who were prevented from using their home languages. In the 1940s, as World War II was unfolding, the persecution of minorities had became obvious, to the extreme of placing in concentration camps hundreds of innocent Japanese immigrants and confiscating their properties. This issue is still highly controversial. Today, after Japanese Americans won a court suit against the federal government by demonstrating that American authorities acted out of prejudice and without any evidence of wrongdoing on the part of the Japanese, there continues to be abuse and hatred against the Japanese in commercial radio programs.

Immigrants' Role in the Economic Development of America

The economic development of America continued to be top priority in the 1950s, and the import of cheap labor from Mexico, which had existed for many years in the Southwest, took on giant proportions. Illegal aliens were being smuggled day and night by the thousands into the country through the Tijuana, Mexicali, Tecate, Nogales, and Juarez borders. With the approval of the Federal Government, more liberal policies were established to bring and protect documented workers from Mexico, as well as from other countries. Many Chinese, who in the 1920s and 1930s had come to work in the railroads, came in larger numbers to the West coast.

By the late 1940s the largest groups of immigrants were no longer European but Mexican, or Hispanics from other countries. Furthermore, these immigrants were often rural, unskilled and illiterate, and they were willing to take jobs and salaries that no American wanted. The migration cycles were clearly marked from Texas to California, to Nevada, back to Texas, and north to the states of Kansas, Illinois, Indiana, Wisconsin and others. Depending on the harvest and planting seasons, migrants were floating from camp to camp in any of the states that needed cheap labor. California was clearly the state that required the most intensive and extended labor, because of its climate that permitted cultivation all year round, and its large agricultural land. Soon the wealth of growers in the Southwest was conspicuously dependent on cheap labor, and the abuses of Mexican and other migrant workers became the focus of public attention. César Chávez, since the 1950s organizer of the famous strikes of farm workers, obtained some concessions to protect these workers' health and acceptable wages. But the ever increasing poverty in the South, and the terrorism in Central America of the 1960s and 1970s was bound to flood the country with thousands of undocumented immigrants looking for jobs.

By the late 1960s the United States launched new efforts 'to regain control of its borders' without attempting to foster the economic development needed in the Spanish-speaking countries to the South. The Spanish-speaking (mostly Mexican) populations in Texas, Arizona, New Mexico and California, on the one hand, and the Spanish-speaking populations in Illinois (Chicago particularly) and New York (both Puerto Rican and Mexican), were matched by the Cuban refugees of the 1960s who landed in Florida and later spread north. The presence of Spanish-speaking people all over the Untied States began to raise concerns in the 1960s and resulted in debates about the use of languages other than English in public schools. Mexican scholars call this phenomenon *la reconquista pacifica del territorio Mexicano* (the peaceful reconquest of the Mexican territory).

The Department of Justice, the Immigration and Naturalization Office, and other federal agencies began to plan strategies to curb the immigration from the Mexican borders. These strategies consisted of intensifying surveillance at the border to prevent illegals from crossing, launching pervasive raids on businesses and industries that were suspected of using illegals, and announcing new naturalization policies offering legal resident status to those immigrants who could prove they had been working in the country for at least for three years before the deadline in mid-1988. Massive deportations took place, children born in this country were separated from their Mexican parents or abandoned because of the raids, and later placed in quasi-correctional schools (hotels in the border areas) waiting for their parents to claim them.

The deterioration of the Mexican economy, the demand for cheap labor, and even the strong support of many California employers who wanted Mexican workers, coupled with the inability of the government agencies to stop the entry of undocumented workers, has resulted in a continuous increase of the Hispanic population in the entire country. If the Hispanic population grew by 61 per cent between 1970 and 1980, the Mexican population grew by 93 per cent in the same period, while the remaining of the US population grew 11 per cent. The most recent population statistics show that Hispanics (particularly in the Southwest) grew beyond everybody's expectations.

In the context of contemporary United States, what is the ethnic, racial, social and cultural future of the country? North America has now, as it always has had, a highly diversified population. Its largest minority is the African American group, descendants from the slaves brought during the previous two centuries. The core of European immigrants who rapidly assimilate is still very large and quite invisible. After the Hispanic population, which is the largest language minority group in the country (and now predominantly urban), the largest immigrant groups are German, French, Italian, British and other European groups. After them the Asian immigrants (Chinese from mainland China and from Taiwan; Korean, Filipino, Hawaiian, Indochinese — Vietnamese, Cambodian, Khmer, Hmong and Laotian) are the fastest growing and rapidly becoming visible minorities. Although there is a great deal of intra-group and inter-group diversity among the Asian populations, Asian Americans are becoming visible because of their overall high performance in schools, businesses and industry. The overwhelming majority of Asians compete well in math and science subjects in college, and succeed in their jobs.

There are still a numerically small communities of Native American Indians who remain highly isolated in reservations or urban areas, after having lost much of their economic self-sufficiency, their cultural traditions, and their control over land. Massive relocations and extermination policies have effectively destroyed many Indian communities and their ability to maintain a sense of peoplehood. The situation of many of the Indians and Eskimos in Alaska is comparable to that of Native Americans in the lower states.

One of the least known minorities is that of African American, the black population, as it is commonly referred to by many. This population is one of the least understood and most highly stereotyped. Anthropologists have conducted studies that persuade them that most African Americans are not genetically poor African, but the result of miscegenation. As in the case of black-white mixed unions in Latin America, the children of such unions were assigned the lower status of black. Miscegenetion in America has been less permissible than in the Latin American countries such as Brazil or Mexico where large numbers of African slaves were brought. In America, racial prejudice against the African Americans has been so strong that even today in more liberal parts of the country, a racially mixed (black-white) couple in which the individuals have similar educational and socioeconomic levels face serious social sanctions when seen in public, or worse if they marry. The sanctions are commensurate with the degree of darkness and the socio-economic level of the potential black spouse.

The 1950s and 1960s marked a clear change in the country. The federal government began to reinforce laws forbidding racial prejudice in transportation, housing and employment. Lynching, beatings or terrorist attacks against blacks by racist groups, such as the KKK, were met with interracial marches in the South and organized economic boycotts against businesses that discriminated against African Americans. The assassination of Martin Luther King and the public condemnation of racist groups (such as White Supremacists and KKK members), opened the door to blacks and resulted in strong legislation in favor of integrated schools and businesses. By the mid-1970s many African Americans moved North and took important positions in state and federal government offices, industries, and businesses.

African Americans in America are today a highly diversified group that shares some phenotypic characteristics, a history, some cultural traits, the English language, the experience of racism, the struggle for democratic principles of equal opportunity for all, and the hope of more active participation in the political machinery of the country. Socially and economically, African Americans are also highly stratified and somewhat isolated across social strata. Upper-class African Americans live in a world that is far removed from poor African Americans. Upper-class minorities, regardless of ethnic background, interact with each other and with mainstream persons more than with lower-class members of the same ethnic group. By the same token, low-income African Americans, Chicanos and whites live in similar conditions and interact with each other more than with any upper classes.

African American males in America are considered to be at-risk, to be a group of individuals with limited chances to survive and succeed. The socialization of African American males in ghettoes, exposed to the drug culture and to the brutality of poverty and intellectual isolation, often results in antisocial collective behavior, gang activity, violence and jail. There may be more school-age African American youngsters in jail than in high schools. African American low-income teen-age girls have a high incidence of pregnancies and become women on welfare who stay on welfare for life. The gang activities among African American girls is growing fast, and the amount of violence, especially related to the drug traffic, is growing more every day.

The demoralization of African American families who come to exist by accident or without the necessary preparation to face the challenges and demands of technological societies, especially the educational demands, is shown in home violence, prostitution, low school achievement, poverty, neglect of children, lack of effort in maintaining property, clean living quarters, personal hygiene and in investing energy in maintaining a job. Competitiveness of African Americans in sports, and competitiveness of selected African Americans in businesses or in professional careers, demonstrates that under the proper conditions African Americans can succeed. How does one explain the overall failure of many African Americans in adapting to the demands of American society? How does the performance of African Americans compare with that of Hispanics? What peculiar social and cultural elements seem to work against the African American families? These issues will be discussed later on. Suffice it to say that socialization of African American youth is beyond the control of the family. The experiences of African Americans in the country, in schools, churches, housing areas, etc., has a great deal to do with the successful adaptation of the few and the overwhelming failure of the others.

The stratification of the Old World, consisting of the different ranking layers of European classes and castes, was not transferable in its identical form to the New World in America. Indeed, while the Spanish colonization had access to special social mechanisms to reinstitute in the New World the Old World castes, England and other colonizers in America had fled oppressive systems in Europe that they did not want to replicate. Nevertheless, they did import the use of slavery, which was widespread in most European colonies. The United States, however, was one of the first to abolish slavery and to do away with formal caste structures. Due to this fact, the abolition of slavery, and the limited miscegenation with both slaves and American Indians, the bulk of the American mainstream population continued to be descendants from European immigrants. Cultural differences between mainstream Americans and African Americans, and the remaining prejudice from colonial times regarding the low status of African Americans, collided with American ideals of cultural democracy and equal opportunity for all. This collision cost the country many lives during the Civil War and continued to cost lives during the Civil Rights struggles of the 1950s and 1960s. Democracy in America is a genuine ideal, but democracy coexists with a social and, in general terms, racial stratification that is changed only gradually and painfully.

While most Americans would strongly support the ideals of cultural democracy, integration, equality and diversity, in real life there is a great deal of opposition to the economic progress of minorities; the reason is that minorities are seen as competing for jobs and scarce resources with mainstream populations. The legal disputes against affirmative action policies, which were established to reach some balance of ethnic representation in employment, have been challenged as reverse discrimination. Economic advantages originally given to minority firms, are now considered unacceptable or unconstitutional. Assistance to minority students, grants to conduct research on minorities, grants to support educational programs in languages other than English, are all viewed as a burden on the general public, and even unpatriotic efforts to create nationalist movements within the country. The result of this backlash of anti-minority feelings is that many of the minority students who had entered college (a small percentage of the total college population) had to interrupt or abandon their studies. The overall rise in dropout rates and in underachievement of minorities is clearly related to the economic realities of low-income families. Education is no longer viewed as a viable means to upward social mobility. Survival through unskilled labor, collective business enterprises, or even illegal activities are more realistic alternatives. Castification is ultimately a social illness that demoralizes individuals who once believed in the American dream.

During the recent L.A. riots of April 29–May 2, 1992, after the initial outburst of anger, looting and destructive fires, the African American and Hispanic communities called the police to recover looted merchandise from neighbors and gang members. They reminded the press that it was African American persons who helped restore order and took care of whites who had been victimized during the riots, and took them to the local hospitals. African Americans stated publically that they wanted to be treated honestly and fairly, and that they needed protection from the gangs. Despite the high unemployment of African American males in the area (near 40 per cent) and the neglect or mistreatment by the police, African American leaders and heads of families, reasserted their commitment to pursue the American dream.

While equity concerns directed the public attention in earlier decades to 'ethnolinguistic' and racial minorities, that is those which were cohesive and recognizable by dominant phenotypic characteristics, more recently the attention has been focused on larger groups of disenfranchised people, groups that are clearly interracial, interethnic and highly visible: the homeless, poor, mental patients, AIDS victims, gay people, and various groups of disenfranchised women. All of the traditional minority groups, immigrant, refugee, racial minorities, etc., are so highly diversified internally and have lost so much their cohesiveness, that they are not seen as necessarily ranking by themselves at the bottom of the social scale. So many of the new minorities are so conspicuously poor, neglected, or in total disarray, that even the recent boat people (Vietnamese who have just arrived) are considered superior and capable of moving up on their own. Indeed, I have worked with recent Indochinese immigrants in the West coast (Vietnamese, Hmong, Khmer, etc.) and they are clean, work very hard, help each other, and in a short time they move up in the social ladder.

The tolerance of American culture and the openness to receive even the most dysfunctional individuals is one reason why these groups proliferate and grow. Poverty is relative, and there is no doubt that recent administration has undermined the infra-structure of upward mobility for some minority groups and low-income whites. Yet, the dysfunctional characteristics of many families and individuals, regardless of their race or ethnicity (but more frequently white or African American, not from other ethnic groups) are a luxury of a rich society who can afford to maintain many people who lost the incentive or ability to work and to be productive. The loss of the working ethos of the commitment to achieve, in many low-income Americans, is so clearly in contrast with the dedication and commitment to succeed on the part of Asian immigrants, including those at the bottom of their social ladder. In fact, schools are a setting in which the work ethics of middle-class white Americans is in clear contrast with that of Asian Americans and new Asian immigrants; Asians not only put many more hours of work per day, but they persist in academic tasks of great difficulty with the profound commitment to accomplish distinction.

There are important qualitative differences in the responses of immigrant, refugee and minority groups to the degradation associated with castification processes. American culture, economic progress, freedom and fortune are always attractive. Why and how do some minority groups successfully shake up the consequences of castification and develop long-term plans to free themselves in order to reach full participation in American cultural institutions? What is the role of schools in which the power relations have changed in order to permit ethnic minority groups to bring about needed reforms? We do not have all the answers, but we have an account that may place us on the right track to find some answers. We know that the empowerment of teachers and citizens requires not only the acquisition of general knowledge about the politics of education, but critical thinking, problem-solving and teacher empowerment. As Popkewitz states it:

> *Critical thinking, problem solving, and teacher empowerment* are key phrases in teacher education programs sponsored by the foundations through local business support. These themes have universal appeal and can support a wide array of assumptions formulated in response to contradictory interests. In the current climate, these key phrases have a mixture of references to functional or useful knowledge that relates to demands of the economy and labor formation, as well as more general claims about social inquiry and social innovation (Popkewitz, 1991:128).

Critical thinking that has no consequence for the reorganization of power relationships does not constitute a significant change in the social epistemology of reform. Woodland has a new structure in which power is clearly shared by ethnic members of the community. The following chapters will present the key elements to understand this radical change in structure. In order to make sense of the more recent developments, however, the next chapter provides a historical (or rather an ethno-historical) account of the people that have lived in Woodland and the surrounding areas.

References

ALVARSSON, J. (1990) 'Ethnicity: Some introductory remarks', in ALVARSSON, J. and HORNA, H. (Eds) *Ethnicity in Latin America*, Uppsala, Sweden: Center for Latin American Studies, Upsala Universitet, pp. 7–14.

BACAL, A. (1990) The emergence of ethno-development in the social sciences', in ALVARSSON, J. and HORNA, H. (Eds) *Ethnicity in Latin America*, Uppsala, Sweden: Center for Latin American Studies, Upsala Universitet, pp. 15–27.

CAMMAERT, MARIE-FRANCE (1986) 'The long road from Nador to Brussels', *International Migration*, **24**(3), pp. 635–50.

COUNCIL OF EUROPE (1986) *L'education et le Developpement Culturel des Migrants*, Final Report on Project 7, Strasbourg, Austria: Council of Europe.

DE VOS, G. and SUAREZ-OROZCO, M.M. (1990) *Status Inequality: The Self in Culture*, Newbury Park, CA: Sage Publications.

FOBLETS, MARIE-CLAIRE (1988) 'Migration to Europe today: International private law and the new challenge of legal pluralism', paper presented at the Symposium on Legal Pluralism in Industrial Societies, Zagreb, Yugoslavia.

GUMPERZ, J. (1981) 'Conversational inference and classroom learning', in GREEN, J. and MALLAT, C. (Eds), *Ethnography and Language in Educational Settings*, Norwood, NJ: Ablex.

GUMPERZ, J. and HYMES, D. (1972) *Directions in Sociolinguistics: The Ethnography of Communication*, New York, NY: Holt, Rinehart & Winston.

HOROWITZ, D.L. (1985) *Ethnic Groups in Conflict*, Berkeley, CA: University of California Press.

MORNER, M. (1990) 'Etnicidad, movilidad social y mestizaje en la historia colonial hispanoamericana' in ALVARSSON, J. and HORNA, H. (Eds) *Ethnicity in Latin America*, Uppsala, Sweden: Center for Latin American Studies, Upsala Universitet, pp. 29–43.

OGBU, J. (1974) *The Next Generation: An Ethnography of Education in an Urban Neighborhood*, New York, NY: Academic Press.

OGBU, J. (1978) *Minority Education and Caste: The American System in Cross-cultural Perspective*, New York, NY: Academic Press.

POPKEWITZ, T.S. (1991) *A Political Sociology of Educational Reform: Power/knowledge in Teaching, Teacher Education and Research*, New York, NY: Teachers College, Columbia University.

ROOSENS, E. (1989) *Creating Ethnicity: The Process of Ethnogenesis*, in BERNARD, H.B. (Ed.) *Frontiers of Anthropology*, **5**, Newbury Park, CA: Sage Publications.

SUAREZ-OROZCO, M.M. (1991) 'Migration, minority status, and education: European dilemmas and responses in the 1990s', *Anthropology and Education Quarterly*, **22**(2), pp. 99–120.

TOMLINSON, S. (1989) 'Ethnicity and educational achievement in Britain', in ELDERING, L. and KLOPROGGE, J. (Eds) *Different Cultures, Same School: Ethnic and Minority Children in Europe*, Amsterdam, Netherlands: Swets & Zeitlinger, pp. 15–37.

TRUEBA, H.T., JACOBS, L. and KIRTON, E. (1990) *Culture Conflict and Adaptation: The Case of the Hmong Children in American Society*, London, England: Falmer Press.

Chapter 3

Woodland in Yolo County

Yali Zou

Physical anthropologists believe that the first human beings to inhabit the American hemisphere arrived from northeastern Asia between 30,000 and 40,000 BC. Archaeological evidence of the human presence in the Southwestern US is recorded between 10,000 and 9000 BC (Willey, 1966:16–29). The prehistory of Yolo County is not well documented. According to oral traditions in the region, the Wintum people came from the north. Archaeological investigations verify that they arrived in northern California around 2000 BC, and in Yolo County about 1500 years ago. According to historians Larkey and Walters (whose work was the very foundation of this chapter) the people who settled here were called Patwin, derived from the Wintum word meaning people, and discovered by Stephen Powers, an ethnographer who studied the area in 1877 (Larkey and Walters, 1987:10).

The Patwin are described by Larkey and Walters as merchants extensively involved in trade with other American Indian groups of the area, as non-agrarian, living in autonomous villages or groups of villages located on elevated ground close to a sources of water (Larkey and Walters, 1987:11). These groups had a chief, a shaman and a council of elders. (For a more detailed description of the Patwin you can consult the work by historians Larkey, 1969, and Larkey and Walters, 1987, especially the latter pp. 10–12).

Explorers and Settlers

Larkey and Walters (1987) describe the first Spanish explorers, Father Narcizo Duran and Lieutenant Luis Argüello, who came in May of 1817, with two ships, the San Rafael and the San Jose. They sailed from Half-Moon Bay, California, on the Pacific coast up the Sacramento River to a point in Yolo County above Elkhorn Slough. Argüello returned to the Sacramento Valley in 1821 with a force consisting of sixty-eight men and 235 horses. They stopped at the Rio de los Putos (Putah Creek) and continued north towards what is today Chico. This expedition covered 900 miles, and it was the last to be ordered by Spain before Mexico's independence in 1821. The first English-speaking person to enter Yolo County was John Gilroy, a British sailor who had been in California since 1814. He arrived with Argüello's expedition on October 23, 1821, and camped near Winters.

Argüello's chaplain, Father Blas Ordaz, described later the unique experiences of the members of the expedition. They saw small villages inhabited by the Patwin. One *rancheria*, Libaytos, had some 400 people. The Spaniards gave the

Figure 3.1   Woodland, California

Source: Peter Manesis

name San Pedro to the river at Libaytos. Most of the Patwin were not hostile; some even asked the Spaniards to take them along. Two Patwin, one from Ululato and another from Canucaymo, accompanied the Spaniards on the trip through the territory (Larkey and Walters, 1987:13–14).

The first *ranchero* in the Yolo region was Francisco Guerrero y Palomares. He arrived in California in 1834, and in 1842, when he was 31-year-old, he married 17-year-old Josefa de Haro. Guerrero acquired a *rancho* near Putah Creed. There, his wife bore him a child. Then he acquired another *rancho*, Corral de Tierra, near Half Moon Bay, south of San Francisco.

According to Larkey and Walters (1987:18), the first American who settled in Yolo County was John Reid Wolfskill. In July 1842 he took possession of 17,755 acres of land near Winters. This land had been granted on May 24, 1842, to John's brother, William Wolfskill, by the Mexican Governor Juan Bautista de Alvarado. John Wolfskill raised cattle and horses and cultivated vines, figs and olives. He founded the local horticultural industry by giving cuttings to newcomers who were soon growing fruit trees on farms throughout Yolo County. The second American to arrive was William Gordon, who came to California in 1842 after living nineteen years in New Mexico. Having become a naturalized citizens of Mexico, he petitioned the Mexican Government for a legal title to obtain land on both sides of Cache Creek to the Rio Sacramento. He was granted only two of the eight leagues (4439 acres per league) of land he requested, and he named his *rancho* Quesesosi (Larkey and Walters, 1987:19).

Another pioneer, William Knight, an American from Baltimore, Maryland, who had lived in New Mexico for many years, settled with his family on the Yodoy Mound next to the Sacramento River in 1843. On May 4, 1846, Knight claimed to have received from Governor Pio Pico ten leagues (45,000 acres) to establish a rancho he named Rancho Carmel after his wife. During the Gold Rush of 1849, Knight left his family and established a ferry on the Stanislaus river midway, at a place later called Knight's Ferry. After Knight's death on November 9, 1849, his family attempted to establish legal ownership of their Mexican land grant, but the petition was rejected for lack of evidence. Other pioneers continued to arrive. Thomas M. Hardy, a Canadian carpenter and shipbuilder who had served in the Mexican navy, obtained six leagues (25,000 acres) and established the 'Rancho Rio de Jesus Maria' in 1843. Hardy's neighbor to the south was John Swartz, a Flemish immigrant who arrived in 1843 and settled on land west of the Sacramento River across from the present-day city of Sacramento.

Several other land grants in Yolo County were given by Governor Micheltorena: Rancho Five Leagues on the Sacramento River to Josefa Martinez and her husband William Mathews in 1844; Rancho Jimeno, north of present-day Knights Landing, to Manuel Jimeno of Monterey in 1844; Rancho Laguna de Santos Calle, named for Jose de los Santos Beryessa, the mayor of Sonoma, to Marcos Vaca and Victor Prudon in 1845; and the huge (40,000 acres) Rancho Canada de Capay in 1846 to the three Beryessa brothers, Santiago, Nemicio and Francisco.

The Beginnings of Yolo County

The Treaty of Guadalupe Hidalgo, which ended the Mexican/American War, was signed on February 2, 1848, and California was transferred from Mexico to the

United States. Two years later, when California became a State, Yolo County was constituted as one of the original twenty-seven counties. It covered 1000 square miles; its total population was barely 1000 people. On November 13, 1849, before California was admitted to the Union, residents held a convention in Monterey where they adopted a state constitution and elected a state legislature. There were two candidates for State Senator to represent the district of Sonoma, which included the area that is now Yolo County. One of them was Jonas Spect, who had founded a tent city he called Fremont on the west bank of the Sacramento River at its confluence with the Feather River. Spect wanted to call this county Fremont County. Opposing him was Mariano G. Vallejo who proposed the name Yolo County, for the Patwin word *Yodoy* which means 'a land abounding in rushes'.

Yolo County is located seventy-two miles northeast of San Francisco and eighteen miles from the State Capitol, Sacramento. Its boundaries are the Sacramento River on the east, Colusa County on the north, the Coast Range on the west, and the Solano County on the south. Yolo has 650,880 acres of land of which about 80 per cent are flat. Subsequent boundary changes gave Yolo County its present land mass of 1034 square miles. From the eastern boundary (the Sacramento River) the land increases in elevation starting below sea level in the delta area to a height of 3046 feet on the summit of Berryessa Peak in the Western Blue Ridge Mountains (Larkey and Walters, 1987:9).

According to historians Larkey and Walters, 'The Gold Rush of 1849–1850 dramatically changed California from an isolated wilderness into an American state' (1987:25). Although Yolo County had no gold mines, it was on a direct path between San Francisco and the northern mines, and it attracted many travelers and settlers who admired its unique environmental characteristics. Yolo County had flat and rich land, easily cultivated. Its weather was not extreme seldom freezing in the winter. It certainly had hot spells in the summer, but generally the nights were cool. It was located in the heart of the Sacramento Valley, almost within sight of the dome of the State Capitol. And most important, Yolo's passengers and freight had access to frequent and inexpensive transportation, for by the early 1850s steamboats were regularly plying the Sacramento River from San Francisco as far north as Red Bluff.

The first settlements in Yolo County were on the Sacramento River, for most of the first settlers arrived by boat, but others settled on the flat lands in the interior of the county. Many were happy to settle wherever they could obtain free land. Some of these newcomers engaged extensively in stock-raising, for beef and mutton brought high prices in the mining camps in the nearby foothills. The breeding of high quality horses became a profitable local business. Yolo had both Mexican cattle and Spanish bronco horses that were gradually substituted by the American breeds which reproduced easily. A Yolo County report of 1852 indicates that there were 1808 horses, 314 mules, 1855 sheep, 2607 hogs, and 9626 head of horned cattle. By 1855 there were 35,000 head of cattle in the County. In 1860, due to a bad winter with terrible winds, rain and snow storms, the cattle in the County were reduced to 23,480. A number of crops were cultivated in Yolo County. Barley had been the first major grain crop grown: 126,076 bushels were produced in 1852. Wheat became the County's dominant crop in the 1860s. (The source of these statistics is the anonymous *The Illustrated Atlas and History of Yolo County, California, Containing a History of California from 1513 to 1850*, etc. published in 1879, p. 40).

The agricultural wealth of the county of the 1860s gave political significance to the choice of county seat. In the early days, securing the county seat was an important issue for merchants, politicians and developers or promoters. The first county seat, in 1850, was Fremont, for it was the only town of any size in the county at the time. After the town was washed away in a flood in 1850, a decision was made to move the seat of government to Washington, where it remained until 1857, when repeated flooding in Washington caused the county seat to be moved to Cacheville (now the town of Yolo) on Cache Creek. Cacheville proved to be too small and isolated from the rest of the county's population, so the county seat was returned to Washington in 1860. The location of the seat of government remained a controversial issue, causing much heated argument on political and economical grounds.

The principal concern was that Washington was too close to the Sacramento River. An election was held in 1862 to decide whether the county seat should remain at Washington or be moved to Woodland. According to the old records, the vote was an overwhelming victory for Woodland: 968 in favor of Woodland; 778 for Washington (Gregory, 1913:98). According to Gregory, the people of Washington, as described in the records, were most unhappy and contentious when they lost to Woodland the distinction they had enjoyed of being the seat of government. They contested this decision before the board of supervisors and legislators, but the county authorities decided not to oppose the will of the majority of the people in the county. Consequently, on May 10, 1862, the County's records were transferred to Woodland, and Woodland has been the seat of Yolo County ever since (Russell, 1940:93–94; Gregory, 1913:98).

Population Increase in the 1850–1940 Period

Population statistics for the nine decades between 1850 and 1940 seem to suggest a rapid increase from 1850 to 1880, and a moderate increase from that year until 1910. The first decade of this century saw the smallest increase in the County. Then there is recovery with fast increases from 1910 to 1940 (see Table 3.1). Overall, in less than a century the county grew from about 1000 to over 27,000 people. Yolo's population began to grow rapidly immediately after World War II. The county grew in population from 27,243 to 139,200 in 1990, with most of the growth occurring in the urban areas. The decade growth rate of the seventies was 39.7 per cent but the decade growth rate of the eighties was 23.5 per cent. This indicates a short term decline (see Table 3.2). Table 3.3 shows the development of minority population in Yolo County. Ethnically, 1980 Census records indicate that 77 per cent of Yolo County's population are white, 11 per cent are Mexican American; 1.2 per cent are African American, 1.1 per cent are Japanese; 0.8 per cent are Chinese; and the remainder are Filipino, and East Indian. Table 3.3 shows us that the ethnic diversity of Yolo County is remarkable. While the white population in 1980 was 77 per cent of the total population, the 1980 Census identified significant numbers of African American, Chinese, Japanese, Indians and Mexicans. Mexicans constituted the largest minority in the county, and by 1980 had increased their numbers to 16,116, or almost 14 per cent of the county's population.

Table 3.1: *Yolo County population growth statistics 1850–1940*

Year	Yolo	Net increase per decade	
1850	1086	—	
1860	4716	33.4 per cent	1850–60
1870	9899	109.9 per cent	1860–70
1880	11,772	18.9 per cent	1870–80
1890	12,684	7.7 per cent	1880–90
1900	13,618	7.4 per cent	1890–1900
1910	13,926	2.3 per cent	1900–10
1920	17,150	23.2 per cent	1910–20
1930	23,644	37.9 per cent	1920–30
1940	27,243	15.2 per cent	1930–40

This table was composed from a number of references. The most important documents are cited below:

United States, Department of Interior, Census Office. 8th, 9th, 10th, 11th, 12th, 13th, 14th, 15th, 16th Census, 1860, 1870, 1880, 1890, 1900, 1910, 1920, 1930, and 1940, *Population of the United States*, Washington, DC: Government Printing Press (Printed respectively, 1864, 1872, 1883, 1895, 1901, 1913, 1922, 1931, 1940. (See complete references at the end).

Table 3.2: *Yolo County population growth statistics from 1940–1990*

Year	Yolo	Increase decade	
1940	27,243	—	
1950	40,640	49.2 per cent	1940–50
1960	65,727	61.7 per cent	1950–60
1970	91,788	39.7 per cent	1960–70
1980	113,374	23.5 per cent	1970–80
1990	139,200	22.8 per cent	1980–90

Sources: US Census: 1950, 1960, 1970, 1980. Population of the United States. 1990 figures taken from *Population Estimates of California Cities and Counties: Report 90-E1*, California State Development of Finance: Population Research Unit and the SACOG Population Model.

Chinese and Japanese Immigrants

Emigration from China in the days of the Gold Rush was encouraged by the stories of 'gold mountains'. Chinese immigrants came to the Western region of the United States, but they could only find low-paying jobs, often unwanted by other persons. The Chinese people, however, were responsible for one of the greatest engineering feats of the century, the construction of the Transcontinental Railroad. The Chinese were also highly instrumental in the development of horticulture, something that placed California among the richest agricultural regions in the world. At that time, the Chinese were praised for their ability to adapt to American society and the value they placed on California in particular: 'They are among the most industrious, quiet, patient people among us' (Wei Min She, 1974).

Table 3.3: Composition and characteristics of the population in Yolo County 1860–1980

Year	Total	White	Per cent of Total	African American	Chinese	Japanese	American Indian	Other
1860	4716	4689	99.4	0	6	0	0	21
1870	9899	9318	94.1	69	395	0	117	0
1880	11,772	11,015	93.6	102	608	0	47	0
1890	12,684	11,912	93.9	122	604	5	41	0
1900	13,618	12,662	93	172	346	410	28	0
1910	13,926	12,518	90	280	198	789	32	109
1920	17,105	15,520	90.7	202	175	1152	42	14
1930	23,644	21,083	89.2	194	251	1423	54	639
1940	27,243	24,613	90.3	211	172	1087	232	928
1950	40,640	38,730	95.3	418	132	551	78	731
1960	65,727	63,330	96.4	607	262	745	244	539
1970	91,788	86,786	94.6	1145	844	1010	476	1527
1980*	109,464	87,298	77	1886	1447	1563	1154	16,116

This table was composed from a number of references. The most important documents are:

United States, Department of the Interior, Census Office, 8th, 9th, 10th, 11th, 12th, 13th, 14th, 15th, 16th Census, 1860, 1870, 1880, 1890, 1900, 1910, 1920, 1930, 1940, 1950, 1960, 1970, 1980. *Population of the United States.* Washington DC: Government Printing Office (Printed respectively in 1864, 1872, 1883, 1895, 1901, 1913, 1922, 1931, 1940, 1952, 1962, 1973, 1982.

1980 Census of Population, Volume **1**: *Characteristics of the Population*, Issued March 1982, US Department of Commerce, Washington DC: Government Printing Office.

* In 1980 Mexicans were no longer counted as whites.

In spite of the general support for the Chinese people, anti-Chinese political agitation and violence increased throughout California during the economic depression of the 1870s. The Chinese were excluded from the American labor movement, especially after the Chinese Exclusion Act of 1882 was passed. Without the political and civil rights granted to other residents and to all citizens, Chinese workers became the favorite scapegoat of demagogues and politicians. Depression, unemployment, and falling wages were repeatedly blamed on the Chinese. People were led to accept the infamous slogan, 'Chinese must go!' Racism and xenophobia motivated Americans to deny jobs to Asians, and forced the Chinese to leave the mines and other companies. The displacement of Chinese in the mines and commercial companies persuaded them to seek employment in agricultural regions of Northern California, such as Yolo. This resulted in additional Chinese population increases during 1870, 1880, 1890 in Yolo County. Chinese were first hired to do all kinds of menial services. White employers quickly became aware of the great value of the Chinese workers, and used them to open restaurants, hotels, canneries, laundries and garment industries. By 1910 Chinese occupied important positions in various businesses. In the twentieth century even labor unions began to court Chinese members. There were slogans such as the following posted throughout Yolo County:

If you want to join a union.
Step in and come along
We'll all be glad to have you.
We're many thousand strong
Come join the CLO! Join the CLO!
(Wei Min She, 1974:29)

Upward mobility motivated the Chinese to leave Yolo County for new jobs in San Francisco and other parts of the country, and other immigrants, such as Hispanics and Japanese, moved in to take their entry-level jobs. In 1890, there were only five Japanese, but by 1930 there were 1423. After the Japanese bombed Pearl Harbor on December 7, 1941, Americans became increasingly distrustful of Japanese living in the United States. They closed their Japanese schools and asked them to leave. Then, on March 27, 1942, President Roosevelt issued Executive Order 9066 which ordered all Japanese, whether alien or US-born, to be placed in detention (concentration) camps. The Japanese had to leave their property within seven days. Many of the Japanese who were former Yolo residents were imprisoned at a camp in Tule Lake California, and remained there until September 7, 1945, when the war was ended by the Japanese surrender following the bombing of Hiroshima and Nakasaki.

Mexican Immigrants

Historically, Yolo was Spanish territory until the Mexican Independence of 1921, and a Mexican territory until the signing of the Guadalupe Hidalgo Treaty in 1848, when California and other Southwestern states became part of the United States. But the Mexican population of California in 1848 was very small. It was not until the first two decades of this century that Mexicans had a significant population increase in Yolo County. This increase is associated with the devastation and brutality caused by Mexican Revolutions and World War I. The economic crisis that followed World War I resulted also in policies restricting the inflow of Mexican immigrants perceived to be in competition for jobs with the already established Anglo-American community. Massive deportations of Mexicans in Texas, Arizona and California were planned and executed, and at times they resulted in the exile of persons born in what is today Southwestern America.

From 1942 to 1965 there is another substantial increase in the numbers of Mexicans coming to California. They were attracted by the *Bracero Program* adopted by the US and Mexico. This program attracted to the US Mexican agricultural laborers protected by contracts and government supervision. After 1965, the Mexican population had been increasing steadily, even after the *Bracero Program* was terminated. The main reason for the growth of the Mexican population in rural California is that many *Braceros* became residents and others stayed in the country illegally. Table 3.4 shows that most minorities in Yolo County were poorer than the majority whites. The living conditions of many minorities were difficult. The authors have witnessed the contemporary practice of single room habitations for entire families, and even the use of temporary shelters for migrant workers. In contrast, however, it is significant that the percentage of minority households that own homes is very high, although whites have a larger number of households living in homes owned by them. Table 3.5 shows the differential

Table 3.4: Population above and below poverty level by race and ethnicity (1980 census) Yolo County

	Population	Above	Below	Percentage
Total	107,188	90,195	16,993	15.1
White	88,890	76,359	12,531	14.1
Black	1930	1374	556	40.4
Indian	1310	981	329	25.1
Asian	4414	3301	1113	25.2
Hispanic	19,989	15,461	3528	17.6

Source: US Census of Population and Housing, 1980: Summary Tape File 3A prepared by the Bureau of the Census (machine-readable data file). Washington, DC: US Bureau of the Census, 1981.

Table 3.5: Households by race and Spanish origin (1980 census), Yolo County

	Households	Per cent of Renters
White	35,331	43.7
Black	725	65.8
American Indian, Eskimo, Aleut	396	62.1
Asian and Pacific Islanders	1427	55
Spanish Origin	5283	55.8
Other	3425	60.2
Total	41,304	46

Source: US Census of Population and Housing, 1980: Summary Tape File 1A prepared by the Bureau of the Census (machine-readable data file). Washington, DC: US Bureau of the Census, 1981.

percentage of rentals among the various county populations. The ethnic diversity of the Yolo county is remarkable. The white population (excluding the Mexican population) was only 77 per cent (see Table 3.3) of the total population. On the other hand, the Mexican population had increased to 16,116 (14.2 per cent) of the total county's population, and the total nonwhite population had increased to 26,076 (23 per cent) of the total county's population. The total number of households (see Table 3.5) in the county is 41,305; of them 35,331 are of whites (85.5 per cent), 5973 of nonwhites (14.4 per cent — including 5283 Mexican households). Clearly, the nonwhite households have a larger number of persons per household.

Schools in Yolo County

There were elementary schools in Yolo County even before statehood. According to May E. Dexter-Henshall, the first school in the county was build in 1847, and was located one mile above William Gordon's rancho on Cache Creek. George W. Tyler was the pioneer teacher in this school. The second one was in the boom town of Fremont in 1849. Miss Matilda McCord taught the children there. There was a private school at Washington (Broderick) in the early days. It was probably the third in the County. But by 1851 only one school remained in the County to

Table 3.6: *Information on Four Yolo County Schools, 1854 and 1855.*

Year	Cache Creek (2 schools)	Washington (1 school)	Cottonwood (1 school)	Total
1854	191	—	91	282 students
1855	278	64	95	437 students
1855	18	11	—	29 orphans
1855*	$333	$77	$114	$524
1855	5	2	4	11 teachers**
TOTAL 1855 school expenditures				$1543.50

* Building, rent and repairs of school houses
** Salaries per month per teacher between $60.00–100.00

Source: Adapted from County Records and information in Gregory, 1913, and composed of information found in *The Illustrated Atlas and History of Yolo County, California, Containing a History of California from 1513 to 1850, A History of Yolo County from 1825 to 1880, with Statistics of Agriculture, Education, Churches, Elections, Lithographic Views of Farms, Residences, Mills, and Color Portraits of Well-known Citizens and the Official County Map.* (Winterburn, 1879) San Francisco, CA: De Pue & Co.

serve seventy-five children. In 1853, there were two schools, one in Washington and the other in Yolo City (now Woodland) with a total enrollment of 143 pupils. In 1854, there were three schools in the county, probably located in Woodland, Washington, and the Reed near Knights Landing (Gregory, 1913:132–133).

In 1855, S.N. Mering was elected County School Superintendent. His report regarding school matters was the first to be preserved in the county school records. It showed that there were four schoolhouses: two in the Cache Creek District, one in Washington and one in Cottonwood. These schoolhouses were built and maintained with local funds. Teachers earned between $60.00 and $100.00 per month. The total Yolo County school budget was $1543.50 with a total student population of 437, a total of eleven teachers, and a ratio of forty students to a teacher. The two schools at Cache Creek had almost twice as many students as the other two schools together (see Table 3.6). According to historian Coil, in 1856, when Mr Nicholas Wyckoff became school superintendent, there were two additional schools in the County. The Cottonwood area had increased its student population and had been divided into two schools. The Woodland school also significantly increased its student population in the second half of the nineteenth century and became the largest in Yolo County (quoted in Russell, 1940:245).

The Foundation of Woodland City

Woodland is situated in the center of the rich Cache Creek delta in the center of the County. Over the years, a number of irrigation ditch systems were built to divert water from Cache Creek to water 15,000 acres of fertile land surrounding the town. Historians (Gregory, 1913; Russell, 1940; Larkey and Walter, 1987; and others) point out the ecological richness and beautiful surroundings of Woodland at the turn of the century. In the 1990s, Woodland remains the center of an extremely productive region conveniently situated one-half an hour from

Sacramento and two hours from San Francisco by car. Interstate I-5, the main north-south freeway, passes through Woodland, and other roads, such as State Road 113, a four-lane, divided highway, connects Woodlands with I-80, the main east-west transcontinental freeway.

Over the last hundred years, the beautiful city of Woodland has become the pride of residents of Yolo County. However, never was the glamour of the city greater than in the mid-1890s when other cities, such as Sacramento, were still very small and did not have some of the cultural attractions of Woodland, particularly its popular opera house.

According to Gregory (1913) white settlers, attracted by the fertile soil and mild climate, came to the bank of Cache Creek more than one hundred years ago. Uncle Johnny Morris and his family were the first to come. The Morris family was fascinated by a beautiful grove of wide-spreading oak trees south of the Creek and decided to make it their home. Probably Morris was the first white man to settle in the Woodland area. Henry Wyckoff was another founder of Woodland. In the Winter of 1853, he opened a store he called Yolo City on what is now Court Street. After that several businesses were established in town. A. Weaver was probably the second man to establish a business in Woodland (Gregory, 1913:94).

Among the early settlers was also Major Frank S. Freeman, who bought Wyckoff's store in 1857. He preempted 160 acres of land bounded by what are now the railroad tracks, Main Street, College Street and Beamer Street, and he offered free lots to persons willing to clear the land and build a home within three months. In 1860, Freeman undertook to lay out a town that he envisioned as a future trading center for one of the richest grain growing counties in the nation, thus establishing Woodland. To promote the building of the city as a great trading center, Freeman established a number of shops: blacksmith, harness and butcher shops, a grist mill, hardware store, tin shop, dry goods shop, and clothing and grocery stores, then, sold them to merchants (Gregory, 1913:94–96).

In 1861, Major Freeman circulated a petition among the inhabitants asking the federal government to establish a post office at Woodland, California. The name Woodland was suggested by Mrs Freeman for the groves of oak trees which dominated the landscape. The oaks which gave charm to the green landscape grew almost as tall as the redwoods of the coast forest. Although only a few of the old oak trees remain, the name Woodland is a reminder of that vanished splendor:

> The site of the city was originally covered by groves of white-oak trees. Their long drooping branches swept the tassels of the wild oats which grew beneath, and gave an indescribable charm to the landscape. They were surpassed in height only by the redwoods of the coast forest. Few of these noble trees remain, but the memory of their vanished splendor survives in the name of "Woodland" bestowed upon the city of Mrs J.S. Freeman, the wife of its founder (Thompson, 1902:3–4).

Major Freeman played a prominent role in the early development of Woodland; he recorded the first plat of the city on June 25, 1863. The northern portion of present-day Woodland was divided into blocks, lots and streets. This plat was the basis for future locations of buildings and homes. Sixth street was designated as the Eastern boundary; College street was the Western boundary; North street marked the Northern city limit, and Main street was the Southern city limit. By

1870, the population of Woodland was estimated at around 1600 residents. By that time, unfortunately, most of the oaks which were the pride of the city had disappeared (City of Woodland, Data Base, December 20, 1988).

According to Woodland historians (Larkey and Walters, 1987, Gregory, 1913 and Russell, 1940) the pioneers of Yolo County almost immediately established churches to provide for the spiritual needs of the settlers. The first service in Woodland was conducted in 1850 under an oak tree by the Rev. Thomas A. Ish, a Cumberland Presbyterian minister. The Cumberland Presbyterians erected a Union Church in 1855 in the center of what is now the Woodland Cemetery. The Union Church was used by other denominations for several years.

The Church of Christ was organized in 1854 by Joshua Lawson, who was its first minister. He was succeeded by the Rev. J.N. Pendegast, who was the church's minister and a civic leader in Woodland for twenty-five years. The congregation worshipped in the Union Church from 1855 to 1968, when they erected a small brick church on the Hesperian College campus on Bush Street. In 1889 a large church was erected at College and Oak streets. This building was damaged in the 1902 earthquake, and was replaced by a new building on the same site in 1919.

The Methodists purchased a store building in 1865 on First Street in Woodland to use as a church. Their building had previously been the county Poorhouse, which they bought for $125. Two years later, the Methodists built themselves a brick church on Main Street, and later built another church at North and Second streets. Finally, in 1925 they built a larger church on the same site that is still in use today.

By the 1880s, there were many churches in Woodland. The United Brethren Church, which had been founded in 1858 on the Sacramento riverbank, expanded into Woodland in the 1860s. The First Congregational Church of Woodland was formed in 1865, and St. Luke's Episcopal Church was established in Woodland in 1872. The Seventh Day Adventist Church was established in 1874, and in 1882 the Baptists built a beautiful church building at College and Lincoln streets. The first Roman Catholic Church was dedicated in 1869 (Russell, 1940:265–277).

Russell described the Woodland of 1869 as a town with 2500 people:

> . . . served by five churches, two schools, including Hesperian College, seven hotels, five livery stables, five boot and shoe stores, six grocery stores, five hardware stores, four barber shops, five blacksmith shops, three photograph galleries, a score of lawyers, several doctors and six Chinese washhouses (Russell, 1940:197).

In 1886, under the leadership of Ann Blake Ryder and Alice Armstrong, a group of local women, united in their love of literature and desire for higher cultural opportunities, began to meet to read aloud and discuss Shakespearean works; their efforts resulted in the formation of the Woodland Shakespeare Club, which was the second oldest women's literary club in California (Gregory, 1913:167). The Woodland Shakespeare Club is still active today. However, the focus is not only on Shakespeare, but also, on other great writers. Club members meet once a month from October to April.

Cultural activities increased as more sophisticated people moved to Woodland. The first opera house was built in 1885 on the west side of Second Street between Main and Court Street. It was a small structure with rich furnishings, four boxes and a sloping floor that gave full view of all parts of a fairly large stage. According to Russell, it was opened on February 16, 1885, with a presentation of Shakespeare's, 'The Merchant of Venice' with a cast headed by Louise Davenport and W.E. Sheridan, then considered the foremost Shakespearean actors in the United States (Russell, 1940:205). The entrance to the theater opened on Second Street, and off the lobby was a tiny oyster shop which became famous in the early life of the community. The theater was constructed by a corporation which maintained it until a fire destroyed the building in 1892. D.N. Hershey then took over the property and built a much larger theater house, the stage being the largest north of San Francisco. A spring floor to place over the seats for dancing parties was also constructed. From that time Woodland enjoyed the best plays and heard the best actors as they passed through on their way to Oregon or to San Francisco. The practice was to make Woodland a stop-over for rehearsal of plays.

High school graduation exercises were also held there. In 1913, during one of these exercises, a woman fell from a window of the opera house and suffered a broken leg. She obtained a $2000 compensation in judgment against the Hershey family. The family refused to pay and closed the opera house. The compensation was later negotiated and a compromise was reached, but the Hershey family refused to reopen the opera house (Russell, 1940:205). In 1971, the Yolo County Historical Society purchased the building, declared it a state historical monument and gave it to the State of California in 1980. The following year, with federal and state grants and private gifts and donations from businesses and individuals, the restoration of the building began. Finally, in January 1989 the Woodland Opera House reopened for public visits.

Movie theaters became popular in the 1920s as movies took the place of road shows and classic plays. The first movie house was established by a Mr. Hunt on First Street between Main and Bush streets. In the 1940s, Woodland had at least three large movie theaters where customers could see the latest Hollywood productions. In the 1990s, there was a triple-screen movie theater on Main Street, and there is a new movie theater at County Fair Mall with six small theaters inside.

Some of the earliest buildings constructed were hotels which housed the many people who visited Woodland for business and pleasure. The first hotel in Woodland was the Exchange, a brick structure located at the corner of Main and Second streets, built in 1862 by E.H. Baker. This burned down in the disastrous fire of 1892 (see p. 66). A year later Dr G.H. Jackson built the old Julian Hotel on the same site. In 1880 Christian Sieber built a second hotel, the Pacific House, devoted to the comforts of working men and the hired help of surrounding farms. Three years later the Byrns Hotel was erected at the corner of Main and College, presently the site of the Hotel Woodland. This was the most imposing building of its day with three stories and a tower, and it was the scene of the most splendid social events in the community. It boasted two bathrooms on each floor and bedrooms decorated and furnished to please the rich. Thirty-five years later, during the influenza epidemic of 1918, this famed old hotel became the flu hospital of Woodland. This was its last public service, because within a few months after the influenza was under control, the hotel was condemned and demolished to make way for the modern Hotel Woodland (Russell, 1940:205–206).

A review of the history of Woodland City needs to include the growth of the Woodland City Government. According to documents dating back to 1871, the City of Woodland, incorporated in 1871, is a general law City under provisions of the State of California Government Code. As such, the citizens of the city regularly elect a five-member City Council to represent them in determining the services and regulations to be probed by the City for its residents. In performing this role for the citizens of the City of Woodland, the City Council holds regular and special public meetings, and investigates various matters pertaining to the health, safety and welfare of all Woodlanders. The City Council employs a full-time City manager to implement and administer Council decisions and appoints a City Attorney as the City's legal advisor. So the City Manager acts as the administrative head of the City organization.

Woodlanders for over 100 years have taken great pride in their public library. The first city library in Yolo County was built with funds from the Carnegie Foundation in 1874. The library was first privately managed and later turned to the city in 1891. The present library, a Mission-style design by William H. Weeks, was built in 1905 with $10,000 provided by Andrew Carnegie. Additions were made to the building in 1915, 1927 and 1985–88. According to historian Gregory (1913:161–164), in 1905 an invalid orphan boy living outside the city of Woodland, who had finished reading all the books in his school library, wrote to the Woodland Library board asking permission to read Woodland Library books without the usual fee charged those living outside the city limits. The County library board solved the problem quickly by paying the fees themselves and granting the youngster free access to all the books. By the end of the following month, however, the board was flooded with a number of similar requests from other County children. It soon became almost impossible to care for all such requests by paying the library fees out of their own pockets. Shortly after, the California Library Association and the State Librarian were informed of the way Yolo County had attempted to meet the reading needs of rural children. They were so impressed that they decided that the people living in distant parts of any county should have libraries if they wanted them. This was the beginning of County Free Library System. It was not until 1909, however, that the first County Free Library Law for the State of California was passed. That law permitted a County Board of Supervisors to contract with city libraries for service, thereby assuming the responsibilities of a county library.

Economic Development of Woodland

The wonderful fertility of the soil and the advantages of mild climate contributed to the pioneers' success in agriculture. Settled as an agricultural community around 1853, Woodland grew into a major business and commercial center for the outlying rural communities in Yolo County. Money earned in the gold fields of California financed the purchases of much of the farm land around Woodland. A variety of crops were grown, such as wheat, rice, barley, tobacco, vegetables and grapes. When Woodland became the seat of Yolo County government in 1862, the town began to grow. In 1869 with the establishment of a bank, where farmers could deposit their money, and the advent of the railroad, the town entered upon a new era of business and social activity. Buildings were erected rapidly, business developed and new people sought a home in the thriving new town. Several wineries produced wine, vinegar and brandy, and there was even a local brewery. The livestock industry also had an important role in the area. The Woodland creamery was organized in the 1880s by citizens who recognized the local need for dairy products.

Woodland has benefitted greatly from the success of the agricultural industry by serving as a center for banking, shops, education and in some instances by housing farmers and their help. Another important impact on the community and industry has been the invention and manufacturing of farming equipment. Local inventions included the centrifugal pump in the late 1800s and the Marvin Landplane in 1936 (at Knights Landing). The Best Tractor was developed by the Best family who lived in Woodland, although the tractor was actually manufactured in Oakland. Today several farm equipment dealers are located in Woodland and provide employment and tax revenue for the city while serving the outlying farms. The railroad played an important role in the development of the community, for it brought improved means for transporting agricultural crops to market and for obtaining goods needed by local residents. The first railroad connecting Davisville (now the City of Davis) to Woodland was constructed in 1869. The line was later extended northeast to Marysville, and in 1875 a northern line was built to Oregon.

On July 1, 1892 the worst fire in Woodland's history had completely destroyed two blocks of business houses and one residential section of the city. The fire broke out in John Elston's Drug Store on Main Street between First and Second Streets. Reconstruction of the city's commercial center was delayed because of a world-wide economic depression for several years. By the turn of the century, however, Woodland's economy had recovered, and the city witnessed a continued expansion in construction and population. By 1930, the city boasted of an area of 1.63 square miles and a population of 5542 persons. This growth continued in the 1940s but was slowed down during the war years. At that time, Woodland was a quiet, prosperous town of about 6637 people (Russell, 1940:207–217).

After World War II Woodland expanded its services considerably. According to Larkey and Walters (1987:96–97), in 1947 the city passed a $400,000 bond issue and enlarged a number of public buildings: city hall, jail, fire station, a community swimming pool. Subsequently, the city produced a master plan, zoning areas for residential and commercial development, and encouraged a number of business to invest in Woodland:

> By 1970 Woodland's population had more than doubled since 1950, to 20,677. During the next decade more city services were developed, the city's master plan was revised, more schools were built, new parks were developed, city hall was remodeled, large shopping centers constructed, and the entire northeast area expanded . . . (Larkey and Walters, 1987:96–97).

One of the most recent and important constructions was the County Fair Mall, which in 1986 became the most important shopping center of the County. Additionally, in the last decade Woodland has become a bedroom community for a number of persons working in Sacramento City, as well as a service area, including hotels and motels, for the larger Sacramento Metropolitan Airport. According to the 1980 Census, 62.8 per cent of Woodland's labor force worked in Woodland and an additional 19 per cent worked elsewhere in Yolo County. Consult Table 3.13 which indicates the geographic area of employment of principal wage earners living in Woodland. Woodland continues to provide employment for a majority of its residents.

Population Diversity and First Chicano Settlers

The city of Woodland is the second largest incorporated city in the County with an estimated population of 39,800 persons as of January 1, 1990. The following tables show the population growth of Woodland from 1870–1990 (see Table 3.7).

Table 3.7: Population growth statistics of Woodland

Year	Woodland	per cent Net Increase per Decade
1870	1600	—
1880	2257	41
1890	3069	36.1
1900	2886	6
1910	3187	10.4
1920	4147	30.1
1930	5542	33.6
1940	6637	19.8
1950	9386	41.4
1960	13,524	41.4
1970	20,677	52.9
1980	30,235	46.2
1990	39,800	31.6

Sources: 1990 figures are taken from *Population estimates of California cities and Counties: Report 90-E1*, published by the California State Department of Finance; Population Research Unit and the SACOG Population Model; 1880–1970 US Census Data.

The opportunity for farming brought many nationalities to the area. The Patwin Indians who were hired or enslaved to work as agricultural workers on the farms were replaced by Chinese laborers who came to Woodland in the 1870s after the construction of the transcontinental railroad was completed. The Chinese worked on levee construction, fence building and farming. Some Chinese settled in Woodland and became moderately successful in the restaurant business and laundry services. Dead Cat Alley, the site of the Chinese laundries in the 1940s became the center of the Chinese community and their commercial activities. After the early 1990s, though, employment opportunities for the Chinese began to dwindle, and the Chinese population declined significantly.

The Japanese were first brought to Byron Jackson's Yolanda Ranch in the late nineteenth century as farm laborers. Some Japanese started their own businesses in town, such as barber shops and secondhand stores. There was a great deal of prejudice, and Japanese felt handicapped by the policies which prevented them from becoming citizens and acquiring land. Some of them, however, acquired land and other properties using their United States-born children's names. World War II marks the peak of discrimination against the Japanese, when Americans witnessed the imprisonment of Japanese (including families and young children born in the United States) in detainment camps. Many were forced to sell their land and possessions overnight to speculators. The Japanese who lived in Woodland

Yali Zou

Table 3.8: Population of Woodland by race/ethnicity — 1980

Race	Number	Per cent
White (Non-Hispanic)	17,923	59
Hispanic (Mexican, Puerto Rican, Cuban, Latin American)	6850	23
African American	339	1.1
American Indian	282	.9
Eskimo	1	.003
Aleut	15	.05
Japanese	168	.6
Chinese	88	.3
Filipino	114	.4
Korean	20	.07
Asian Indian	106	.4
Vietnamese	27	.09
Hawaiian	18	.06
Guamanian	4	.01
Samoan	1	.003
Other	4276	14.1
TOTAL	30,235	

Source: The City of Woodland Data Base, December 20, 1988. Consult also the Bureau of the Census for 1980 (see full reference at the end).

Table 3.9: Composition and characteristics of the population in Woodland

Year	White	African American	Chinese	Japanese	American Indian	Other	Total
1940	5872	96	0	0	0	669	6637
1950	9006	152	0	0	138	90	9386
1960	13,251	136	60	37	26	14	13,524
1970	19,870	234	51	98	111	313	20,677
1980*	17,923	339	88	168	282	11,329	30,235

* In 1980 Hispanics were no longer counted among the Whites.

Table 3.10: Persons of Spanish origin in Woodland — 1980

Origin	Number	Per cent
Woodland population	30,235	100
Mexican	6101	20.2
Puerto Rican	58	.19
Cuban	57	.19
Other Hispanic	634	2.13
Total Hispanic	6850	22.71

Source: 1980 Census of Population, Volume 1, Characteristics of the Population, Issued March 1982, US Department of Commerce. Washington, DC: Government Printing Office.

Table 3.11: Employment by industry in Woodland

Industry		Per cent of Total
Agriculture, forestry, fisheries and mining	1020	7.8
Construction	664	5.1
Non-durable goods manufacturing	1015	7.8
Durable goods manufacturing	759	5.8
Transportation	608	4.7
Communications and other public utilities	356	2.7
Wholesale trade	682	5.2
Retail trade	2294	17.6
Finance, insurance, real estate	780	6.0
Business and repair services	514	4.0
Personal, entertainment, recreation services	375	2.9
Health services	1113	8.6
Education services	1312	10.1
Other professional and related services	535	4.1
Public administration	995	7.6
Total	13,022	100.0

Source: *The City of Woodland Data Base*, December 20, 1988 (see complete reference at the end of the chapter).

lost everything, and very few of them returned to Yolo County. (See Tables 3.8, 3.9 and 3.10).

The 1950s and 60s were years of increased agricultural activities. Filipinos first and later Mexican hired hands provided much of the farm labor needed. The *Bracero Program* during World War II and throughout the 1950s, brought large numbers of Mexican Nationals into Yolo County to work on the farms and orchards. Many became permanent residents and raised their families in Woodland, Winters, Davis and Sacramento Valley. Today, Hispanics account for approximately 20 per cent of the city's population. According to the Census data of 1980, in a total city population of 30,235, the Hispanics of Woodland have increased to 6850, of whom 6101 are from Mexico. Thus Hispanics in 1980 constituted about 23 per cent of the total city population, and the white population was over 70 per cent of the total.

The Woodland residents who are employed (and alluded to later in Table 3.13) are divided into two categories: those working inside of the Sacramento Metropolitan Area (including Yolo, Sacramento and Placer counties), and those working in areas outside of the Sacramento Metropolitan Area (Solano County, Stockton, Oakland, and elsewhere).

The 1980 Census indicated that Woodland had a labor force of 14,557 persons (civilians 16-years-old and over who were either at work, with a job but not at work, or unemployed). From the total labor force 13,022 persons were employed, and 1535 persons (or 10.5 per cent) were unemployed. (Table 3.12 indicates employment per industry in Woodland in 1980.)

Persons employed in Woodland industries are presented in Tables 3.11 and 3.12. The largest number of jobs are administrative (clerical and managerial); many are employed in county and school offices. There are a substantial number of service jobs (protective, household, repair, etc.). The number of persons who work outside Woodland and live in Woodland has increased steadily in recent

Table 3.12: Occupations of employed members of labor force in Woodland — 1980

Occupation		Per cent of Total
Executive, administrative, managerial	1394	10.7
Professional specialty	1343	10.3
Technicians and related support	351	2.7
Sales	1352	10.4
Administrative support (clerical)	2397	18.4
Private household	48	0.4
Protective service	269	2.1
Service except protective and household	1511	11.6
Farming, forestry and fishing	786	6.0
Production, craft and repair services	1682	13.9
Machine operators, assemblers and inspectors	803	6.2
Transportation and material moving	645	4.9
Equipment cleaners, helpers and laborers	441	3.4
Total	13,022	100.0

Source: *US 1980 Census*, which also indicates the geographic area of employment of
principal wage earners living in Woodland. Woodland provides employment for
62.8 per cent of its residents, while most others work in Davis or the remainder
of Yolo County.

years. One reason for this is that home prices in Woodland have tended to be
substantially lower than in the neighboring communities of Davis and Sacramento
(see Table 3.13 next page). The first Americans and Mexicans settled in Yolo
County in the 1840s when the area was under Mexican rule. Some of the early
Mexican settlers came from New Mexico, which was then Mexican territory.
Among these individuals were Juan Manuel Vaca and Juan Felipe Peña and their
wives and children, who in 1843 were awarded land south of Putah Creek called
Rancho los Putos by the Mexican government. The same year Francisco, Santiago
and Demesio Berryessa were granted Rancho Canada de Capay in the Capay
Valley.

After the US-Mexican War, despite the provisions of the treaty, the land
grants had to be confirmed by the US government. Many of the land grants
issued in the 1840s were never recognized 'resulting in injustices and hardships for
many of California's earliest Spanish-speaking settlers' (Larkey, 1969:15). Other
land grants were lost to squatters who had come to Yolo County after the Gold
Rush. Furthermore, some Mexicans lost their land due to boundary disputes.

The loss of land titles by some of the original Mexican settlers and the development of agriculture in Yolo County had a significant impact on the County's
Mexican population. They went from owning land to becoming hired hands. The
Yolo County area became a significant wheat producer in Northern California
during the 1870s and 1880s, and it required additional manual labor. 'Seasonal
demand of the wheat crop was so enormous that outside help/labor was needed
to supplement regular year-round supply; several Mexicans were hired as cooks
or field hands' (McGowan, 1961:250).

The Mexican population of the area was not only relegated to menial jobs at
that time, but was also discriminated against. Nativism, a philosophy which states
that Anglo Saxons were 'entitled to the first fruits of the land and other groups

Table 3.13: Place of employment of population of Woodland — 1980

Area	Number	Per cent
A. Inside Sacramento SMSA*		
(Yolo, Sacramento, Placer Counties)		
Woodland	7813	62.8
Davis	847	6.8
Remainder Yolo County	1524	12.2
Sacramento City	727	5.8
Remainder Sacramento County	248	2.0
Placer County	50	0.4
Subtotal	11,209	
B. Outside Sacramento SMSA		
Fairfield	41	0.3
Vacaville	21	0.2
Remainder Solano County	112	0.9
Stockton SMSA	13	0.1
Oakland	18	0.1
Other San Francisco-Oakland SMSA	24	0.2
Worked elsewhere	195	1.6
Subtotal	424	
Place of work not reported	809	6.5
Total	12,432	100

Source: The City of Woodland Data Base, December 20, 1988 (see complete reference at the end of the chapter).

* SMSA = Standard Metropolitan Statistical Area.

should be content with the leftovers' (McGowan, 1961:321), was persistently practiced in Yolo County. This attitude was practiced during the gold rush years through the Foreign Miners Tax law, which placed a special tax on non-Anglos and '. . . was enforced primarily on Mexicans and Chinese' (McGowan, 1961:321). The Mexican population of Yolo County, it appears, experienced many of the same injustices as other Mexicans in California, as described by Estrada, Garcia, Macias, and Maldonado:

> By the turn of the century, Mexicans had been largely dispossessed of their property. Relegated to a lower-class status, they were overwhelmingly dispossessed, landless laborers, politically and economically impotent . . . long-term residents of the region were reduced to being aliens in their native land. The common theme that united all Mexicans was their conflict with Anglo society. The dominant society, profoundly racist, found it entirely reasonable to relegate Mexicans to a colonial status within the United States, 1981:109).

Mexican Migration (1900–1930)

The Sacramento Valley, and Yolo County in particular, became an important agricultural center in Northern California. Estrada, Garcia, Macias, and Maldonado report that agriculture played an important '. . . procreative role. It helped create industries for the processing, canning, packing and crating of agricultural products' (1981:111). Canneries and irrigation changed the face and economy of the Sacramento Valley during the last decade of the nineteenth century and first decade of the twentieth (McGowan, 1961).

The economic conditions created by the advancements in agriculture and two world events accelerated the migration of Mexicans into the Sacramento Valley, and Yolo County in particular, between 1910 and 1930. The Mexican population began to appear in Yolo County in substantial numbers during the second and third decades of the twentieth century. The emigration of Mexicans to the United States was a direct result of two events. Mexico was devastated by a civil war and revolutions between 1910 and 1921, and the United States became involved in World War I.

A significant number of people left Mexico and migrated to the United States in order to avoid the social, economic and political chaos created by Mexican Revolutions. The United States welcomed such immigration because the country was in desperate need of hand labor. The demands and losses created by the war and the rapid agricultural development in the Southwest required additional agricultural workers to staff advancement projects in California. McGowan, reports that 'With the introduction of irrigation, orchards, sugar beets and tomatoes, the problem of farm labor became more serious' (1961:203). The Sacramento Valley, including Yolo County, experienced an agricultural labor shortage in 1918. This shortage, however, was relieved by the importation of Mexican workers. 'Mexicans formed a third group, which began to appear in the Valley in substantial numbers during the 1919 harvest. By 1930 the census counted 9695 in the Valley, with 4624 in Sacramento, and 1984 in Yolo county' (McGowan, 1961:308).

The new Mexican immigrants to Yolo County and the Sacramento Valley faced discriminating practices against them. 'Mexicans were thought to be inferior beings and inherently unassimilated, and were forced into a dual wage system . . . received low wages' (Estrada, *et al.*, 1981:112). McGowan describes the racist sentiments of the area and era in the following way:

> Nativism, ever a feature of California society since 1850, took a new twist after 1884 . . . racism in the Sacramento Valley had been previously a matter of agricultural labor, although in the beginning it seems to have arisen from cultural differences. Attitudes toward the various nationalities or racial groups seems to have depended on the economic advantage that could or could not be derived from them (McGowan, 1961:141).

As stated earlier, the conditions that Mexicans faced in the Sacramento Valley and Northern California were not very hospitable nor positive. Newspaper stories about the Mexican community during the period of time are almost nonexistent. However, the very few that do exist are very negative in nature. During 1929 and 1930, the *Woodland Democrat* several times referred to Mexicans in the context of crime and drug abuse, for example, the front page headlines on July 25, 1929: 'Mexican Arrested After Battle', on November 22, 1929: 'Mexican Killed in Lodi Knife Battle'; on November 23, 1929: 'Mexican Denies Willow Robbery' and on January 14, 1930: 'Mexican Stabbed in Liquor Fight'. The Anglos who became involved in criminal or illegal activities during the same period of time are not identified as such by the newspaper. Mexicans, blacks, Chinese and Filipinos who became involved in illegal activities are, however, identified by nationality or ethnic group either in the title of the article or in its content. This phenomenon illustrates the regional social attitudes of mainstream populations at the time, and the hardships endured by law-abiding Mexican families.

It is during this period (1918–1930) that the Mexican community in Yolo County, particularly around the Woodland area, began to make its presence known. Mexican immigrants included whole families, not just single males. The beginning of a Mexican community emerged during this period of time. It is reported that several original Mexican families settled in or near Woodland during this period. Some of them were as follows: Guerrero, Tafoya, Sosa, Lucero, Pico, Pena, Contreras, Montoya, Medina, Zaragoza, Martinez, Losoya, Espinoza, Rico, Sanchez, Sandoval and Casas. Some family members found employment as laborers in agriculture, others were employed in the railroad and sugar beet industries. In the following years other families continued to immigrate to the Woodland area. The social life in the Mexican community in and around Woodland evolved around family and cultural activities. The *compadrazgo* system was well at work; it was reported that they baptized each others' children, served as godfathers in marriages, attended social gatherings at each others' homes to celebrate birthdays, baptisms, marriages, or Mexican holidays. It became a very closed, family-oriented community.

With this preliminary and brief introduction to the Mexican community, we approach our ethnohistorical and ethnographic account of an immigrant Chicano community in Woodland, that is, an account that will present, from the perspective of the members of the Chicano community, the social, cultural and political reality of Chicanos in Woodland, especially in their attempts to enter the mainstream Woodland community. The study in the following chapters provides a longitudinal, broad interpretation of critical events in the life of the Chicano families leading to the critical role they played in Woodland politics and education. The link between the past and present Chicano communities is understandable in the analysis of the organizations that permitted Chicanos to survive culturally, understand the political process, and play a significant role in decision-making and policy formulation. The focus of our study is primarily on the political transformational process that changed the status of Chicanos from castelike to active members of the city and even its leaders.

References

CALIFORNIA STATE DEPARTMENT OF FINANCE (1990) *Report 90-E1* Population Research Unit and the SACOG Population Model.
City of Woodland Data Base, December 20, 1988, Woodland City Council, Woodland Planning Commission, Community Development Department.
ESTRADA, F.L., GARCIA, F.C., MACIAS, F.R. and MALDONADO, L. (1981) 'Chicanos in the United States: A history of exploitation and resistance', *Daedalus Journal of the American Academy of Arts and Sciences*, **110**(2), pp. 103–31.
GREGORY, T.J. (1913) *History of Yolo County, California*, Los Angeles, CA: Historic Record Company.
LARKEY, L.J. (1969) *Davisville 68: The History of the City of Davis, Yolo County California*, Davis, CA: Davis Historical and Landmark Commission.

LARKEY, J.L. and WALTERS, S. (1987) *Yolo County Land of Changing Patterns*, Sacramento, CA: Windsor Publications, Inc.

McGOWAN, J. (1961) *History of the Sacramento Valley*, **II**, New York, NY: Lewis Historical Society.

RUSSELL, WILLIAM C. (Ed.) (1940) *History of Yolo County: Its Resources and Its People*, Woodland, California.

THOMPSON, R.A. (1902) *Woodland, Yolo County, California*, Reprinted from *Out West*, July, 1902.

UNITED STATES BUREAU OF THE CENSUS (1984) *1980 US Census*, Current Populations Report, Washington, DC: Government Printing Office.

UNITED STATES, DEPARTMENT OF COMMERCE, BUREAU OF THE CENSUS (1982) *Twentieth Census: 1980*, Characteristics of the Population, Washington, DC: Government Printing Press.

UNITED STATES, DEPARTMENT OF COMMERCE, BUREAU OF THE CENSUS (1973) *Nineteenth Census: 1970*, Characteristics of the population, Washington, DC: Government Printing Press.

UNITED STATES, DEPARTMENT OF COMMERCE, BUREAU OF THE CENSUS (1952) *Seventeenth Decennial Census: 1950*, Census of Population, Washington, DC: Government Printing Press.

UNITED STATES, DEPARTMENT OF COMMERCE, BUREAU OF THE CENSUS (1962) *Eighteenth Census: 1960*, Characteristics of the Population, Washington, DC: Government Printing Press.

UNITED STATES, DEPARTMENT OF INTERIOR, CENSUS OFFICE (1864) *Eighth Census: 1860*, Population of the United States, Washington, DC: Government Printing Press.

UNITED STATES, DEPARTMENT OF INTERIOR, CENSUS OFFICE (1872) *Ninth Census: 1870*, Population of the United States, Washington, DC: Government Printing Press.

UNITED STATES, DEPARTMENT OF INTERIOR, CENSUS OFFICE (1883) *Tenth Census: 1880*, Population of the United States, Washington, DC: Government Printing Press.

UNITED STATES, DEPARTMENT OF INTERIOR, CENSUS OFFICE (1895) *Eleventh Census: 1890*, Population of the United States, Washington, DC: Government Printing Press.

UNITED STATES, DEPARTMENT OF INTERIOR, CENSUS OFFICE (1901) *Twelfth Census: 1900*, Population of the United States, Washington, DC: Government Printing Press.

UNITED STATES, DEPARTMENT OF INTERIOR, CENSUS OFFICE (1913) *Thirteenth Census: 1910*, Population of the United States, Washington, DC: Government Printing Press.

UNITED STATES, DEPARTMENT OF INTERIOR, CENSUS OFFICE (1922) *Fourteenth Census: 1920*, Population of the United States, Washington, DC: Government Printing Press.

UNITED STATES, DEPARTMENT OF INTERIOR, CENSUS OFFICE (1931) *Fifteenth Census: 1930* Population of the United States, Washington, DC: Government Printing Press.

UNITED STATES, DEPARTMENT OF INTERIOR, CENSUS OFFICE (1940) *Sixteenth Census: 1940*, Population of the United States, Washington, DC: Government Printing Press.

WEI MIN SHE LABOR COMMITTEE (1974) *Chinese Working People in America: A Pictorial History*, San Francisco, CA: United Front Press.

WILLEY, R.W. (1966) *An Introduction to American Archaeology: Volume One, North and Middle America*, Englewood Cliffs, NJ: Prentice-Hall, Inc.

WINTERBURN, J. (1879) *The Illustrated Atlas and History of Yolo County, Containing A History of California from 1513 to 1850: A History of Yolo County from 1825 to 1880, with Statistics of Agriculture, Education, Churches, Elections, Lithographic Views of Farms, Residences, Mills and Color Portraits of Well-known Citizens, and the Official Country Map*, San Francisco, CA: De Pue & Company.

Chapter 4

Chicanos in Politics: Learning to Participate and Organize

Cirenio Rodriguez

This chapter documents the socio-historical transformation of an immigrant Mexican community in a Northern California rural town; it describes the dynamic process whereby the Mexican community gradually develops its own organizations and learns to function in the town's social and political system. The relative success of the Chicano community can be better understood from a socio-historical and ethnographic perspective. The Mexican community went from a politically and economically dispossessed and powerless position to a socially organized and politically empowered one. We describe and analyze critical events in the life of the Mexican community which contributed to its social, cultural, economic, and political transformation.

The presence of Mexicans in Yolo County predates the Mexican-American War, however, there were very few (see Chapter 3). The new settlers faced a foreign and hostile environment. One of the original settlers reported that Mexicans were not welcomed in the area and that some were refused housing rentals within the city limits, forcing them to live in the unincorporated rural areas of the city. *Compadrazgo* functioned as a civil and religious mechanism to maintain community cohesiveness and eventually developed, along with other cultural institutions, into a political instrument, thus encouraging Mexicans to participate actively in the decision-making processes and to take calculated risks in collective economic and political adventures.

The Depression: Deportations, Hardships and Resistance

The cohesiveness and continuity of the Mexican community was disrupted by the 1929 nation wide depression. Some of the Mexican families were repatriated to Mexico, and those that remained had a difficult time. A member of one of the original families reported that the depression caused many hardships among the families: 'There was no work; my husband and brother would buy and sell vegetables to the families in town and the women made bread and tamales and would also sell them' (Interviewee I, July 18, 1990).

The great depression caused many problems for the Mexican communities in the United States, including the Sacramento Valley. Estrada (*et al.*) (1981) reports that Mexican workers were singled out and blamed for the ills of the period.

Cirenio Rodriguez

Between 1929–1934 over 400,000 Mexicans, many of whom were US citizens, were repatriated to Mexico. 'Shipment to Mexico was a clear violation of both their civil and human rights' (Estrada *et al.*, 1981:118). *The Woodland Democrat* acknowledged on its editorial page on September 16, 1932, the practice of repatriation of US citizens, '. . . Many American-born children are being taken to their parents' motherland without any choice of their own' (p. 5). The Mexican workers who remained faced many difficult challenges. The cohesiveness of the Chicano community, their ingenuity, and resourcefulness made it possible for those who were left to overcome the hardships. It was reported that Mexican families helped themselves and the *compadrazgo* system was helpful and productive as well.

The depression in the Sacramento Valley hit the migrant workers the hardest; the problem was complicated by the significant increase of dust bowl migrants. 'The migrant workers were indeed in a sad state in the middle 1920s. A study of 753 migratory families indicated that as a family unit they had earned $381 in 1930 but only $289 in 1935' (McGowan, 1961:269).

There were some attempts to organize members of the Sacramento Valley Mexican and Spanish-speaking communities. The Cannery and Agricultural Industrial League attempted to organize migrant and farm workers from Yolo and Solano counties. It was reported that one of the strategies that such organizations used was to provide food to needy migrant and farmworkers. A common practice was to identify some local individuals with access to the local community. For example, in Woodland a Mexican person by the name of Mr Pancho Reynosa was involved in such activities. The conditions created by the depression and unemployment in the Sacramento Valley resulted in labor strife in 1932. One of the first labor disturbances that was reported occurred in the summer of 1932 near Winters. Over 300 unemployed fruit pickers camped in Putah Creek participated in a hunger march led by two students from the University of California at Davis and other members of the Cannery and Agricultural Industrial League. The Winters incident was forcefully suppressed by the local authorities, leading to the arrest and conviction of the leaders. It is interesting to note that some of the leaders were identified as outside agitators (*Woodland Democrat*, July 16, 1932). The conviction of the Winters Hunger March leaders was protested by its supporters. It was reported that soon after the convictions were announced, fourteen fires were started. The local newspaper reported them as 'revenge fires' (*Woodland Democrat*, July 21, 1932). It is interesting to note that some of those arrested and identified as possible leaders in Winters reappeared in a much publicized labor strike in Vacaville in November-December of 1932. One of the individuals arrested in Winters, John Lopez, was a resident of Vacaville, and reappeared as one of the key leaders in the Vacaville labor strike.

A group of farm workers from Vacaville (Solano County) organized a chapter of the Cannery and Agricultural Industrial League. The workers were unhappy with the working conditions and demanded an eight-hour day, a pay increase from $1.25 to $1.50 per day, and free transportation to and from work. The farmers refused, resulting in violent confrontations and accusations that Communists had infiltrated the union. Several Spanish surname individuals were reported to be involved. John Lopez was accused of stabbing a strike breaker and was arrested. He was also identified as one of the main organizers of the labor strike. The striking workers met in front of John Lopez's house to organize and hold a demonstration. The *Woodland Democrat* on December 5, 1932 reports a 'March led by a group of young girls carrying banners and chanting $1.50 an hour, 8 hours, and free transportation' (*Woodland Democrat*, Dec. 5, 1932, p. 1). Other Spanish surname individuals, residents of Vacaville, were reported to be present during the meetings/march and some were arrested: Max Rodriguez, A. Espinoza, James Melgar, and John Lopez were some of the Spanish surname individuals. The Vacaville labor strike was also suppressed and the blame was put squarely on the outside agitators' . . . who caused the impressionable Spanish workers and youth to join the union and participate in the labor disputes' (*Woodland Democrat*, December 9, 1932, p. 1).

Chicanos in Business and Social Institutions (1920–1930)

During the late 1920s and early 1930s, the Mexican community began to interact with American business, educational, legal and social institutions. It also coincides with the birth of a Mexican middle class. Some members of the Mexican community went into business by buying acreage, growing sugar beets and other agricultural products; others became labor contractors and provided lodging and meals to single male migrant workers. One of the surviving members of the original Mexican families describes how her family went into business: 'Mr. Tafoya provided a sugar beet field to my husband. In 1937 my husband bought a piece of land for $900. He was a labor contractor and had a labor camp in 1937.' The *Woodland Democrat*, in its October 16, 1929 issue, reported that a new cafe serving Mexican food was opened by N. J. Espinosa.

The sons and daughters of the Mexican immigrants attended public school as well as Catholic school. A member of one of the original families indicated that most of her brothers and sisters went to Catholic schools because her father thought that the public school system did not provide a good education. Public schools '. . . would not prepare us for college . . . if you were female, you took clerical and home economics courses. If you were male, you took workshop and mechanics . . . they never gave you a chance to better yourself as a Mexican.' The *Woodland Democrat*, on January 22, 1930, reported that twenty-nine children received grammar school diplomas (8th grade) and one of the graduates had a Spanish surname, Angelo Pinto. During this period of time the Woodland High School offered 'Americanization' classes to its immigrant community during the evenings.

On December 9, 1932, the local newspaper reported a meeting of the Woodland High School Spanish club. Several members of the Mexican community were identified as members of such organization. They included Jess Ramos, A. Lucero, and Thora Sosa. This article had several interesting features: it identified the Mexican community as Spanish celebrating Spanish cultural traditions, '. . . old Spanish customs will be observed tonight. Spanish dishes will be served. . . . Mrs. Marie Acosta, a local Spanish woman, will show students how to prepare enchiladas' (*Woodland Democrat*, Dec. 9, 1932, p. 1). Neither the students, the customs, nor the participants were recognized as Mexican, but as Spaniards. It is also important to note that the sons and daughters of some of the Mexican families were participating in organizations based around cultural activities.

Organizational life of the Mexican community in and around Woodland evolved around *El Comité de Beneficiencia Mexicana*. It was organized in 1937 by members of the original families that settled in the area in the 1920s. The purpose of *El Comité*, as it became known, was to provide protection for the Mexican community when one of its members died. It was reported that a person by the name of Lucio Perez started the first *Comité* in Santa Helena in 1936; the second chapter was organized in Knights Landing, and the third chapter in Woodland, California under the direction of Don Jose Sosa and Eusebio Rico in 1937. The *Comité* became one of the oldest and most successful organizations of the Chicano community. The *Comité* in Woodland evolved into a very significant organization. The organizational leadership was shared among several members of the Chicano community. In 1972 the president of the organization was Al Sosa, son of Jose Sosa, its founder. Under the direction of Al Sosa the *Comité* became involved in activities and issues other than providing fiscal assistance when one of its members died. It allotted a $250 scholarship to Mexican students in cooperation with *Comite Pro-Fiestas Patrias* and provided support to young Chicanos involved in the high school student MECHA organization and other groups (*Daily Democrat*, May 18, 1973, p. 10).

The Woodland *Comité* was part of a network of Mexican mutual aid organizations in Sacramento Valley and the Southwestern United States. Hernandez (1983) reports that these mutual aid societies '. . . grew into powerful political machines as Mexican-Americans were forced to seek new ways to protect their deteriorating economic and political conditions' (Hernandez, 1983:3). Rudy Acuña (1972) claims that the Mexican Mutual Aide societies are the oldest social organizations from which Mexican political organizations and trade unions were born. Certainly in Yolo County the *Comité de Beneficiencia Mexicana* is the oldest Chicano organization which still functions to the present day. It is interesting to note that it served the same social, political, and organizational function as that observed by Hernandez (1983) and Acuña (1972). Other Chicano groups that emerged during this period were *Las Guadalupanas* and *Comité Pro-Fiestas Patrias*. The purpose of the *Comité Pro-Fiestas Patrias* was to celebrate Mexican civic holidays. This organization planned dances and beauty pageants within the Mexican community.

Las Guadalupanas is a religious Catholic organization that provided the Mexican women with a social activity outside of their home lives. The activities were religious in nature; however, as the organization developed, it evolved into a successful fund raiser for the church and provided scholarships to the Chicano community. It is one of the more active and visible Chicano organizations still functioning and is the only Chicano organization that owns its own building.

Participation by members of the Mexican community in business, educational, and social institutions played a significant role in the development of the Mexican community. Those individuals who went into business were the first members of the Mexican middle class in Woodland. They also became a link between the Anglo and Mexican communities. These individuals also began to interact with legal and social Anglo institutions. In order to open a business, they obtained licenses and permits from city, county, and state agencies. They were also required to pay taxes and submit labor and/or employment reports to state or local agencies. A review of city archives indicates that some members of the Mexican community who owned property and building permits were obtained to either improve their properties or construct new buildings. In order to be successful in dealing with institutions from the dominant society, members of the Mexican community learned the rules, regulations, customs, and language of the host society.

The involvement of Mexican youth in school extra-curricular activities is of significance. They learned organizational and leadership skills by participating in the Spanish Club. It is also interesting to note that it was the Spanish language that provided the organizational and leadership opportunities. It must be pointed out, however, that the members and activities of the organization were referred to as Spanish and not Mexican — A reflection of the anti-Mexican sentiment of the area and era. The *Comité de Beneficiencia Mexicana* not only provided the adult members of the Mexican community with organizational and leadership opportunities, but it also linked them with social and legal institutions of the host society. The *Comité* had to function in accordance with local and state regulations, and forms and reports needed to be submitted to legal authorities. The Mexican community developed and formed their own business and social organizations. The nature of these activities was a reflection of the group linguistic and cultural background. However, they also served to acquaint and link the Mexican community with social, legal, and cultural customs of the host society.

Mexican Migration in the 1940s and 1950s

The Sacramento valley experienced significant social, economic, and demographic changes during the 1940s and 1950s. These changes were a result of innovations in the agricultural industry and by the demands of World War II, which also contributed to the increase of the Mexican population in Sacramento valley, particularly in and around Woodland. Scruggs (1988) reports that World War II changed the nature of seasonal farm labor in the USA. The war created the demand for a greater production of food, while at the same time local workers joined the US Armed Forces. Under the USA and Mexico agreement, the *Bracero* program was initiated. Mexican farm workers arrived in the area in significant numbers. 'Mexicans came not only under contract, but in circumvention of the laws of the two neighboring nations' (Scruggs, 1988:151). The number of Mexican seasonal farm workers in California increased from 36,000 in 1944 to 100,800 in 1956, and numbered 93,100 in 1957 and 92,400 in 1958. In Yolo County in 1958 there were 10,144 Mexican seasonal farm workers, which represented over 10 per cent of those reported statewide. It was reported that many of the Mexican farm workers who came as *Braceros* never left the area; some married local Mexican girls while others went to Mexico and brought wives back with them.

Contributing to the growth of the Woodland Mexican population were the births of children to the Mexican families who had settled in the area in the 1920s and 1930s. One such indicator was the growth of school-age children. Douglas (1949) reports that in 1933–34 there were seven Mexican children enrolled in the Woodland school district. The number increased to 36 in 1937–38, 47 in 1942–43, 95 in 1943–44, 208 in 1948–49, and 259 in 1949–50. Most of the parents of these children were born in Mexico and only three in the USA. According to Douglas (1949, p. 27), 'The parents spoke mostly Spanish at home and their occupations was entirely of the unskilled class . . . a few were independent farmers . . . a few labor contractors. These individuals, Douglas claimed, '. . . have financially made a great deal of progress and are making strides toward complete Americanization.'

Douglas (1949) further reports that the family was the center of social activities and that about 50 per cent of the Mexican community owned their own homes and live in '. . . certain areas of the community' (p. 27). It seems that the Mexican community lived in segregated housing tracts. This phenomenon is consistent with statements made by one of the first Mexican settlers (1920s) who claimed that Mexicans faced housing discrimination.

The growth of the Mexican community, due to the *Bracero* program and birth rates among Mexican families, had a significant impact on the organizational, political, and social development of the Mexican community. The significant increase of single male Mexican farm workers provided the local (established) Mexican residents with opportunities for upper mobility. Members of the families who arrived in the 1920s and 1930s became labor contractors, and others joined the ranks of growers, while some found employment as field supervisors. Some worked in the railroad, sugar beet refinery and canning/packing industries. Others also joined the business community; the increase of Mexican migrant workers provided an excellent opportunity for members of the local Mexican community to open restaurants, stores, bars, and barber shops. The following are some of the businesses: La Villa Restaurant (1950), El Sombrero Tortilleria (1960), Tafoya's Grocery Store (1949), and Rick's Barber Shop (1949–50).

Such opportunities increased the number of individuals who joined the Mexican middle class. It must be pointed out, however, that contrary to what Douglas claimed, (see p. 79), they did not make strides to complete Americanization, which is interpreted to mean they rejected their language, customs, and culture. On the contrary, Mexican cultural, civic, and social organizations continued to flourish. *El Comité de Beneficiencia Mexicana, El Comité Pro-fiestas Mexicanas,* and *Las Guadalupanas* continue to function. Members of the Mexican community bought a piece of land in the outskirts of town and held dances for their own community. The dances were held in the open, 'Just a concrete slab. They used to call it *Al Aire Libre.*' In addition, several new organizations serving the Mexican community emerged, the Pan American Men's Club, the Yolo Athletic Club, and the Yolo Mother's Club. The leadership for these organizations came from those individuals who had become more successful; they were the bilingual, bicultural individuals from the Mexican community.

During World War II the Mexican community in and around Woodland not only contributed to the war efforts by working in many of the industries that supported the war, but some of their children joined the armed forces. Estrada *et al.* (1981, p. 120) reports that '. . . war industries provided the semblance of occupational opportunity for many. . . . the rigid tie between class and ethnicity seemed somewhat weakened.'

Response to Racial Discrimination

The statewide growth of the Mexican population, however, exacerbated the relationship between the Mexican and Anglo community. Chicanos throughout the state faced several challenges. Intergroup relations between Anglos and Mexicans were not at their best. Racial discrimination was widespread resulting in '. . . ugly confrontations between Mexicans and Anglos. The press, for its part, helped to raise feelings against Mexicans' (Estrada, *et al.*, 1981, p. 120). The Chicano community in Yolo County also experienced racial discrimination. It was reported that some of the business establishments in Woodland would not serve Mexicans.

An active member of the Chicano community claimed that discriminatory practices against Mexicans were a reality. 'In those days they wouldn't let you rent a hall or go into a bar or restaurant . . . we started the barber shop because nobody could get a haircut here. The Mexicans could not, they had to go to Sacramento.' Discrimination was directed against the Mexican national and the seasonal farm worker; a member of one of the original families reported that her father told her of incidents where Mexicans were discriminated against. In one instance she claimed that her father was getting a haircut and the barber (an Anglo) refused to cut the hair of a Mexican national. Her father confronted the barber and told him that he was a Mexican and then walked out of the barber shop.

Statewide discrimination and abuse of Mexican seasonal laborers (*Braceros*) was a common practice and large-scale abuses were frequent; the Mexican government sought to protect its citizens from unequitable wages and overt discrimination in working conditions (Estrada, *et al.*, 1981). A member of one of the most respected Woodland Mexican families described a personal experience of how she became involved in protesting the abuse of Mexican seasonal laborers. As a young lady she complained about the working conditions and the lunch that the *Braceros* were receiving. She was helping her father and noticed that some of the workers would not eat their lunches or take time to rest. She and her cousin confronted the manager and threatened to call the newspaper and the Mexican consulate to expose the problem. The manager quickly responded and in the afternoon of the same day '. . . here comes a caravan of vans with hot chocolate and Mexican bread to the fields. By the end of the week these vans would come every day' (Interviewee J, July 17, 1990). Feldman and Callum (1983:26) describe the manner in which a Yolo County walnut grower characterized Mexican farm workers as a '. . . water spigot you turn it on when you need it and turn it off when you don't . . . we don't pay any social attention to them . . . that is almost slavery.'

As the Mexican community grew during the 1940s and 1950s, the need for recreational activities also grew. However, the Woodland Mexican community experienced discrimination in this area as well. A member of one of the original families claimed that 'There was nothing available for the Mexicans. The Mexicans came and they united; they are the ones who started things that were for Mexicans.' Another Chicano reported that in those days (1940–1950) . . . they would not let you rent a hall or go into a bar.' The Mexican community in and around Woodland formed their own organizations in order to participate in social, recreational, and sports activities. The Yolo Athletic Club, the Yolo Mother's Club, and the Pan American Men's Club were organized during this time. The purposes of these organizations were primarily social and athletic. The founder of one of the groups claims that, 'We started the Pan American Club [1950] in hopes of at least giving our people a chance to compete in athletic activities . . . they [Mexicans] could compete, but they [Anglos] would not invite them to; it was only one here and one there.' This particular group had over 100 members in 1950–1951. Some of their activities were organizing baseball, softball, and basketball games; sponsoring a team to participate in the California Central Valley League; sponsoring dances for Mexican young adults, and celebrating Mexican independence. The Pan American Club also provided the Mexican community an excellent opportunity to develop organizing skills. Several of the members became involved in political organizations in later years. It is important to note that several of the members of the Pan American Club were World War II veterans.

The growth of the Mexican population was beginning to concern local educators. They were puzzled by the Chicano student populations' low scores in Achievement and Intelligence Tests; at the same time many students scored near the top in curriculum-based tests. A leading educator in the area claimed in a masters thesis that '. . . in the school system there are a great many Mexican-American children who consistently seem to obtain low test scores in Intelligence and Achievement Tests' (Douglas, 1949, p. 1). The administrators and teachers were concerned about such conditions and when asked to explain this phenomena, they indicated that it was due to the children's '. . . inability to understand English . . . and because of retardation.'

In the review of the literature for his studies, Douglas (1949) wrote that most studies have concluded that Mexican-American children presented special problems for the schools. He divided the literature into four categories: 1) Hereditary status, 2) environmental status, 3) lack of selection/unsuitability studies, and 4) language handicapped studies. In his study of Mexican children in the Woodland Joint Unified School District, Douglas (1949:104–105) concluded that Mexican-American students in the Woodland Joint Unified School District faced problems due to their '. . . numerous handicaps of language and environment'. In order for these children to succeed and compete with the '. . . normal American child', they 'would have to have higher IQs'. The Mexican students developed academic gaps in fundamental subjects after the third grade. It was also noted that education and school environment have little impact in the IQ of the Mexican children. The author (Douglas, 1949) implied that unless the Mexican children in the Woodland Joint Unified School District had above-average intelligence, they would fail, due to their numerous handicaps, and that education and school environment have little effect on the students' IQs. In other words, in order for Mexican students to succeed, they need to be gifted.

This study is very important because it describes the conceptual basis for the education of Mexican children in the 1940s and 1950s. It is an example of the Classical Assimilation Theory which blames the students' cultural/linguistic background and their home environment for the low IQ scores and low achievement results. The study helps to understand the educational conditions, policies, and procedures to which Mexicans were subjected at that time. It must be pointed out, however, that Mr Douglas was convinced that the Mexican children '. . . had more capabilities than they were showing on the Intelligence Achievement Tests'. He wanted to demonstrate that the Mexican students had normal intelligence just as the white students had. It was reported that he was a friend and advocate of the Mexican children.

It is clear that one of the main functions of the educational system was to assimilate the Mexican students. There were no special programs to deal with some of the issues identified by Mr Douglas in his 1949 study. Furthermore, in a 1990 interview, he claimed that '. . . if you were ten-years-old, you started in first grade if you did not speak English . . . they did not have any junior high school classes for bilingual students at all. The only problem . . . was the language handicap.' In his study, Douglas (1949:32) reports that in 1949–50 only forty-seven Mexican children out of 259 had attended kindergarten and twenty-seven of those were retained. Retention of Mexican children in the Woodland Joint Unified School District was prevalent. 'Retention . . . in at least one grade is very common

... 53 per cent have been retained at least once and 8 per cent in two grades.' Furthermore, he reports that 73 per cent were above the normal grade level.

The Mexican children in Woodland faced some difficult challenges both in and out of the classroom. Most of these children attended two elementary schools, Beamer and Dinglé. It seems that at Beamer school the student population consisted of sons and daughters of Mexican agricultural workers and sons and daughters of members of the affluent Anglo community. An influential member of the Mexican community describes her experiences in the school system during this period of time claiming that the Mexican children were discriminated against by the Anglo and affluent students '. . . I always felt that maybe they did not include me as much as the others because I used to watch. They would be invited to birthday parties and I was not, and I always felt it was because we did not have the money and I was Mexican.' Another member of the original families reported that the educational system discriminated against Mexican children; 'There were three girls (Mexican) all brilliant in grammar school — brilliant, but not one of them ever won an award or a scholarship.'

Members of the Mexican community confronted such discriminatory practices either as individuals or as an organized entity. The Pan American Club was created in response to the discriminatory practices in sports and recreation. The significance of this critical event is that the Mexican community responded in an organized manner with their own institutions in order to provide the Mexican youth with opportunities to participate in sports and recreational activities. This organization is also important because some of the members were (first generation) sons of the original families; others were World War II veterans. The Mexican community in Yolo County acted similarly to other Chicano communities throughout the Southwest by creating its own organizations in response to hostility and exploitation (Estrada, *et al.*, 1981).

Chicanos in Politics (1950–70)

The Chicano community in and around Woodland experienced an organizational and political transformation during the decades of the 1960s and 1970s. It went from a loosely organized community around social, recreational and cultural activities to a more politically action-oriented community. The organizational and political activities are characterized by protesting against injustices committed against its members and demanding that those injustices be rectified. It was during this period of time that Chicano political and activist organizations, such as Mexican-American Political Association, Mexican-American *Concilio*, United Chicano Student Organization, *Movimiento Estudiantil Chicano de Aztlan* (MECHA), and the Brown Berets surfaced.

Members of the Chicano community also participated in the local electoral process by running for the Woodland City Council, Woodland Joint Unified School District Board of Education, and Yolo County Board of Supervisors. Some Chicano community members were also appointed to several Woodland Advisory committees. It must be pointed out that the political and organizational activities of the Chicano community were partly influenced by the politics of the era. The civil rights movement, war on poverty, and the Chicano movement had a profound impact on the organizational and political development of the Chicano community. The Chicano community continued to grow during the 1960s and 1970s. The *Bracero* program was terminated in 1964, and many of the farm workers opted to stay in the area. Some married local women while others returned to Mexico and then came back with their families. A member of one of the original families claims that '*Braceros* started coming in with the war and alot of them never left . . . some left and some just stayed. Every year new families would come.'

The growth of the Mexican community also brought about the creation and nurturing of Mexican cultural organizations. *El Comité Pro-Fiestas Patrias, Las Guadalupanas*, and *Comité de Beneficiencia Mexicana* continued to function. *Los Caporales*, a Charro organization, was founded by Ramon Tafoya; this organization celebrated Mother's Day by sponsoring parades and dances each year. There were other cultural groups that surfaced; one was *Asociacion de Charros La Regional*. This group was led by Isaac Fletes and held several cultural celebrations every year (The *Daily Democrat*, Woodland-Davis, July 3, 1973, p. 8). Another cultural group was a Mexican folk dance group led by Mrs. Daniel Moreno who organized the group in 1967 and 'attempted to instill in the Chicano youth a true appreciation of Mexican folk dances' (The *Daily Democrat*, February 28, 1969, p. 4).

The politics of the era had a significant impact in the political development of the Chicano community. The Mexican-American Political Association was created in the mid-1960s and became very active in electoral politics. The war on poverty also had a significant impact on the Chicano community as well. As a result of federal legislation, the Equal Opportunity Commission was created in Yolo County. Its original intent was to help organize poor people to help themselves. One of the functions of the Yolo County EOC was to provide leadership and organizational training to the local indigenous and poor communities. It hired local leaders and they, in turn, organized around issues in their own communities.

In 1969, the EOC hired as its executive director, Domitilio Vaca. His tenure as chief executive officer of EOC was short-lived. He was terminated by the County Board of Supervisors. The public reason given for his termination was that Mr Vaca '. . . was accused of failing to provide adequate administrative leadership for the EOC program in the county, along with other charges' (The *Daily Democrat*, Editorial, April 1, 1969, p. 16). The firing of Mr Vaca as executive director of EOC created a major conflict in Yolo County. The Chicano community was at the center of such conflict. Some members of the Chicano community supported the actions of the Board of Supervisors to fire Mr Vaca, while many others opposed it. The supporters of Mr Vaca claimed that the Board fired the EOC executive director because he was being effective in empowering members of the Chicano community and because he was involved in supporting some controversial issues. At the March 18, 1969, meeting of the Equal Opportunity Commission, Mr Vaca was accused of leading some protestors '. . . in a confrontation two months ago with administrators of the high school and supporting a grape boycott resolution passed at a meeting Monday night of the Mexican American Political Association (MAPA) and with at least knowledgeable efforts to organize the Brown Berets in the area' *Daily Democrat*, March 19, 1969, pp. 1 and 14).

The accusation of his involvement at the high school with MAPA and the Brown Berets came from two members of the EOC Commission representing the Mexican-American Political Association. The president of MAPA, Rick

Gonzalez, came to the defense of Mr Vaca claiming that 'Vaca went along to the meeting at the high school to find out what type of program the Mexican kids were having . . . I went too. We went as individuals, not representatives of the EOC' (The *Daily Democrat*, March 19, 1969, p. 1). Other EOC staff and board members were also present at the high school meeting and defended their actions by claiming that 'We are all involved in the war on poverty and this is part of it . . . we are concerned with the social setting in Yolo County. How can we conduct a war on poverty unless we become involved with the problems' (The *Daily Democrat*, March 19, 1969, p. 14). This incident caused some division in the Mexican community. On March 26, 1969, at a meeting of EOC, a group of seventy to seventy-five poor people 'most of them Mexican-Americans showed . . . to voice their support of EOC Director Domitilio Vaca' (The *Daily Democrat*, March 27, 1969, p. 1). Members of the Chicano community circulated a petition with sixty-five signatures in support of Mr. Vaca. Among those listed in the petition were members of the original Mexican families who settled in Woodland in the 1920s and 1930s, such as members of the Zaragoza, Sosa, Ramirez, Rico, and Montoya families (The *Daily Democrat*, March 28, 1969, p. 7). Other supporters of Mr. Vaca included the United Chicano Students, a group of Woodland high school students. The president of this organization, Earl Villarreal, said that, 'From my point of view, Domitilio Vaca should not be fired as director . . . the rich people may agree with the Board of Supervisors in their discharge of Mr Vaca . . . the poor people do not. Dom is serving the people, not the rich' (The *Daily Democrat*, April 1, 1969, p. 3).

Some members of the Anglo community came to the defense of Mr Vaca; a member of the Davis Human Relations Council (DHRC) claimed that Mr Vaca was not given a fair chance to perform and that some members of the EOC board opposed his hiring because '. . . middle class members of the commission wanted a candidate other than Vaca' (The *Daily Democrat*, April 2, 1969, pp. 1 and 18). It was suggested that the Anglo community power structure was opposed to the empowerment of the low income community. 'The pressure of poor people to find solutions to their own problems through group action will always bring about this kind of response . . . from the supervisors and other aspects of the power structure' (The *Daily Democrat*, April 2, 1969, pp. 1 and 18).

Supporters of the Board of Supervisors included some members of the Mexican community who claimed that EOC was not helping the poor because most of the funds were 'used for salaries, travel for the staff . . .' (The *Daily Democrat*, March 31, 1969, pp. 1 and 9). Others claimed that EOC under Vaca was '. . . no better than that of the previous administration' (The *Daily Democrat*, April 17, 1969, p. 1). Other supporters of the Board of Supervisors included the Yolo County Tax Payers Association and The *Daily Democrat* who claimed in its editorial page of April 1, 1969, that the poor 'are being used' (The *Daily Democrat*, April 1, 1969, p. 16). Domitilio Vaca was eventually terminated as executive director of the Yolo County Equal Opportunity Commission. The *Daily Democrat*, in its April 17 edition, reported that Mr Vaca was fired and replaced by an interim director. In the opinion of some members of the Mexican community such action was to be expected. A Chicano organizer for the war on poverty claimed that Domitilio Vaca was fired because he fought for poor people and supported Cesar Chavez; 'That's why they fired him'. The decision of the Mexican-American Political Association in March, 1969, to support the grape boycott played a significant role in the Chicano community. Members of the Mexican community claimed that such action by MAPA was one of the principle reasons for the firing of Domitilio Vaca, which resulted in a conflict between the Yolo County Board of Supervisors and some Chicano organizations. It also created a rift within the Chicano community leading to the dismantling of MAPA and the creation of the Yolo County Mexican-American *Concilio* in the early 1970s.

Another significant event in December, 1968, was the action of members of the Mexican community to meet with officials from the high school. The purpose of this meeting was to discuss the lack of programs, counselors, and problems that the Mexican students had. There were two Mexican student organizations: one was the United Chicano Students and the other was the Mexican-American Youth. Members of both groups complained of having problems with the school. A staff member of EOC reported that 'Mexican-American students at the school had been encountering problems' (The *Daily Democrat*, March 20, 1969, p. 1). The Director of EOC met several times with students and parents to discuss their problems with the high school. It resulted in '. . . several subsequent and peaceful meetings with school officials, some of which included parents of students involved' (The *Daily Democrat*, March 20, 1969, p. 8). Some of the requests made by the Mexican students and parents included 'a change in emphasis in the hiring of Chicano counselors and in curricular activities' (The *Daily Democrat*, March 20, 1969, p. 8).

A member of the Chicano community who was involved in the meetings with the high school administrators indicated that the school had received some federal funds but the curricular services were not reaching the students. It appears that the Mexican community had not been informed that the district had received federal funds for a bilingual program. As a result of the complaints by members of the Mexican community, the local school district hired some bilingual aides, some of whom were members of the original founders who settled in the 1920s and 1930s. It is interesting to note that during the 1960s, the number of Chicanos hired as teachers or counselors by the school district was minimal. Woodland Joint Unified High School, however, attempted to respond to the needs of the Mexican community; it offered Back-to-School-nights in Spanish and called them Spanish nights.

During the decade of the 1970s, some members of the Yolo County Mexican community became more politically aware and involved. The Mexican-American Political Association ceased to function effectively at the end of the 1960s due to the support of the grape boycott. The Chicano community also lost some control of the Equal Opportunity Commission. These two incidents prompted the Mexican community to form a new organization, the Mexican-American *Concilio*, in the early 1970s. The founders of this new organization were many of the same individuals involved in EOC and had remained with MAPA. The purpose behind organizing Concilio was to provide the Mexican community with the means to help themselves and not depend on governmental handouts. 'Taking charge of one's destiny was the key philosophy offered by the founder of the Mexican-American *Concilio* in Yolo County, the Reverend Daniel Casey' (The *Daily Democrat*, February 11, 1983, p. 1).

The *Concilio* became involved in several issues; however, it appears that organizational efforts dealt primarily with discriminatory practices in employment and/or the lack of Chicano representation in public agencies or private companies.

In 1974, the Yolo County Mexican-American *Concilio* filed a suit against the Yolo County Board of Supervisors accusing them of discrimination in employment. this suit was later '. . . combined with a class action suit filed by twelve women and Blacks, most of whom were represented by Legal Services' (The *Daily Democrat*, May 10, 1983, p. 2). The county was ordered to change its affirmative action plan and to pay $150,000 to the plaintiffs in the suit and put aside $620,000 for 'women and Blacks who could show they were hurt financially by the county's employment policies' (The *Daily Democrat*, May 10, 1983, p. 2). Members of the activist Chicano community claimed that the victory over the county showed the community power structure that the Chicano community was organized and capable of winning battles.

Politics and Education in the 1970s

Another significant issue pursued by the *Concilio* was in the area of education. On May 1, 1972, members of the Chicano community appeared before the Woodland School Board accusing the school district of being unresponsive to the needs of the Chicano students in the district. The District's priority goals did not meet the needs of Chicanos. Mr Louie Lucero, a member of one of the original Mexican families and a third-year University of California, Davis, law student, cited statistics claiming that 22.4 per cent of the student population in Woodland was Mexican-American but only one percent of the teachers employed by the district were Spanish surname. He claimed that students should be given an opportunity to study about their people, and he added that only through hiring of Spanish surnamed teachers could this be accomplished. Ricardo Gonzalez, a community activist and recent city council candidate, said, 'In the 22 years I've lived in the community, I've noticed you do not have the personnel these people seek' (The *Daily Democrat*, May 2, 1972, p. 1). The school district eventually appointed Rick Gonzalez to an advisory committee that would review and submit a recommendation on the goals of education. 'The committee . . . is to be composed of representatives from each social, economic, political, and racial group' (The *Daily Democrat*, May 2, 1972, p. 1).

At the June 5, 1972, meeting of the Woodland School Board, the Superintendent of Schools recommended that the Board adopt a policy for the recruitment and hiring of Chicano teachers. '. . . if fully qualified Mexican-American teachers are available, the Woodland Joint Unified School District, within the next five years (1972–77), will endeavor each year to add Mexican-American teachers to its staff in order to attain a goal of 20 per cent of the certified staff, (The *Daily Democrat*, June 6, 1972, p. 18). The policy was formally adopted by the school board on June 19, 1972 (The *Daily Democrat*, June 20, 1972, p. 18). The Chicano community not only requested that the district hire more Chicano teachers but suggested that representatives from their community serve on the interviewing teams along with district personnel. One of the Chicano activists and a member of the *Concilio* described the involvement of the Chicano community in the recruitment and selection process of teachers. '. . . We went in and they allowed us . . . to interview the Hispanic teachers and out of fourteen who came forward, seven were hired. We were more advocates of people getting jobs in the proper places' (Interviewee A). The assistant superintendent for personnel, Harold Douglas, claimed that the Mexican population had increased significantly and that the recruitment and hiring of Chicano teachers was done because '. . . it was the federal government putting pressure on the schools . . . we had to keep up with all the reporting and show we tried.'

The district, in fact, hired a good number of Chicano teachers in the years that follow the confrontation with the Mexican community. Several Chicano teachers were hired in 1973. Among them were Reinaldo Genera who was assigned to teach first grade at Plainfield Elementary School, Evelia Genera, assigned to teach second and third grades at Willow Springs, and Velma Villegas-Gonzales who was hired as a bilingual kindergarten teacher at Gibson School (The *Daily Democrat*, Sept. 20, 1973, p. 20). These three individuals would eventually assume leadership roles in the 1980s within the school district. Mrs Genera became the head counselor at the high school, Mr Genera became an elementary principal, and Mrs Villegas-Gonzales became bilingual coordinator, principal, and associate superintendent for curriculum.

The involvement of the Chicano community in school issues in the early 1970s seemed to deal primarily with the employment of Chicanos and, to a lesser degree, with curriculum issues; however, bilingual education was a definite issue that some members of the Chicano community pursued. On November 11, 1971, at Deganawidah Quetzacoatl University in rural Yolo County, a conference on bilingual/bicultural education sponsored by the Northern California Head-Start Directors Association was held. The focus of the conference was 'The Mexican-American Child'. The conference was attended '. . . by dozens of officials and teachers who hoped to turn educational affairs around for Spanish-speaking children' (The *Daily Democrat*, November 12, 1971, p. 1). Some of those who presented at this conference were bilingual staff from the California State Department of Education, faculty from the Bilingual Teacher Program, at California State University, Sacramento, and Dr Ernesto Galarza, a noted Chicano scholar.

In the Woodland Joint Unified School District, bilingual education had been offered since the late sixties; however, it was not until the early seventies with the hiring of bilingual teachers that the program assumed its own identity. In an unpublished report by two University of California students (Joyce and Landis, 1974), the Woodland School District Bilingual Program was discussed. The authors of the study wanted to get the perceptions from teachers (elementary/secondary), central office administrators, and school principals about the district's bilingual programs. One of the major findings in this study was that the district did not have a bilingual coordinator, which contributed to the lack of '. . . communication between bilingual/bicultural teachers . . . with the exception of teacher's meetings at the individual schools' (Joyce and Landis, 1974, p. 4). The authors also found support for the district bilingual program among the elementary school bilingual teachers — both Chicanos and non-Chicanos — as well as some opposition from some non-bilingual teachers. 'Some were definitely against the program and thought it was a waste of time and money; this could be due to the fear of being replaced by a bilingual/bicultural teacher' (Joyce and Landis, 1974, p. 4).

Parents were involved in the program from the beginning since they had to approve their children's participation in the program; however, the authors claimed that participation varied from school to school and whether or not Spanish was used as a means of communication. 'They had greater participation from Spanish-speaking parents than in previous years. Generally speaking, Chicano parents stayed away from PTA meetings . . . if, however, a Mexican-American organization was started, the parents seemed more interested and attendance grew steadily' (Joyce and Landis, 1974, p. 9).

The school principals were, for the most part, supportive of the district bilingual programs and looking forward to the bilingual coordinator who was hired by the district. This study is important because it documents, to some degree, the nature of the education that Chicanos were exposed to and, to some degree, the impact that Chicanos' organizing efforts had on the district. Bilingual education became an issue within the Woodland Joint Unified School District during the 1970s. Some district staff members supported it, while other opposed it. The coordinator of the district's bilingual education claimed that such a program would provide Mexican students with a quality education and equal opportunity. Furthermore, she stated that Mexican children needed to be given an education which equaled that given to Anglo children regarding equal time, intensity and reality (The *Daily Democrat*, January 12, 1977). An elementary school teacher objected to the school district's continued participation in a federally funded bilingual program. She labeled the program as anti-English language. The program coordinator defended it by claiming that such programs helped students foster respect and appreciation for both cultures of the world (The *Daily Democrat*, October 29, 1977).

The Woodland Joint Unified School District had a significant and continuously growing number of limited English-speaking children. Many of the children were also identified as migrant since their parents worked in agriculture in Yolo County. The Woodland Joint Unified School District provided bilingual education to the children under an ESEA Title VII federal grant; however, the district also participated in a migrant education program. Perhaps one of the major contributions of bilingual, and certainly migrant, education was the empowerment of parents. Both programs required that parents be involved in the decision-making process. Parents (both migrant and parents of Limited English Proficiency (LEP) children) received extensive and comprehensive training and information. The information and skills received by the parents were very valuable; many of these parents became involved with the education of their children and became strong supporters of bilingual and migrant education. Some of the parents became involved in school district issues outside of bilingual and migrant education.

The Mexican community in Yolo County in 1971 demonstrated their interest in education and promoted a literacy campaign when some families assisted the Yolo County Library to choose books and films in Spanish. Some of those that participated were Mr and Mrs Adrian Vidales, Mr and Mrs Jose Ramirez, Mr and Mrs Jose Zuniga, Mrs Isabel Jimenez, Mrs M. Cazarez, Mrs I. Marquez, and Mrs Rita Cital (The *Daily Democrat*, December 17, 1971, p. 5). In the Spanish section of The *Daily Democrat*, April 6, 1973, it was reported that over 100 adult Mexican students were enrolled in English as a second language courses. However, only about 50 per cent attended classes because there was only one certified teacher and a teacher assistant. The district had been unaware of this need when it was brought to their attention. The interesting aspect of this article is that a significant number of adults wanted to learn English, but because of the lack of teachers, only a few could benefit. It also refutes the belief by some that the Mexican community was not interested in learning English. This attitude was expressed in a Letter to the Editor by a Yolo County resident who claimed that Mexicans '. . . segregate themselves into class and culture and ideological groups speaking a foreign tongue . . . it is time he becomes American or return to his native land and speak Spanish or think Mexican to his heart's content' (The *Daily Democrat*, November 26, 1971, p. 9).

Participation by Chicanos in Electoral Politics

The Mexican community in Yolo County, and Woodland in particular, participated in the local electoral process by running its own candidates for the Woodland Joint Unified School Board, Woodland City Council, and Yolo County Board of Supervisors during the 1970s. The Chicano community also challenged the county's system of selecting voter registrars. In November, 1971, members of the Yolo Mexican community appeared before the supervisors charging the county clerk with discrimination in the selection of voter registrars. They claimed that while the Chicano population was 20 per cent, only one of the county's 100 deputy voter registrars was Chicano (The *Daily Democrat*, November 16, 1971, p. 1). On November 19, 1971, the first three Mexican-American voter registrars were deputized. It was reported that a minimum of ten would come forward, but that more than ten would be needed to cover remote areas of the county. Mr Apodaca, spokesperson for the group, was warned by the county clerk not to use the voter registrars for partisan purposes. 'If they strayed from a strictly non-partisan approach, the groups' interest would be in danger' (The *Daily Democrat*, November 20, 1971, p. 2).

Members of the Woodland Chicano community ran for local public offices on several occasions during the 1970s. Ricardo (Rick) Gonzalez, one of the founders of Pan American Club, MAPA, EOC, and *Concilio* ran for the city council several times. In the 1954 city council elections his name appears as a write-in candidate. He also ran unsuccessfully in 1960, 1968, 1972, and 1974. He came very close to winning in 1972 and 1974, losing by three votes in one year and 42 votes in another. Several other members of the Woodland Mexican community ran unsuccessfully for the Woodland City Council; in 1970, Mr Guerrero; in 1972, Mr Garcia; in 1978, David Armendariz; in 1980, Richard Verdugo; in 1983, Xavier Tafoya, and in 1986, Vince Revelles. All but one, Xavier Tafoya, lost the elections. Additionally, in 1966, Eulogio Guerrero and Ralph Lara ran for Woodland constable. Three members of the Yolo County Spanish-speaking community ran unsuccessfully for the County Board of Supervisors during the 1970s and 1980s. Al Sosa ran in 1970, Pedro Villarreal in 1974, and Xavier Tafoya in 1986. They ran for the third district, which included Woodland. The first successful member of the Mexican community to be elected to public office was Jack Losoya; he was elected to the Winters city council in 1969 and as mayor in 1970.

Members of the Woodland Mexican community also sought election to the Woodland School District Board of Trustees. In 1973, Michael Bojorquez, a twenty-one-year-old student at California State University, Sacramento and son of a Chicana activist, ran for the school board. Mr Bojorquez's campaign was supported by members of the activist Chicano organizations. He was not successful; however, his candidacy is important because he was the first Chicano to run for the school district. Furthermore, during this election three other candidates with what appears to be Spanish or Portuguese last names also ran. They were

Luduvina, Orejel, and Rodrigues. The combined votes for these candidates numbered over 1200. The possibility exists that the Mexican community might have split their votes, thereby denying Mr Bojorquez a seat on the Woodland Joint Unified School Board.

During the 1975 school board elections two other members of the Mexican community ran for the school board; the two candidates were David Armendariz and Ted Ramirez. Dr Ramirez, a dentist, was elected to the school board. He was the first person of Mexican descent to serve on the Woodland Joint Unified School Board. Mr Armendariz was supported by the Woodland Chicano activist. Dr Ramirez's tenure on the school board, according to some Chicano activists, was marked by a more conservative philosophy than their own. Many of the gains made by the Chicano community in employment of certificated Chicano teachers reached a plateau by the end of the 1970s; however, it must be pointed out that some members of the bilingual staff that were hired in the early 1970s were promoted to administrative positions. Velma Villegas-Gonzales was appointed to bilingual coordinator and principal; Reinaldo Genera was also appointed principal. They became the first Chicano administrators in the Woodland Joint Unified School District.

The 1960s civil rights movement, the war on poverty, and the Chicano movement had a significant impact on the organizational development of the Chicano community. In Yolo County, particularly in Woodland, the Chicano community was transformed; it went from a loosely organized community around cultural recreational and sports activities into a more activist, militant, and politically oriented community. Browning, Rufus, Marshall and Tabb (1984) claimed that the war on poverty created a new arena where the concern of the minority, in this case Chicano, population received close attention. The 'new game' involved several interest groups such as public bureaucrats and politicians, and it 'stimulated the emergence of new players . . . offering new bases of power . . . and directly or indirectly generating political activity' (p. 214). Such was the case with the Yolo County Chicano community.

Some of the salient events that surfaced during the late 1960s and early 1970s in the Chicano community were the conflict with the Yolo County Board of Supervisors in 1969; the support of the Chicano community for the grape boycott and of MAPA as a viable political organization. The organizations that surfaced in the early 1970s, such as *Concilio, MECHA*, etc., were much more activist and militant in nature. Estrada, *et al.* (1981:122) describes these organizations as '. . . activists and sometimes radical . . . these organizations came to be known collectively as the Chicano movement. Often very critical of certain basic assumptions of US society, they sought fundamental transformation in the distribution of power in the United States . . . they were looking . . . for a radical and equitable transformation of a racist society.'

An area of concern that the activist Chicano organizations (such as *Concilio*) pursued was affirmative action, or the lack of Chicanos as employees in public agencies such as the county and local school district. The Chicano community put pressure on the local school district which responded, in part, due to the demands and protests by Chicanos, but also because it did not want to lose the funding that it was receiving from the federal government (as it was explained by a school official of the era). The Chicano community during the 1960s and 1970s had not yet experienced a political victory in the electoral process. However, in

1975, a Mexican-American was elected to the schoolboard. Members of the Chicano community did not consider this person an activist. It must be pointed out that the first administrative appointments of Chicanos occurred during his tenure. The hiring of Chicano certificated personnel in the early 1970s, the several unsuccessful attempts by Chicanos to seek public office, and the political activism of the 1960s and 1970s were the seeds planted for a future and successful harvest.

Conclusion

Estrada, *et al.* (1981) claim that the history of Chicanos in California is marked by exploitation and resistance. This description fits the experiences of Chicanos in Yolo County, particularly in and around the city of Woodland. Chicanos resisted the discriminatory practices of the host society in several ways: 1) by cohesiveness of community; 2) formation of own organizations; 3) maintenance of culture; 4) demand and protest; and 5) political mobilization and incorporation. Chicanos refused to be totally assimilated into the Anglo-Saxon society. The Mexican community did incorporate itself into the mainstream culture but always maintained its own identity by forming and participating in Mexican social, cultural, recreational, economic, and political organizations. This phenomena was made possible by the constant influx of Mexican immigrants for much of the twentieth century and the refusal of some Anglo members of the community to fully accept the Mexican community as equal members.

The early years (1920s–1930s) in the life of the Mexican community were marked by a cohesiveness among the several original families. The familial ties kept the Chicano community together in the face of difficult and antagonistic times. The *compadrazgo* system (fictive kinship) played, and continues to play, a significant role in the Chicano community. The practice of making family members friends and incorporating friends into the family by becoming godparents to each other's children and/or becoming godparents to each other in matrimony, baptism, etc. created a community of families, each related to one another. As the families grew and more Mexicans moved into the area, it became necessary to form their own organizations such as *El Comite de Beneficiencia Mexicana*, a mutual aid society. This was the first formal organization in the Mexican community. It provided the organizational skills and experiences for future generations. This organization also served a political function as Rivera (1984), Acuña (1972), and Hernandez (1983) claim.

During the 1940s and 1950s Chicanos formed other cultural and recreational organizations. Of particular importance is the Pan American Club which was formed in direct response to discriminatory practices in sports as experienced by the Mexican community. It is also important because the sons and daughters of the original families were coming of age; some fought in World War II and came back home to face discrimination. This organization was not political in nature, but it did make a political statement and provided an organized mechanism by which Chicanos could participate as equals and excel in an organized activity (i.e., sports). Another significant aspect of this organization is that one of its founders and future Chicano activist, emerged as a spokesperson and leader of the Mexican community.

One could argue that the creation, development, maintenance, and nurturing of Chicano organizations is not a function of a separatist attitude but a function of adaptation strategies of an immigrant community for successful incorporation into mainstream society. The Chicano organizations functioned within the framework of the dominant society. They had to conform to the rules and regulations of the host community. Chicanos learned how to function and succeed by learning organizational, social, economic, and political skills while participating in their own organizations. They also learned how to play the game of the host society. They incorporated successfully into the mainstream and participated without losing their ethnic, linguistic, and cultural identity.

The Chicano community in Woodland grew from less than a hundred persons in the 1920s to 6850 in 1980. The Chicano student population for the Woodland Joint Unified School District was 2709 (33 per cent) in 1989–90. The size and the percentage of the Chicano population is a significant rich resource that cannot be ignored. The Chicano community has a rich organizational and political experience; the first organizations were social and cultural in nature, later to be augmented by political and advocacy organizations, such as MAPA, *Concilio*, etc. This rich organizational life contributed to the political success of Chicanos in the latter part of the 1980s.

Chicanos have a rich history of involvement in the political electoral process in Woodland. Chicanos ran for the city council, county board of supervisors, and the local school board during the 1950s, '60s, '70s. Although many of the elections were not successful, they provided the organization and training skills for future elections. The political empowerment of the Mexican community was influenced by its organizational experience and the cohesiveness of the Mexican families in early years. It did not become openly involved in the political process until the 1960s and 1970s. The civil rights movement, the War on Poverty, and the Chicano movement had a significant impact on the organizational development of the Chicano community. During this time the Chicano community became more militant and political and advocacy organizations emerged. It was a period of nationalistic sentiment, self-respect, and cultural renaissance. These organizations fought for equality in education, employment, housing, and social and political justice.

The 1960s and 1970s could be described as a period of 'demand and protest', aptly described by Browning, *et al.* (1984). Some gains were made during this time; however, significant and sustained gains were not made until the mid-1980s as a result of political incorporation. Browning, *et al.* (1984) suggest that significant and sustained gains cannot be made by a minority community unless and until such community incorporates itself in the political system, that is, until one of its members is elected into a public body as a member of the dominant coalition (which is the subject of next Chapter).

References

Acuña, R. (1972) *Occupied America: Chicano Struggle Towards Liberation*, San Francisco, CA: Canfield Press.

Browning, R., Rufus, P., Marshall, D. and Tabb, D. (1984) *Protest is not Enough: The Struggle of Blacks and Hispanics for Equality in Urban Politics*, Berkeley, CA: University of California Press.

Douglas, H.R. (1949) *Intelligent Quotients and Achievement of Mexican American Children in Grades One Through Twelve*, unpublished Masters Thesis.

ESTRADA, L., GARCIA, C., MACIAS, F., REYNALDO, X. and MALDONADO, L. (1981) 'Chicanos in the United States: A history of exploitation and resistance', *Daedalus Journal of the American Academy of Arts and Sciences*, Spring 1981, pp. 103–31.

FELDMAN, J. and CALLUM, D. (1983) 'Strangers in a promised land', *Sacramento Magazine*, 9(10), pp. 24–40.

HERNANDEZ, L. (1983) 'Concilio's founder urges Hispanics to work together', The *Daily Democrat*, February 11, p. 1.

JOYCE, P. and LANDIS, K. (1974) 'Project for Chicano politics', unpublished manuscript, Davis, CA: University of California at Davis.

McGOWAN, J. (1961) *History of the Sacramento Valley (Volume II)*. New York, NY: Lewis Historical Publishing Co.

RIVERA, J. (1984) *Mutual Aid Societies in the Hispanic Southwest: Alternative Sources of Community Empowerment*, Research Report submitted to Alternative Financing Project, Office of Assistant Secretary for Planning and Evaluation. Washington, DC: US Department of Health and Human Services.

SCRUGGS, O. (1988) *Braceros 'Wetbacks' and Farm Labor Problem: Mexican Agricultural Labor in the United States (1947–1954)*, New York: Garland Publishing, Inc.

The *Daily Democrat*, February 28, 1969, Woodland, CA.

The *Daily Democrat*, March 19, 1969, Woodland, CA.

The *Daily Democrat*, March 20, 1969, Woodland, CA.

The *Daily Democrat*, March 27, 1969, Woodland, CA.

The *Daily Democrat*, March 28, 1969, Woodland, CA.

The *Daily Democrat*, March 31, 1969, Woodland, CA.

The *Daily Democrat*, April 1, 1969, Woodland, CA.

The *Daily Democrat*, April 2, 1969, Woodland, CA.

The *Daily Democrat*, April 17, 1969, Woodland, CA.

The *Daily Democrat*, November 12, 1971, Woodland, CA.

The *Daily Democrat*, November 16, 1971, Woodland, CA.

The *Daily Democrat*, November 20, 1971, Woodland, CA.

The *Daily Democrat*, November 26, 1971, Woodland, CA.

The *Daily Democrat*, December 17, 1971, Woodland, CA.

The *Daily Democrat*, May 2, 1972, Woodland, CA.

The *Daily Democrat*, June 6, 1972, Woodland, CA.

The *Daily Democrat*, June 20, 1972, Woodland, CA.

The *Daily Democrat*, April 6, 1973, Woodland, CA.

The *Daily Democrat*, May 18, 1973, Woodland, CA.

The *Daily Democrat*, July 3, 1973, Woodland, CA.

The *Daily Democrat*, September 20, 1973, Woodland, CA.

The *Daily Democrat*, January 12, 1977, Woodland, CA.

The *Daily Democrat*, October 29, 1977, Woodland, CA.

The *Daily Democrat*, February 11, 1983, Woodland, CA.

The *Daily Democrat*, May 10, 1983, Woodland, CA.

The *Woodland Democrat*, October 16, 1929, Woodland, CA.

The *Woodland Democrat*, January 22, 1930, Woodland, CA.

The *Woodland Democrat*, July 16, 1932, Woodland, CA.

The *Woodland Democrat*, July 21, 1932, Woodland, CA.

The *Woodland Democrat*, September 16, 1932, Woodland, CA.

The *Woodland Democrat*, December 5, 1932, Woodland, CA.

The *Woodland Democrat*, December 9, 1932, Woodland, CA.

Chapter 5

Political Gains of the Chicano Community: Taking and Using Power

Cirenio Rodriguez

In this chapter we describe and analyze the political incorporation (empowerment) of the Mexican community manifested in the election of one of its activist members to the local school board. The condition of underclass or castelike in which Mexicans had lived for many decades was broken through a series of gradual changes that ultimately resulted in the public acceptance of Mexicans as leaders of the community. Implied in this change was the notion of Woodland society in which ethnic minorities were viewed as worthy of public office, competent and committed to the common welfare of the larger community. The various steps towards the emancipation of Mexicans were obviously of the type alluded to by Popkewitz in his discussion of social transformation and control (1991:195–198). The earlier stages of critical thinking were followed by skillful handling of the 'administrative efficiency' often used by mainstream members to control 'deviant' interests and sociopolitical orientations (Popkewitz, 1991:196), especially in ethnically diversified settings. The democratic process worked, and the shift of political power took place. This shift in power is precisely what reform is all about (Popkewitz, 1991:22–27). In the final analysis:

> The cultural values that drive the construction of institutional practices contribute significantly to current reform proposals. Possessive individualism and instrumental rationality establish a belief in a meritocracy and a consensus of goals in a society that is, in fact, culturally, ethnically, and economically differentiated (Popkewitz, 1991:164).

The dynamics of change and reform in Woodland are a complex combination of the internal forces guiding the Mexican community to maintain their language, culture and institutions, while at the same time adapting to the American way of life, and at the same time encouraging the mainstream community to change its cultural values away from the active segregation of ethnic minorities to a democratic multicultural society that opens its ranks to all ethnic groups.

This election result impacted the school district's policy, program, and personnel practices benefiting the Chicano community. During the 1980s, the Chicano community experienced some significant positive changes. Two of its members were elected to public office. Several new organizations were created and the Chicano community made significant gains within the educational system. The decade of the 1980s is marked by political incorporation of the Chicano community and responsiveness and openness by the local school system to the demands and protests of the Chicano community.

Browning, Rufus, Marshall and Tabb (1984) developed a theory of political mobilization and incorporation by black and Latino communities — a responsiveness and openness by local municipal government to the demands and protests of the minority communities. This theory explains why some black and Latino communities were much more active and why much more was achieved in some cities than in others. It describes the conditions under which some communities were able to elect their own representatives to locally elected offices and under what conditions the local government agencies responded to the needs and demands of the minority communities. These authors were able to document '. . . the existence of a widely diffused movement in which demands for group access and representation and for governmental responsiveness are prominent and intense' (Browning, *et al.*, 1984:240). The demand/protest phase of political mobilization by minority communities was directly influenced by the civil rights movement and by the response of the national government which 'initiated programs directed at the problems of poverty, racial inequality and discrimination' (Browning, *et al.*, 1984:5).

The theory of political incorporation identifies a period of political mobilization by minority groups characterized by demand and protest followed by electoral mobilization, incorporation into the dominant liberal coalition and policy responsiveness by governmental agencies to the interests of the minority community. The demand/protest phase may contribute to electoral mobilization and to . . . some measurable gain in responsiveness from city government, the incorporation of the group yields much more (Browning, *et al.*, 1984:240). Incorporation is defined as having direct influence on the policy-making body. It 'refers not only to representation but also to the position of minority representatives *vis-à-vis* the dominant coalition on the city council' (*Ibid.*, p. 18). Political incorporation by the minority community is a function of the group's resources. These resources are characterized by:

1 The size of the minority community.
2 The support that this group receives from the electorate (both Anglo/ Chicano).
3 The organizational development and experience of the minority community.

Political incorporation by the minority group results in sustained and significant gains in areas of employment, programs, and policy which benefit such population. In turn, political incorporation by the minority groups and positive responsiveness by the governmental bodies are subject to other political factors. 'Conservative coalitions tend to resist minority demands and to oppose their efforts to gain access to city government; liberal coalitions tend to co-opt . . . we emphasize the relevance of ideology. Conservative and liberal coalitions responded very differently to minority mobilization and demand' (Browning, *et al.*, 1984:241). In order for a disenfranchised minority community to achieve a position where sustained and strong influence can be exercised, its members must be elected, must become members of a coalition, and the coalition must be the dominant force and be able to shape public policy.

The openness and responsiveness by the local governmental agency (the school district) to the interests of the Chicano community is characterized by policy changes which result in employment and programs that benefit the Chicano community. The theory of political incorporation advanced by Browning, *et al.*, summarized above can help us understand, describe, and analyze the relationship between the Chicano community and the Woodland Joint Unified School District during the 1970s and 1980s.

On September 25, 1981, a group of concerned Chicano parents appeared before the Woodland School Board listing incidents of racism and discrimination toward members of the Mexican student population. In an open letter to the Board of Trustees, members of a group called *Latinos Unidos Para Mejor Educacion* (LUPME) requested that their concerns be put in the School Board agenda for the following meeting. At the October 8, 1981 School Board meeting, LUPME presented a series of concerns. Ramon Ramirez, the spokesperson for LUPME, listed the following concerns of the group:

1 Discriminatory treatment of Latino/Chicano students in suspensions and disciplinary actions.
2 Discriminatory practices and policies (tracking) that adversely effect the educational opportunities of Chicano/Latino students, resulting in a low rate of college attendance for this population.
3 Significant number of Latino/Chicano students placed in special education classes.
4 A perception by Chicano parents and students of racist attitudes by district administrators and teachers.
5 The lack of Latino/Chicano counselors, teachers, and administrators in the district.

On February 25, 1982, the School Board approved the formation of a Minority Concerns Committee to study the concerns expressed by LUPME, and review district policies, procedures, and practices. The committee was charged with the task of finding out if 'minority students are being treated differently than other students in similar circumstances' (The *Daily Democrat*, February 26, 1982, p. 1). The group was asked to submit recommendations in areas where discriminatory practices were found. The composition of the committee included representatives from a broad spectrum, not 'only the Spanish-speaking community' (The *Daily Democrat*, February 26, 1982, p. 1). The committee was to submit a report to the School Board by May 15, 1982.

Members of the Chicano community who brought the complaints before the School Board were assisted by the Northern California Legal Assistance and the Yolo County Mexican-American *Concilio*. The group used interesting strategy which resulted in legal and political/advocacy pressure put on the school district. The critical event between the School Board and the Chicano community was continuation of the demand/protest phase between the Chicano community and the school district. It was also important because the concerns of the Chicano community were much more comprehensive than in the past and included other topics besides employment and bilingual education. This critical event led to improvement in the relationship between the Chicano community and the school district in years to come.

After months of study, the committee submitted a list of finds to the School Board. 'In all, 43 concerns were brought up by the committee, and the district had a response for each one' (The *Daily Democrat*, September 8, 1982, pp. 1–16). The findings and recommendations submitted by the 'Minority Concerns Committee' were divided into four categories:

1 Counseling
2 Supervision and Discipline
3 Staffing
4 Special Education

Each area was studied by a subcommittee which submitted its own findings and recommendation to the entire committee for approval and submission to the board. (The *Daily Democrat*, September 8, 1982, p. 1).

School district officials reviewed the committee findings and recommendations and submitted a reply to each of the concerns. The following are some of the committee's recommendations and the district's responses:

1 To recruit, hire, and promote Chicanos as bilingual teachers, counselors, and administrators.
2 To involve limited-English speaking students in mainstream extracurricular activities.
3 To provide inservice programs for staff and parents that develop awareness and sensitivity to the cultures of ethnically diverse populations.
4 To recruit and staff special education with proper bilingual special education credentials.
5 To involve Mexican and non-English speaking parents in school issues by conducting the meetings in the primary language of the parents.

Members of the Chicano community responded positively to the recommendations made by the Minority Concerns Committee and to the district's response. A representative of *Concilio* indicated that the committee performed '. . . a tremendously important task . . . but perhaps even more impressive . . . is the leadership, sensitivity, and fairness that Robert Watt, School District Superintendent, has shown' (The *Daily Democrat*, September 10, 1982, p. 1). Jesse Ortiz, a future School Board member, claimed that 'similar concerns were brought up . . . [1972], and we were pacified with a bunch of jargon. This report appears to be more than that, and I hope it is' (The *Daily Democrat*, September 10, 1982, p. 1).

There are several important results that surfaced from the conflict between the school district and the Chicano community: the recognition by the School Board that the district had problems with their Mexican student population and the positive response by members of the Mexican community to the district's actions. The second major outcome is that the superintendent, Bob Watt, emerged as a 'sensitive and fair leader', as one Chicano described him. This fact is very important, because the superintendent played a significant role in future years. The third major consequence is that Jesse Ortiz surfaced as an advocate of the

Chicano community. He also played a significant role in future years in the relationship between the school district and the Chicano community.

Political Climate and Mobilization in the 1980s and 1990s

It is important to explain the political climate of the school district and of the Chicano community in the early 1980s in order to better understand the dynamics of the phenomena studied here. The Woodland Joint Unified School District was experiencing a classical incumbent defeat/superintendent turnover/outside successor phenomena (ID/STO/OS), as explained by Iannaccone and Lutz (1970), and subsequent verificational studies on school district policy realignment. Some members of the Woodland School Board were recalled in 1981. The incumbent superintendent was fired and a new one from outside the district was brought in. As predicted by Iannaccone and Lutz (1970), the district experienced policy, organizational, personnel, and programmatic changes as a result of the recall of School Board members, superintendent turnover and the hiring of a new superintendent from outside the district. In fact, the school district went through a realignment and, at times chaotic period for about three years. The top district administrative team was replaced and some policy and programmatic changes were made.

It is during this period of time that the Chicano community struck at the district, accusing it of discriminatory practices. Some changes were made in 1982–84, but, in general not much was accomplished, due to the district policy and administrative instability. However, during the 1983 School Board election, two of the Board members elected in the 1981 recall election were defeated. Two new Board members were elected, Bob Horel and Donna Rae Hays. The election of these two individuals brought some stability and continuity to the policy and administrative system, and to the district in general. The new School Board members played a significant role in the relationship between the Chicano community and the school district in the years to come.

The political, cultural, and mutual aid organizations of the Chicano community continued to function during the 1980s. *Concilio* found itself involved in some fiscal problems but continued to operate on a limited basis. *Comité de Beneficiencia Mexicana*, *Las Guadalupanas*, the Charro group, and the MECHA student organizations also functioned during this time. However, several new organizations began to emerge, and gains were made in the political electoral arena by the Chicano community. Two Ballet Folklorico groups were formed during the 1980s. One was led by a Beamer teacher and bilingual instructional aide; this group was reorganized and became known as the Ballet Folklorico of Beamer School. Its members consisted mainly of Beamer Elementary School students and alumni. The other group, Ballet Folklórico Latino de Woodland, was sponsored by the Hispanic Chamber of Commerce.

In 1983 through the efforts of the Mexican-American *Concilio* and other members of the Mexican community, the Hispanic Chamber of Commerce was founded. The organizers of the new organization felt that the Woodland Chamber of Commerce was not in tune with the needs of the Hispanic small business community, therefore, there was a need for the creations of the Hispanic Chamber of Commerce (The *Daily Democrat*, April 1, 1983). It must be noted that among the organizers of the new Chamber of Commerce were Xavier Tafoya, city council member, and Rick Gonzalez, a member of *Concilio*. Another organization that surfaced in the 1980s, the Association of Mexican-American Educators (AMAE), was organized in 1984. One of the first tasks of this organization was to advocate for many of the changes that the Minority Concern Committee recommended in 1982, and the board supported as a result of the actions taken by LUPME in 1981–82. AMAE was concerned with what appeared to be lack of commitment by the School Board. In an article in (The *Daily Democrat*), June 13, 1984, the district bilingual education coordinator claimed that local schools would feel the impact of statewide shortages of bilingual teachers and the district recruitment efforts were failing to solve the problem.

The AMAE leadership also expressed concerns with the lack of administrative hires and promotions by the school district. The chairpersons of *El Concilio*, AMAE, and a representative of the Hispanic Chamber of Commerce expressed their concerns to School Board members and to the Superintendent of schools. The groups were critical of the school system; a series of meetings between representatives of *Concilio*, AMAE, and School Board members were held, targeting the two individuals elected in 1983. The importance of AMAE is that the Chicano district employees had internal organizations through which changes could be advocated and recommended. Simultaneously, an outside group, *El Concilio*, also put pressure on the school district. It must be pointed out that AMAE was born out of an education committee of *El Concilio*. Several meetings were held in 1983 and 1984 to discuss the status of the education of Chicanos. This was in response to the 1981–82 conflict between the Chicano community and the school district. The conclusion reached was that an organization which represented the voice, interest, and knowledge of Chicano educators had to be organized. Such was the birth of AMAE in 1984.

The 1982 elections for the Woodland City Council brought an electorate victory to the Chicano community; Xavier Tafoya was elected to a four-year term. He was the first person of Mexican descent ever elected to the city council. There had been other attempts, especially by Rick Gonzalez, who lost by a very small margin in the 1970s. The election of Mr Tafoya served to convince many outside and inside the Mexican community that a Mexican could get elected to public office in Woodland. It is interesting to note that Mr Tafoya is a member of one of the original Mexican families. During the latter part of the 1980s, the Chicano community made significant gains with the Woodland educational system. Relationships between the school district and the Mexican community were at their best. Under the leadership of its Superintendent and Board of Education, the Woodland Joint Unified School District responded positively to the educational demands and needs of the Chicano community. Some of the Chicano educators hired in the 1970s became educational leaders and played an important support and advocacy role. The Mexican community, however, in 1987, elected one of their own to the School Board. This is very important because the Chicano School Board member was an activist and vocal supporter of the needs of the Chicano community.

In 1985 Jesse Ortiz, a native of Woodland, challenged the incumbents in Trustee Area Four of the Woodland joint Unified School District. Ortiz, a veteran of the Marine Corps and a graduate from Woodland High School, ran a strong campaign. His educational philosophy included the belief that all children have the right to grow to their fullest potential and claimed that all schools should and could become effective. He also made the dropout problem in the district, particularly as it impacted Chicano students, a cornerstone of his campaign (The *Daily Democrat*, November 3, 1985, p. 8). The challenger, Ortiz, indicated a strong commitment to the Woodland community and listed a number of organizations that he had been a part of, such as special olympics, the Yolo County *Concilio*, the Yolo County Mental Health Council, and the Yolo County Association of Mexican-American Educators (The *Daily Democrat*, August 16, 1985). He had the support of a wide spectrum of the community at large, including most of the Chicano community. The election was held on November 5, 1985, and the election results were disappointing to the Chicano community in general and to candidate Ortiz in particular; he lost by three votes.

The election results were disappointing, however, there was a silver lining to it. Some members of the Chicano community claimed it was a functional equivalent of a win. He had almost defeated an incumbent School Board member. The campaign had been 'a clean one', as one of the challengers put it, 'it was a very good, clean campaign. I was rather surprised there wasn't more letter writing and mud slinging' (The *Daily Democrat*, November 6, 1985, p. 8). The fact that it was not a hotly contested anti-incumbent campaign was evidenced by Mr Ortiz's political appeal with the voters. The incumbents usually have an advantage over the challengers, especially during a campaign when they are not the focus of attention. The voters had given Mr Ortiz a very strong vote of confidence.

The experience and the political organization of the 1985 School Board election campaign paid dividends in 1987; Jesse Ortiz competed for one of two seats on the Woodland Joint Unified School District Board of Education. An incumbent School Board member decided not to seek re-election; it was important to fill this vacancy with someone supportive of the educational needs of the Chicano community. The retiring incumbent School Board member had shown a strong support to the Chicano community. This individual was elected in 1983 and played a significant role in stabilizing the school district and provided leadership in opening the educational system to the Chicano community.

During the 1987 School Board election, there were five candidates — four challengers and one incumbent — seeking two seats on the School Board. The issues that surfaced during this election were: '1) Woodland growth vs. inadequate funding, 2) rising student dropout rates, 3) overcrowded classes, 4) low teachers' salaries, and 5) school board/community relations' (The *Daily Democrat*, October 26, 1987). Mr Ortiz ran a proactive campaign emphasizing strengthening the home, school, community partnership, implementing more comprehensive remedial and recovery programs in grades 9–12 to lower the dropout rate, and exploring various methods used by other districts in handling growth (The *Daily Democrat*, October 22, 1987, p. 1). The school district dropout rate, the education of limited English-proficient children, and bilingual education also surfaced during the 1987 campaign. Mr Ortiz claimed that the dropout rate was a district and community problem. Mr Ortiz was supported by a wide spectrum of individuals and organizations, including the local newspaper which endorsed him and claimed that:

> Jesse Ortiz impressed us with his deep-seated commitment to our educational system . . . [and] is committed to the community and its young people. His involvement in numerous local organizations shows the

dedication that we believe is needed on the school board . . . It is for this commitment, his caring attitude toward the community, and the skills he brings to the tasks at hand that we recommend a vote for Jesse Ortiz (The *Daily Democrat*, November 1, 1987).

The election results this time were different — Mr Ortiz received 1768 votes and won a seat on the Woodland Joint Unified School District. Also re-elected was Bob Horel, an incumbent, and a strong supporter of the Chicano community. The election of Mr Ortiz to the School Board is extremely significant for several reasons. First, it provided a direct voice for the Chicano community at the policy-making level. Second, it provided continuity to the policies of the School Board which benefitted the Chicano community. Third, it provided the Chicano community with a much awaited victory in electoral process in the educational arena. And fourth, it provided the Chicano community with a positive role model in a public and visible position.

Meir and Stewart (1991) make a strong case for the election of Chicanos to local school boards, and claim that Hispanics are denied access to educational institutions, in part due to the lack of representation on school boards. 'Second generation educational discrimination' exists because Hispanics lack the political power to prevent such actions. School districts with greater Hispanic representation on the School Board and among teaching faculty experience significantly less 'second generation discrimination against Hispanic students'. They claim that the elections of Latinos to local school boards leads '. . . to greater Hispanic representation in administrative positions which leads to more Hispanic teachers'. The increase of Hispanic educators, they contend, produces '. . . educational policies that benefit Hispanic students'. The education of Mexican-American students, for example, '. . . are a function of their political resources. Where they have extensive political representation, they have been able to reduce the level of discrimination. Where they do not, they are a subordinate racial minority' (Meir and Stewart, 1991, p. XV).

Second generation educational discrimination is defined by Meir and Stewart as:

> . . . [T]he use of academic grouping and discipline in a discriminatory manner so that Hispanic students are separated from Anglos. With this separation, Hispanic students are denied educational opportunities that are offered to Anglo students (Meir and Stewart, 1991:1).

According to these authors, second generation discrimination by the educational system results in high drop-out rates, low levels of educational attainment and inferior educational programs; the election of Chicanos to local school boards will result in educational policies that benefit Chicano students (Meir and Stewart, 1991). The impact that Chicano representation had on school boards is manifested in educational policy changes that can be measured by looking at three criteria: academic grouping, discipline, and educational attainment. Academic grouping is characterized by homogeneous and/or ability grouping at the elementary level and curriculum tracking in secondary schools. Homogeneous ability grouping and curriculum tracking deny equal educational opportunities to minority students. This type of second generation educational discrimination produces low academic achievement in minority students. Students can be discriminated against in

disciplinary procedures if these procedures are not consistently applied. 'Much literature supports the conclusion that discipline is used for purposes other than to maintain order. By selectively punishing minority students, they can be discouraged from attending school or from engaging in certain behaviors' (Meir and Stewart, 1991:24). The authors argue that researchers must study the disciplinary procedures of Hispanic students by educational institutions.

Hispanic students who are subjected to academic grouping and discriminatory disciplinary practices are more likely to be denied access to the best educational experiences that the school district has to offer. They might consequently pursue one of three options:

1 Drop out of school altogether.
2 Continue to attend school but become disinterested, fall behind, and never graduate.
3 Stay in school, graduate from high school but receive an inferior education compared with that received by Anglo students.

Dropout and high school graduation rates are recommended as indicators of educational attainment. The authors suggest that further research on the quality of education that minority students receive needs to be pursued (Meir and Stewart, 1991:25, *passim*).

It is clear that the involvement of the Chicano community in the politics of education of the Woodland Joint Unified School District and the election of a Chicano to the School Board produced educational policies that benefited Chicano students. In presenting and analyzing the data, the categories proposed by Browning, *et al.* (1984) and those proposed by Meir and Stewart (1991) will be used. These categories are gains in employment by Chicanos, improvement of educational programs, academic grouping, discipline rates, drop-out rates, college attendance rates and academic recognition awards. The school district's priorities and policies towards the Chicano community were radically transformed during the late 1980s and early 1990s, in part as a result of political incorporation and representation of a Chicano on the Woodland Joint Unified School Board and, in part due to the responsiveness of the school district. A Chicano educator and long term employee of the district contends that the election of Mr Ortiz to the School Board played a significant role; 'It is critical to have a Chicano [on the school board]. I think it [the School Board] has a real vested interest in the Hispanic community. It is important; . . . the community has to feel that it has representation.'

This individual indicated that having Mr Ortiz on the School Board made a significant difference because he was concerned with the education of Chicano children and always made the rest of the School Board members and administrators aware of the issues. Such concern was translated into policies that benefited the Chicano community. For example, during the 1990–91 academic year, the School Board adopted a ten-point list of priorities. The number one priority was bilingual education; number two, opportunity program; number three, cultural diversity; number nine, the Elementary Schools Math, Engineering and Science Achievement Program (MESA); and number ten, a counselor for at risk students. The significance of the Board's priorities is that dollars were committed and did not just receive lip service.

The district's commitment to bilingual education is significant because the number of LEP students grew from 707 in 1981 to 1171 in 1990. The district commitment is clearly evident in the number of bilingual certificated staff. The district's bilingual office identified fifty-eight bilingual certificated personnel for the 1990–91 school year, working in several of the schools (forty-seven in elementary schools, six at the junior high level, and five at the high school level). It must be pointed out that eighteen of those identified were not Chicanos, though they were bilingual (Spanish/English). This was possible due to the School Board's policy of sending district representatives on recruitment trips throughout the Southwest in order to hire bilingual and minority personnel. A common practice was to offer contracts to bilingual personnel at the site of the recruitment efforts. The bilingual program curriculum was also strengthened at both the elementary and secondary level. The district aggressively pursued federal grants for its bilingual programs. During the 1980s, it received three different Title VII grants; one was in cooperation with another school district in Yolo County in the area of computers, another focused on the LEP high school students, and the third was a math and science curriculum for two elementary schools (Beamer and Grafton) in collaboration with faculty from California State University, Sacramento and Stanford University.

A district administrator indicated that the district has made significant improvement in curriculum areas for limited English-speaking students. 'There have been lots of changes, clearly more of a commitment to improve the curriculum and providing district money . . . at the junior high level.' Bilingual education was the Board's number one priority in 1990. The school district also implemented an innovative program at Beamer Elementary School. At the request of both Anglo and Chicano parents, under the leadership of the school's principal, the School Board approved a Spanish immersion program which was implemented in 1984. The salient feature of this program is that it served monolingual English-speaking students and monolingual Spanish-speaking Mexican students. This is a variation of most other Spanish immersion programs which serve primarily the monolingual English-speaking community. This program has been recognized as a model program, and personnel from other districts have visited the school to see it in operation.

The school district also demonstrated its commitment to a quality education for all children, in particular for those students who have traditionally been underrepresented in math, engineering, and science careers, by implementing and fiscally supporting the Math, Engineering and Science Achievement program (MESA). This program was implemented at all levels of the school district (elementary, junior high and high school). The Woodland Joint Unified School District is one of the very few districts statewide that implemented a MESA program at all levels. The K-12 MESA program was one of the top ten priorities of the School Board for the 1990–91 academic year. The School Board was faced with a significant fiscal shortage; the Superintendent and School Board made it very clear that MESA was off the negotiating table and would not be cut. This is significant, because in a crisis most School Boards would have cut such programs. The fact that this district did not cut MESA is very important. It must be noted that the majority of the students in MESA are Chicanos.

The district's high school has been nationally recognized for a model vocational program whose purpose is to integrate the academic and vocational curriculum.

Table 5.1:   *Employment gains by Chicanos (1981–1990)*

Year	Chicano students per cent	Chicano teachers per cent	Chicano pupil personnel per cent	Chicano administration per cent	Chicano classified staff per cent
81–82	30	8	11	12	21
84–85	31	9	16	12	26
89–90	33	14	17	19	28

Source: California State Department of Education CBDS Data Collection (1981–1990).

Table 5.2:   *Certified personnel hired per year (1986–1990)*

Year	White (per cent)	Chicano (per cent)	Other Minority (per cent)
1986	26.55 (69.8 per cent)	9 (23.7 per cent)	2.5 (6.6 per cent)
1987	34.75 (67.9 per cent)	11 (21.5 per cent)	5.4 (10.6 per cent)
1988	34.75 (67.1 per cent)	13 (25.1 per cent)	4 (7.8 per cent)
1989	28.75 (63.6 per cent)	14.5 (32 per cent)	2 (4.4 per cent)
1990	37.75 (68.9 per cent)	12 (21.9 per cent)	5 (9.1 per cent)

Source: Woodland Joint Unified School District (October 25, 1990).

The program has also been credited with increasing the number of students attending institutions of higher education. In a February, 1991 report to the School Board, a high school administrator reported that, 'In five years since the career opportunities paths in education, the drop-out rate at the high school has plummeted . . . the number of students going on to higher education increased . . . attendance rates climbed [and] suspension rates fell (The *Daily Democrat*, February, 16, 1991, pp. 1, 8).

As suggested by Browning, *et al.* (1984), an indicator that the school district is responsive to the interest of the Chicano community is gains in employment by the Chicano community within the school district. It is also an indicator of the political influence of the Chicano community. Table 5.1 shows the gains that Chicanos made from 1981 to 1990. The table lists the Chicano students, teachers, administrators, pupil personnel, and classified staff in the Woodland Joint Unified School District during the 1980s. It also shows the gains by Chicanos in each category. The actual gains by the Chicano community in areas of employment occurred from 1986 to 1990 as reported by the school district personnel office to the School Board on October 25, 1990. Table 5.2 shows the growth of Chicanos in certificated personnel hired from 1986 to 1990.

This data is significant because the district made a concerted effort to hire Chicanos and other minorities proportionate with their student population. The combined minority student population for 1989–90 was 36 per cent, with Chicanos accounting for 33 per cent. The district shows a combined minority certificated hire rate for 1990 to be 31 per cent which is close to the 36 per cent minority student population. The district has not by any means reached parity with its minority population, in general, nor with Chicano community in particular. The data, however, demonstrates a commitment by the School Board and the administration to hire certified personnel who reflect the makeup of its student body.

It is important to note that for the 1991–92 academic year, Chicanos were represented at all levels of the policy and administrative areas of the school district. There was one Chicano on the School Board, which included one black female, two white males, and three white females. At the administrative level, a Chicana served as the Associate Superintendent for Curriculum, a Chicano served as Director of Bilingual Programs, five Chicanos served as principals, one Chicano and one Chicana served as vice-principals at the three secondary schools, and a Chicana was the head counselor for the high school. The number of Chicanos in administrative and leadership positions increased from five in 1989–90 to eight during the 1991–92 academic year; Chicano principals increased considerably from two in 1990–91 to five in 1991–92.

Obviously, the appointment of Chicanos to key positions in education represents one of the most drastic changes in education policy. Popkewitz reminds us, however, that these seemingly drastic changes reflect some central control manifested in the language of change, and that the 'discussion of universal standards juxtaposed against a local *determination* of strategies presupposes centralized definitions' (1991:165). Consequently:

> The reform reports legitimate the transformation occurring and are involved in the processes related to production. The policy formulations articulate particular interest-bound responses to social and economic transformations . . . The resulting practices are neither neutral, disinterested nor without social consequences. This framing of discourse patterns with institutional practices cannot be read as either a theory of conspiracy or the voluntary practices of a misguided people . . . (Popkewitz, 1991:165).

The information obtained in Woodland supports the positions of Meir and Stewart (1991) as well as Popkewitz (1991) that 1) Chicano representation at the school board level, in administrative and teaching positions ultimately produces educational policies that benefit the Chicano community; and that 2) the political compromises arrived at by the Chicano and mainstream communities are the result of cultural changes in both communities. It must be pointed out, however, that the appointment of Chicanos to leadership and teaching positions is not a function of political patronage, but a function of the political resources of the Chicano community which leads to policy transformation by the School Board. Meir and Stewart (1991) argue that the election of Chicanos to the School Board results in policies that benefit the Chicano student population. These policies deal with academic grouping, discipline, and scholastic achievement. The authors label these categories as 'second generation educational discrimination.' The participation of Chicanos at the policy-making level, the authors claim, reduces or eliminates such discriminatory practices leading to the improvement of scholastic attainment by the Chicano student population.

Table 5.3 illustrates Woodland High College Prep courses by ethnicity for academic year 1990–91; Anglo students accounted for 71 per cent, Chicanos 24 per cent, and others 5 per cent of those students enrolled in A–F requirements for entrance in the University of California. The total Chicano student population at the high school for 1990–91 was 29 per cent of which 24 per cent were enrolled in college prep courses. One may argue that Chicanos enrolled in college bound courses have not yet reached parity in proportion to its total population, however,

Table 5.3: Students enrolled in college prep (CP) classes (1990–1991 academic year)

Year	Anglo	Chicano	Other
1990–91	71 per cent	24 per cent	5 per cent

Source: High School College Preparation Courses by Ethnicity, 1990–91 Academic Year.

Table 5.4: High school Student suspension rate (discipline)

	Student population		Students suspended		
Year	Total students population	Chicano student population	Total	Chicano	Other students
1986–87	1510	380 (25 per cent)	322	120 (37 per cent)	202 (63 per cent)
1989–90	1501	490 (33 per cent)	115	39 (34 per cent)	76 (66 per cent)
1990–91	1519	447 (29 per cent)	73[a]	24 (33 per cent)	49 (67 per cent)

Note: [a]Six months
Source: 1990 High School Accountability Report Card and 1986–87, 1991 Student Suspension Reports.

they are much closer to parity than they are away from it. It must be pointed out, however, that the high school staff has a task to do in order to improve such rate. It is interesting to note that Woodland Joint Unified High School significantly increased the senior graduates completion average of A-F requirements. It went from 18.8 per cent in 1985 to 40.2 per cent in 1990. It surpassed the state average in 1990 which was 31.1 per cent. In 1985, Woodland was below the state average (25.4 per cent). The following table (Table 5.4) illustrates the high school student suspension rates for academic years 1986–87, 1988, and 1990–91 (six months only). It is interesting to note that in 1986–87, 21 per cent of the student population was expelled; of those 322 expelled, 120 or 37 per cent were Mexican students. The Chicano student population, however, was 25 per cent. It is clear that Chicanos were slightly overrepresented in this category. It could be argued that this particular year, Chicanos were discriminated by the high school disciplinary policies and practices as postulated by Meir and Stewart (1991).

Woodland Joint Unified High School students were suspended at an average of twenty-seven per month and Chicanos at an average of ten per month in 1986–87. However, the expulsion experienced a sharp decrease during the 1989–90 and 1990–91 academic years. In 1989–90, 115 students were suspended and thirty-nine (34 per cent) were Chicanos. The monthly average suspension rate for the school was 9.6 per cent, while for Chicanos it was 3.2 per cent. During the first six months of 1990–91 academic year, a total of seventy-three students, or an average of twelve per month, were expelled. During the same period, twenty-four (33 per cent) Chicano students were suspended — an average of four per month.

The rate of suspensions for Chicano students during the 1989–90 and the first six months of the 1990–91 academic year also showed a reduction when compared with the 1986–87 rates. Chicano students were expelled disproportionately in 1986–87. However, in 1989–90 and 1990–91 this rate of suspension approximates its

Table 5.5: High school academic award recognition

Year	Total number of students	Number of whites	Number of Chicanos	Awards given	Number of Chicanos recognized
1969	N/A	N/A	N/A	120	4 (3 per cent)
1983	N/A	N/A	N/A	240	37 (15 per cent)
1987	1510	1078 (71 per cent)	380 (25 per cent)	190	30 (16 per cent)
1989	1462	988 (68 per cent)	414 (28 per cent)	161	25 (15 per cent)
1990	1501	968 (65 per cent)	490 (33 per cent)	168[a]	39 (23 per cent)
1990	1501	968 (65 per cent)	490 (33 per cent)	97[b]	38 (39 per cent)
1991	1519	1011 (65 per cent)	447 (30 per cent)	292	55 (19 per cent)

Note: [a]Awards; [b]Scholarships
Source: District Award Assembly Lists — *Daily Democrat*, 1969, 1983, 1987, 1989, 1990, 1991

Table 5.6: Students inducted into National Honor Society

Year	Total inducted	Spanish surname students inducted
1971	54	1 (2 per cent)
1990	37	7 (19 per cent)

Source: *Daily Democrat*, 1971, 1990.

enrollment rate for both years. It could be argued that Chicanos are not disproportionately suspended; therefore, they do not experience second generation educational discrimination.

Several indicators of scholastic achievement will be discussed. They are academic recognition, high school drop out rate, and college going rates (Tables 5.5 to 5.7). One of the indicators of scholastic achievement that the high school utilizes is 'recognition for academic achievement.' The high school recognizes its students on a regular basis, during an awards assembly. The list of the honor students is printed by the local newspaper. Table 5.5 shows the academic recognition of Chicano students for 1969, '83, '87, '89, '90, and '91. In 1969, there were 120 students recognized for academic achievement; however, only four (3 per cent) of Chicano students received awards; the Chicano high school student population was around 20 per cent. The number and percentage of Chicanos recognized for academic achievement reached a high of 23 per cent and 19 per cent for 1990 and 1991 respectively. However, the percentage of Chicanos awarded scholarships in 1990 was 39 per cent. The data demonstrates that Chicanos experienced a significant increase in academic recognition since 1969. This percentage is not proportionate with their population. It could be argued that Chicano experience a degree of second generation educational discrimination in scholastic attainment since their recognition rate is not proportionate to their population rate. However, it is safe to say that the discriminatory aspect has been drastically reduced when compared to the 1969 recognition rate. Chicanos in 1990 received a significant number of scholarships. There were 97 given in this year and Chicanos received 39 per cent, while their population was 33 per cent; one can only conclude that Chicanos are doing much better academically than 1969.

Table: 5.7: *High school drop-out rates (1988–1989)*

Year	Average	Whites	Chicanos
	State rates		
1988	22 per cent	17 per cent	31 per cent
1989	20 per cent	16 per cent	29 per cent
	Woodland high school rates		
1988	10 per cent	9 per cent	13 per cent
1989	10 per cent	8 per cent	15 per cent

Source: California State Department of Education CBEDS Data Collection (1988–1989).

Table 5.8: *High school college attendance rate*

Year	Anglo students	Chicano students
1985	42 per cent	22 per cent
1986	54 per cent	51 per cent
1988	38 per cent	51 per cent
1989	47 per cent	37 per cent

Source: California Post-Secondary Education Commission (1985–89).

Another indicator of improvement in scholastic achievement by Chicano students at Woodland Joint Unified High School is the number of students inducted into the National Honor Society. Table 5.6 shows that in 1971 only 2 per cent of those inducted were Chicanos; however, by 1990 (19 per cent) of the inductees were Spanish surname students. Their number is not yet proportionate with their population (31 per cent), but the dramatic increase from 1971 to 1990 must be noted. It demonstrates a reduction in the second generation educational discrimination phenomenon as described as described by Meir and Stewart (1991). It supports their hypothesis that it is a function of the participation of Chicanos at the policy-making level.

The data on Table 5.7 shows an overall low dropout rate in 1988 and 1989 for the high school. Mexican students were dropping out at a higher rate than white students during both years; however, their rate was significantly lower than the state average for their group. The slightly higher drop-out rate among the Chicano students is and has been a concern of local educators, the Chicano community, and the Chicano School Board member as reflected in his election campaign. It is a concern of the high school head counselor and administrators which they claim needs to be constantly addressed. It must be pointed out, however, that the rates reported in Table 5.7 do not include the dropout rate for the continuation high school.

Table 5.8 lists the college-attendance rate for Woodland Joint Unified High School graduates for 1985, 1986, 1988, and 1989. The data clearly demonstrates some significant gains made by the Chicano high school graduates. Their overall attendance rate increased from 22 per cent in 1985 to 51 per cent both in 1986 and

1988 and to 37 per cent in 1989. The increase is significant due to the fact that in 1980 the US Census reported that in Yolo County only 4.4 per cent of the adult Chicano population had completed one to three years of college.

The school district officials reported that the number of Chicanos attending the University of California system increased considerably in 1990. The Chicano graduating class of 1990 consisted of seventy-nine students, fourteen of which (18 per cent) attended the University of California system. It is a significant increase from seven in 1989. The rates for the California State Universities and community colleges were not yet available. However, it was reported by school district officials that in 1990, Woodland had the second highest minority MESA populations attending college in Northern California. This report was made in regards to the impact that MESA has had on the college-attendance rate of Chicano students.

District officials have provided several reasons for the relative success of Chicano students. The MESA advisor claimed that the services offered by the MESA High School program contributed to the high college-attendance rate of Chicano students (The *Daily Democrat*, July 3, 1990). An administrator in charge of vocational education reported to the School Board that the Model Career Paths Vocational Program also contributed to such success (The *Daily Democrat*, February 16, 1991, pp. 1–8).

Another Chicano educator claimed that the success of the school district could be attributed to several factors:

1 The pressure by the Chicano community in 1972 and 1982 which forced the school district to analyze itself.
2 The hiring of some educators in 1972–73 as a result of the first confrontation between the Chicano community and the school district. "Woodland has been in the forefront in hiring minority educators . . . who were really prepared . . . some of these individuals . . . are very strong in their commitment . . . they are articulate, well versed . . . have been able to establish tremendous credibility in the district."
3 The district implemented a number of innovative programs at the elementary level which provided the students with ". . . real strong feelings of self concept and ability because there are a lot of resources, role models, and activities to promote."
4 The election of a Chicano to the School Board, the Board's willingness to improve the education of Chicanos.
5 The leadership provided by the Superintendent.
6 The support of the School Board was also mentioned as some of the factors which contributed to the success of Chicanos in the school system.
7 The support and actions of the Woodland School District teachers.

Although there seemed to be some relative successes, school officials and members of the Chicano community are not totally satisfied with the outcomes. Of great concern to some has been the number of Chicano students who receive a 2.0 or lower at the secondary schools and the percentage of Chicano students enrolled in college prep courses. A group of Chicano parents are also concerned with the quality of education that their sons and daughters are receiving at the junior high schools. They are concerned that Chicano students are not being challenged enough and that the junior high curriculum (1991–92) may, in fact, be tracking Chicano students into less academically challenging and low quality classes. A series of meetings was held during the 1991–92 academic year between the parents, administrators, counselors, and teachers. The significance of this phenomena is that members of the Chicano community are not just discussing affirmative action, bilingual and/or discipline problems, but are expressing concerns with the 'lack of high level and challenging curriculum'. The school district policy makers are also discussing such issues.

In a January 1990 article, the local newspaper reported the conditions of Chicanos in the Woodland system were adequate but could be better (The *Daily Democrat*, January 18, 1990, p. 1).

A local Chicano activist claimed that the Woodland Joint Unified School District was going in the right direction but that much needed to be done. A professor at University of California Davis claimed, 'Beamer School is an example of how teachers work with minority students who have a language barrier . . . that is a good model of what can happen. It is doable' (The *Daily Democrat*, January 18, 1990, p. 16).

Conclusion

The Mexican community experienced an organizational and political transformation from its inception in the early 1920s to the late 1980s and early 1990s. As documented in the previous chapter, the Chicano community went from a politically dispossessed and economically powerless position in the 1920s to a relatively socially and politically empowered one, eventually electing its own members to locally elected governmental bodies, thereby making an impact in the school district's policy, programmatic, and personnel practices that benefit the Chicano community.

The data confirms the theories posited by Browning, *et al.* (1984) and Meir and Stewart (1991). During the 1970s and early 1980s, the Mexican community, influenced by the civil rights movement, experienced the 'demand protest phase' in its political development, aptly described by Browning, *et al.* (1984). The Chicano community made some gains in the employment of some of its members and implementation of educational programs; however, the gains were not significant nor sustained. It was not until Chicanos were elected to local elected political bodies (City Council, 1983, and School Board, 1987) that real, significant, and sustained gains were made. Browning, *et al.* (1984) labeled this phenomena as political incorporation, having direct influence on the policy-making body. Political incorporation of the Chicano community is a function of the group resources, such as:

1 The size and percentage of its members;
2 Organizational and political experience of its members;
3 Pressure of an informed and active middle class;
4 The support that it received from the Anglo community, especially the responsiveness by members of the power structure (School Board and administrators).

The Chicano community grew from a few families in the 1920s and 1930s to a significant critical mass in the late 1980s and early 1990s; in 1989–90, Chicanos represented 33 per cent (2709) of the K-12 school-age population. Chicanos learned to organize and function within the framework of the dominant society without losing their own identity. Chicano organizations were created, and some individuals from the Mexican community participated in institutions and organizations of the host community. Several Chicanos ran unsuccessfully for public office, finally electing their own to City Council in 1983 and to the School Board in 1975 and 1987.

The emergence of a Mexican middle class started in the late 1920s and 1930s when some of the original settlers operated business enterprises. Such phenomena continued in the 1940s through the 1960s. This Mexican middle class was joined by a group of professional Chicanos in the late 1970s and 1980s. The hiring of bilingual/bicultural educators by the school system played a significant role. Many of those Chicanos hired in the early 1970s assumed leadership positions within the school system. The Chicano community could rely on an internal advocacy group. In 1984 this group assumed its own identity and formed their own organizations, Association of Mexican American Educators (AMAE). This organization complimented several Chicano organizations, *Concilio* and *Latinos Unidos Para Mejor Educación* (LUPME), which had pressured the school district in prior years.

The gains that the Chicano community experienced in education would not have been possible without the support received from individuals of the Anglo community, such as members the School Board, district administrators and teachers. The election of two individuals to the School Board in 1983 played a significant role. It provided stability and direction to the school district. The district Superintendent with the support of the Board responded positively to the needs of the Mexican student population. The election of a Chicano to the School Board solidified such support. It must be pointed out that the Chicano School Board member enjoyed significant support from the Anglo community as well as the Mexican community.

Meir and Stewart (1991) suggest that the election of Chicanos to the School Board resulted in the promotion of Chicanos to administrative and teaching positions, eventually leading to the development and implementation of policy and programs which lead to the elimination of discriminatory practices and the academic improvement of Chicano students. In contrast with the claims of previous generations of social scientists that research on social issues must be neutral, the authors, based on the information presented here, claim that the only way to understand the nature of the social and political changes in Woodland is to engage not only in objective or descriptive efforts, but in efforts to explain what these changes mean to the minority community:

> Social amelioration efforts of social science were supposed to be politically nonpartisan. The ideology of the social sciences was only supposed to describe how *things* work; that knowledge could be used by any group or interest to provide direction for social progress. Evolutionary and piecemeal change was emphasized. Functional qualities, individuality, and rational organization had priority. Planning was intended to promote social progress as well as to ward off radicalism (Popkewitz, 1991:228).

Today however, as was the case in Woodland, researchers feel a moral obligation to pursue studies which have emancipatory value and produce an implementation of democratic principles, along the lines suggested by Popkewitz (1991) and Apple (1989, 1990). It is precisely in the context of cultural changes permitting members of a society to exercize fully their democratic rights, that the 'ethnogenesis', or the creation of ethnicity (Roosens, 1989) can take place without major disruptions in public life, and without enslaving individuals who lack the power to defend themselves. Castification (Ogbu, 1978; Suarez-Orozco, 1991) is rejected by members of ethnic groups on the grounds that their rights are being violated. Empowerment is enacted, when these members of minority groups go a step further and pursue elected offices which carry a great deal of power.

References

APPLE, M. (1989) *Teachers and Texts: A Political Economy of Class and Gender Relations in Education*, New York, NY: Routledge.

APPLE, M. (1990) *Ideology and Curriculum*, New York, NY: Routledge.

BROWNING, R., RUFUS, P. and MARSHALL, D. and TABB, D. (1984) *Protest is not Enough: The Struggle of Blacks and Hispanics for Equality in Urban Politics*, Berkeley, CA: University of California Press.

CALIFORNIA POSTSECONDARY EDUCATION COMMISSION (1985) *College Going Rate for Selected Schools*, Sacramento, CA: State Department of Education.

CALIFORNIA POSTSECONDARY EDUCATION COMMISSION (1986) *College Going Rate for Selected Schools*, Sacramento, CA: State Department of Education.

CALIFORNIA POSTSECONDARY EDUCATION COMMISSION (1988) *College Going Rate for Selected Schools*, Sacramento, CA: State Department of Education.

CALIFORNIA POSTSECONDARY EDUCATION COMMISSION (1989) *College Going Rate for Selected Schools*, Sacramento, CA: State Department of Education.

CALIFORNIA BASIC EDUCATIONAL DATA SYSTEM COLLECTION (1981–82) *Enrollment and Staff in California Public School Districts*, Sacramento, CA: California State Department of Education.

CALIFORNIA BASIC EDUCATIONAL DATA SYSTEM COLLECTION (1984–85) *Enrollment and Staff in California Public School Districts*, Sacramento, CA: California State Department of Education.

CALIFORNIA BASIC EDUCATIONAL DATA SYSTEM COLLECTION (1989–90) *Enrollment and Staff in California Public School Districts*, Sacramento, CA: California State Department of Education.

IANNCCONE, L. and LUTZ, F. (1970) *Politics, Power and Policy: The Governing of Local School Districts*, Columbus, OH: Charles E. Merrill Publishing, Co.

MEIR, K and STEWART, JR., J. (1991) *The Politics of Hispanic Education: Un paso pa'lante y dos pasos pa'tras*, New York, NY: State University of New York Press.

OGBU, J. (1978) *Minority Education and Caste: The American System in Cross-cultural Perspective*, New York, NY: Academic Press.

POPKEWITZ, T.S. (1991) *A Political Sociology of Educational Reform: Power/knowledge in Teaching, Teacher Education and Research*, New York, NY: Teachers College, Columbia University.

ROOSENS, E. (1989) *Creating Ethnicity: The Process of Ethnogenesis*. Newbury Park, CA: Sage Publications.

SUAREZ-OROZCO, M.M. (1991) 'Migration, Minority Status, and Education: European Dilemmas and Responses in the 1990s', *Anthropology and Education Quarterly*, **22**(2) pp. 99–120.

The *Daily Democrat*, February 26, 1982, Woodland, CA.

The *Daily Democrat*, September 8, 1982, Woodland, CA.

The *Daily Democrat*, September 10, 1982, Woodland, CA.
The *Daily Democrat*, April 1, 1983, Woodland, CA.
The *Daily Democrat*, June 13, 1984, Woodland, CA.
The *Daily Democrat*, August 16, 1985, Woodland, CA.
The *Daily Democrat*, November 3, 1985, Woodland, CA.
The *Daily Democrat*, November 6, 1985, Woodland, CA.
The *Daily Democrat*, October 22, 1987, Woodland, CA.
The *Daily Democrat*, October 26, 1987, Woodland, CA.
The *Daily Democrat*, November 1, 1987, Woodland, CA.
The *Daily Democrat*, January 18, 1990, Woodland, CA.
The *Daily Democrat*, July 3, 1990, Woodland, CA.
The *Daily Democrat*, February 16, 1991, Woodland, CA.
WOODLAND JOINT UNIFIED SCHOOL DISTRICT (1990) *Teacher Recruitment and Hiring Report*
    (Board Report), Woodland, California.

Chapter 6

A School in Change:
The Empowerment of
Minority Teachers

José Cintrón

Beamer Park Elementary is a K-6 school and was built in the mid-1940s. The name of the school is real, however we have used fictitious names for the principal and the teachers, most of whom are still working at the school. It is located in the southeastern quadrant of the city of Woodland, California. The school is situated approximately three blocks from the downtown business area of the community. Beamer is one of three neighborhood schools in the Woodland Joint Unified School District (WJUSD). It sits in an older middle-class section of the city, and is surrounded by moderately priced to upper-medium priced homes. Beamer is one of two original elementary schools in the city of Woodland. It has historically served the Mexican migrant population and many of the upper income students of the school district as well.

Sociocultural Environment

Beamer is the only Spanish immersion school in the Woodland Unified School District and is currently one of only two in the Yolo County region — the other elementary Spanish immersion school is located in Davis, California, a neighboring community about ten miles away. The facilities of the Beamer school take up one complete city block not far away from downtown Woodland. Approximately two-thirds of the property is dominated by a grass and asphalt playground area that is encompassed by chain-link fencing that surrounds the entire play field. In turn, two baseball diamonds, one an official Woodland Little League field, and another smaller one for the Beamer students, take up most of the space. The remaining play area consists of six basketball hoops, four tetherball poles, a large jungle-gym arena, two swing sets with monkey bars and slides, a large grassy area for soccer and football games, and an asphalt section for outdoor lunching and bike racks. There is an additional smaller play area for the kindergartners alongside the primary grades wing; it has several swings and a smaller jungle-gym set.

The school is comprised of four red brick structures of varying sizes and two permanent long and narrow portable classrooms. These buildings are grouped in the northwestern upper hand corner of the square sized property. The placement of the six structures gives Beamer school a basic configuration similar to a reversed letter C. Two long narrow structures or wings house the lower grades and the upper grades; a larger rectangular structure houses the administrative offices and the library; the largest structure houses the cafeteria, gymnasium, and band rooms; and the portables contain two upper-grade classrooms. The lower-grade (K-3) classrooms are housed in the northeastern wing of the school along with the offices and classrooms of the Chapter I Resource Specialist and the English as a Second Language Specialist. The southwestern corner of the school contains the upper primary grades (4,5,6) as well as the computer lab and storage areas for curriculum materials. Approximately in the middle of these two bordering structures sits the administrative wing, which contains the principal's and nurse's office, a counselor's room, and a moderate sized reception area for two secretaries. In addition, this structure contains the library, teacher/staff lounge, and a work area with duplication, ditto, and paper-cutting equipment. A teacher/staff soda machine and paper supply area also take up space in this wing. Each wing is independent and unattached but joined by asphalt and concrete walkways. The portable classrooms sit approximately in the southeastern corner of the site next to the faculty/staff parking lot. One contains a fifth the other a sixth grade classroom. An additional sixth grade Gifted and Talented Education (GATE) program classroom is attached to the outside of the gymnasium building.

The largest structure on site is the combination multipurpose building. A moderate-sized wooden floored gym takes up much of the space in this structure. On one wall folding bleachers with twenty rows of seating face a curtained and raised stage of the same dimensions on the opposite wall. In a corner of the building there is a small cafeteria with glass-covered dispensing bins. There is no cooking of meals on site; however, lunches are brought in daily from a district kitchen and given or sold to the students, faculty and staff. Nevertheless, the cafeteria does have a kitchen containing several stoves and ovens that are made available to individual classrooms for fund-raising functions (bake sales, for instance) or light food preparation during holidays (warming hot chocolate in winter, for example). Students eat their lunches on portable tables inside the multipurpose room during the winter season, and outside on picnic benches when weather permits. In addition, the multipurpose building houses the music and physical education teachers' classrooms and storage for gym equipment and musical instruments. Custodial supplies and equipment are also stored in various locations throughout the building.

The interior and exterior of Beamer school can simply be described as clean and well kept. Because of the age of the buildings, the maintenance is generally very conscientious. The principal continually encourages the staff, faculty, and student body to take pride in the cleanliness of their school, and apparently it works. A walk through the hallways shows walls free of markings or vandalism; the school grounds are generally clean and litter free. In fact, the principal specifically asks faculty, staff, and students to pick up paper or debris around school property, and often we have observed students and faculty picking up litter from hallways or outside walk areas. Similarly, restrooms are clean and graffiti free, as are the exterior walls of the structures.

Going through the halls of Beamer gives visitors a positive feeling. In contrast with other elementary schools in which teachers shout at students, or where children are wandering about, or are in class uninvolved in instructional activities,

Beamer reflects an a cheerful and very active group of teachers who enjoy their job and children who genuinely enjoy their school. The interior hallways are always decorated with student-produced art pieces or educational themes of classroom projects. Teachers also are encouraged by the principal to maintain clean and orderly classrooms and to teach students to respect the school building and playgrounds. Overall, classrooms are inviting, bright and colorful. Walls are decorated with posters, bulletin boards, student poetry and pictures, art pieces and memorabilia, and other teaching regalia. Several faculty have fish, baby chicks, rabbits, mice, and even lizards as room pets and use them as instructional aides for science and health unit demonstrations.

According to one of the Hispanic teachers, Beamer is an oasis because:

[I]t (Beamer School) has a unique instructional environment; it has diversity in terms of students, faculty, ethnic groups. So when you have diversity, you have respect for different cultures and ethnic groups and their self-determination. You come here and see Nicaraguenses, Mexicanos, Chilenos, and others.

Ms. Maria Hernandez, the senior immersion teacher on staff, commented, 'The respect for diverse cultures is clearly stated and promoted, and that's something we [faculty] have talked about doing.' Ms. Liliana Herrera, another immersion teachers concures and states, 'It is a stated goal to have diversity in Beamer, and to transfer that spirit to the children; a goal stated by the principal and fellow teachers.'

The principal's office is attractively decorated, albeit small and modest. There is a comfortable couch and several chairs with two or three stuffed animals strewn about for the children; the desk and walls exhibit many personal mementos and photographs. The door is usually open, inviting easy access by teachers, students and parents. One of the virtues of the current principal (Linda Segura) is that she makes everyone around her feel comfortable.

The office reception area is moderate in size, and upon entering and immediately to the left, there is a bulletin board where student art work and other school-wide achievements are displayed. This reception area is well lighted and busy. The two secretaries (both English/Spanish bilinguals) are energetic and friendly and their positive rapport with students and parents enhances the feeling of welcome that exudes from this office space.

Composition of Faculty and Students

The staffing at Beamer Elementary during school year 1990–91 continued a familiar pattern established three to four years ago by the principal and the faculty, specifically the Spanish immersion/bilingual faculty. In fact, the long-term goal of establishing a K-6 grade immersion program is almost realized, and beginning with fall 1991 school year, Beamer will have immersion classrooms in all but one grade level. During the 1990–91 school year however, the school had fifteen classrooms with five Spanish immersion rooms, two bilingual (English/Spanish) rooms, and eight English language rooms. The immersion rooms comprised grades K-4 and the bilingual grades 5 and 6. The English dominant classrooms were in grades

Table 6.1: Faculty and staff ethno-racial composition of Beamer Park Elementary —
1990–1991

Faculty		Staff		Total
Anglo:	7	Anglo:	6	13
Male	1	Male	1	2
Female	6	Female	5	11
Hispanic:	7	Hispanic:	10	17
Male	2	Male	1	3
Female	5	Female	9	14
Cape Verdean:				1
Female	1			

Source: Beamer Park Elementary Handbook, 1990–1991.

K-4 with one 5/6 grade combination and two Gifted and Talented magnet rooms
with a 4/5 combination and a sixth grade. Currently the Spanish immersion/
bilingual rooms and the English dominant rooms are almost evenly split — seven
Spanish eight English. However, plans for the fall 1991 semester call for the addition
of another grade level to the immersion sequence, making the program a K-5
experience. Moreover, it would become the only Spanish immersion program of
its kind in the surrounding service area, including the Davis Immersion Program.

Ethno-racially the faculty and staff of Beamer Elementary is almost evenly divided among Hispanic (Latinos) and Anglo Americans (white, Euro-Americans).
Currently there are no African American or Asian American employees, nor have
there been any during the last three years, since the researchers became involved
with the school. There are seven Hispanic, seven Anglo, and one Cape Verdean
on the faculty. (See Table 6.1). The Anglo staff column in Table 6.1 includes the
librarian, three instructional aides, the reading specialist and the day custodian.
The 1990–91 principal of Beamer, Mrs. Linda Segura is an Anglo woman married
to a Hispanic and also is included in this count. The Hispanic staff column includes
the two front office secretaries, five English/Spanish bilingual instructional aides,
two English/Spanish resource specialists and the night custodian.

There are only three male classroom faculty members at Beamer, one Anglo
and two Hispanics. In addition, the physical education teacher is an Anglo male,
and the music teacher is a Hispanic woman. However, these two positions are
normally not counted as full-time. Other support personnel, including the nurse,
school counselor, and psychologist are Anglo.

The ethnoracial distribution of the student population at Beamer is similar to
that of the teaching staff. Mexican and other Hispanic children predominate; they
represent 55 per cent of the total student population (Segura, L. and Associates,
April 1991). This is down two points from fiscal year 1989–90, when there were
253 Hispanic students (57 per cent), according to the Consolidated Program
Evaluation Report completed in June 1990. In the same report, Anglo students
numbered 158 and represented 36 per cent of the total student population. The
Asian population was 3 per cent (fifteen students), African American students
were 1.5 per cent (five students), and the five East Indian students represented 2
per cent. The total number of students enrolled at Beamer during spring semester
1991 was 440 (Segura, L. and Associates, April 1991).

Table 6.2: Categorical consolidated programs of Beamer Park Elementary — 1989–1990

Program	Funding
Limited-English Proficient	$33,509
School Improvement Program	$45,879
Chapter 1	$45,156
Miller Unruh	$21,900
Chapter 2	$2579
Total	$149,023

Source: Beamer Park Elementary School, Consolidated Program Evaluation, 1990–1991.

A substantial number of Beamer students are from homes with low incomes, as shown by the number of children who participated in the two lunch programs available at the school. During the 1989–90 school year 45 per cent, or 197 students, were enrolled in the free lunch programs, and an additional 67 or 15 per cent qualified for reduced lunches.

Programs at Beamer

Beamer is often referred to as *the* bilingual elementary school (typically by non-Beamer faculty/staff) in the WJUS District. The reference is due in large measure to the number of categorical programs and externally funded programs that exist and thrive successfully at the school. Outsiders — teaching colleagues at other schools, for example — have a perception of Beamer as the school that gets everything. This district-wide perception is clearly understood and shared by many of the Beamer faculty as well. Notwithstanding, the faculty of Beamer strongly believe that they have earned these resources and acknowledge that they make a more concerted effort to solicit these alternative or supplemental monies as compared to other schools in the district (see Table 6.2). In addition to the district and federally funded programs listed in Table 6.2, Beamer has consistently and successfully competed for external funding resulting in the incorporation into the Beamer instructional plan, of several innovative and important curricular ideas, as well as staff development and growth. During 1990–91 Beamer participated in many external and extra-curricular programs. Among these are: an Adopt-a-School program with Mobil Chemical Company — now in its seventh year; Choose Well Be Well which is an educational program with emphasis on food selection and eating habits, in its first year; Early Intervention for School Success program, in its first year; a school-wide Physical Education Program, in its second year; Eisenhower Math and Science; a music program; *Matemáticas para la familia* (Family Math), in its second year; and a Math, Engineering, Science Achievement program (MESA) — the sole elementary chapter in the district — in its second year.

Staff development is an important on-going element in the empowerment scheme for the immersion/bilingual teachers at Beamer. A very significant effort began several years ago during the summer of 1987 when two teachers and the principal participated in a seminar hosted by Title VII and Stanford University on Complex Instruction and the Finding Out/*Descubrimiento* (FO/D) science and math curriculum. Seven more faculty again participated during summer 1988 in the FO/D training, and every summer through 1991 Beamer faculty received training in the curriculum. In addition, during Summer 1990 two Beamer faculty and one of the resource specialists were certified as FO/D Trainers by Stanford and are now providing in-services to teachers throughout the school and district. During summer 1989 one of the immersion teachers participated in a series of workshops on Children's Spanish Literature in Spain. During the summer of 1988 eight Beamer faculty participated in a week long Biliteracy Seminar hosted at the University of California, Santa Cruz. Beamer's administration and faculty reputation for being risk takers in the district fosters a certain noticeable pride among the faculty and staff that work there. Faculty feel it is a school that gets things done, where people are free to try new and innovative programs and classroom applications.

The principal, faculty and staff take pride in the reputation of the school, and the faculty work diligently to maintain this image. When we asked several teachers about the Beamer image, where this image was fostered or whence it came, the response from one of the immersion teachers was typical, 'other teachers say to me that we get everything (programs)'. Maria Hernandez, the kindergarten immersion teacher, was more specific in her response. She commented, 'Beamer works for everything! Beamer tries! We're willing to stay here until seven at night every day to work on things and get things off the ground . . . and I don't see that at other schools.' The prevailing attitude among the teachers and staff at Beamer is that they work for and aggressively solicit these additional programs or projects. Proposal writing for some of the supplemental funding sources takes on a team approach. Local university faculty, School Board members, school faculty, resource personnel, and the principal usually team to write a local or state proposal for a particular project or funding source. A genuine commitment and responsibility to the children motivates these efforts along with a strong desire to be on the cutting edge of pedagogic innovations and/or program implementation.

Spirit of Cooperation

The Spanish immersion and bilingual teachers interviewed for this study represent a group of faculty with a visible, powerful, and important role to play at Beamer. All members of the Immersion/Bilingual Team (I/BT) have as a common goal the implementation and effective use of Spanish language in instructional delivery. This team represents the incarnation and vehicle of power — for Hispanic issues, specifically — and the mechanism for voice within the school and ultimately throughout the Woodland school district. The I/BT consists of all the teachers in the immersion and bilingual classrooms, subsequently the majority are Hispanic. However, other faculty and staff who are interested in the goals and philosophical orientations suggested by the team are invited to participate. Teaching in an immersion/bilingual classroom or having proficiency in Spanish are not prerequisites for participation by other interested school personnel. Interestingly, the principal and several other non-Hispanic faculty participate actively as I/BT members. The two GATE teachers, who are Anglo, have varying proficiencies in Spanish, they have studied the language and various Hispanic cultures (via travel and study abroad), and understand the underlying tenets, philosophies, and goals of bilingualism and multiculturalism and their significance and importance in US

Table 6.3: Immersion/bilingual faculty descriptions of Beamer Park Elementary —
1990–1991

Name	Ethnicity	Sex	Grade	Years Teaching
María Hernández	Cape Verdean	F	K-I*	5
Graciela Poza	Chilean	F	1-I	3
Robert Barrios	Chicano	M	2-I	3
Liliana Herrera	Mejicana	F	3-I	1
Javier Gonzales	Chicano	M	4-I	2
Sara Rogers	Chicana	F	5-B*	2
Angela Escobar	Nicaraguan	F	6-B	3

* I = Immersion Classroom
  B = Bilingual Classroom

Source: Researcher Personal Interviews, 1990–1991.

society. They are strong voices within the I/BT ranks and are both perceived as allies, advocates, and friends by the majority of the I/BT members.

The I/BT teachers represent a close approximation of the Beamer community and the city of Woodland in terms of ethnicity, years of teaching experience, and ethnoracial breakdown (see Table 6.3). The I/BT members are fairly young (early 30s to early 40s) and are individuals whose teaching experience spans a relatively short period of time. The most experienced, Maria Hernandez, has been teaching five years, and the least experienced, Liliana Herrera, has just completed her first year of full-time teaching. The others have two or three years in the classroom.

Maria Hernandez, the Cape Verdean immersion kindergarten teacher and one of the original immersion program veterans, was team leader during the 1990–1991 school year. Javier Gonzales, a young Chicano and second-year fourth grade immersion teacher, is presently team leader. The team leader is charged with scheduling and facilitating meetings as well as preparing the year-long school calendar with events and activities (social or academic) that directly impact the immersion/bilingual program. Other responsibilities include delegating duties to the members during these planned activities and, more importantly, serving as the team advocate or representative at school functions, district meetings, and community activities.

During our conversations with I/BT members over the last three years, we have been impressed with the noteworthy sense of pride and dedication they engender at the school. Their position and status at Beamer is often visible and strong, while on other occasions subtle and restrained, but ever-present. All of these individuals share a strong sense of self-worth, effectiveness and motivation to change schools for the benefit of all students, but most especially for the linguistically and culturally different children. The ethnic identification of teachers is important to them, and they are proud to state it. Maria Hernandez is Cape Verdean, Sara Roger is Chicana, Graciela Poza is Chilean, Liliana Herrera is Mejicana, Javier Gonzalez is Chicano, Robert Barrios is Chicano, and Rosa Vargas is Nicaraguan. All teachers feel very proud of their ethnoracial affiliation. The Mexican migrant student population is the largest at Beamer, and it appreciates the fact that they have Hispanics of various ethnic groups in the school. I/BT faculty have warm and close relationships among themselves; they truly form a team. They help each other and teach children to do likewise.

The majority of the faculty at Beamer have high levels of expectation and commitment to student learning. The I/BT teachers have especially high expectations for their students, and they make strong and consistent efforts to challenge students academically. The level of involvement in the immersion/bilingual classroom activities is intense and genuine. The interest of students is shared as a response to the efforts made and time spent by these teachers preparing academically challenging activities, attending and participating in a myriad of after-school meetings, week-end leisure time dedicated to school fund-raising functions, and attending professional training workshops.

A recent activity highlights the dedication and commitment of the immersion/bilingual teachers to better serve the needs of their students. Last year Beamer adopted a program entitled *Matemáticas para la Familia* or (Family math). Three of the immersion/bilingual teachers volunteered to participate as after-school instructors for interested parents. A small stipend was paid to the teachers to participate in the Family Math Program. Parents and teachers met several evenings per week for two semesters. The focus of the program was to train participating Spanish-speaking parents in the at-home teaching of simple math concepts to their children. During the 1991–92 school year the stipend was eliminated, and the original volunteer teachers continued to participate in the parent-training sessions gratis.

Another example is the Math, Engineering, Science Achievement Program (MESA), a math and science club aimed at encouraging minority students to develop an interest in the sciences. In this program volunteer students are asked to participate in after-school math and science activities that culminate in a year-end science fair/competition with neighboring school districts. Several I/BT faculty help administer the program and also participate as volunteers in the program. This is the only MESA Program at the elementary level in the entire Woodland district and one of only a handful in the surrounding area. The response by participating teachers, students, and parents has been overwhelmingly positive and supportive. Other activities include planning and facilitating the immersion/bilingual program openhouse, preparing and staffing several Sunday *menudo* (Mexican tripe stew) breakfasts, planning and coordinating *Cinco de Mayo* activities, and the *Dia de las Madres* celebration. These teacher-student/community activities engender a bond between the school and the community it serves. Seeing the teachers so fully involved creates a sense of reciprocal learning between teachers, students and their parents.

The I/BT faculty is a highly dedicated and motivated group of individuals. They meet monthly to plan upcoming year-long multicultural activities, I/BT program fund raisers, to decide on new instructional approaches or staff development opportunities, and whenever it is necessary, to address a specific school-wide or district-wide issue. As an example, at the recent final meeting of the year (Spring 1991), concerns regarding Linda Segura's successor were discussed. The team was hopeful that the new principal would understand their I/BT perspective. In addition, the team discussed the upcoming school year focus area. 'Multicultural infusion' was proposed as a possible year-long focus along with on-going teacher and staff inservice conducted by a university faculty. A number of recommendations were made in order to improve instructional approaches, and the quality of the learning environment at Beamer. These suggestions have been implemented during the academic year of 1991–92.

One of the more important elements of the success of the immersion/bilingual teachers in their strides towards empowerment is the principal, Mrs Linda Segura. Mrs Segura is a low key, soft spoken, high energy administrator. She effectively delegates many of the decision-making responsibilities to competent and trusted faculty. In the process she instills a growing sense of self-governance among many of the faculty and in particular, the immersion/bilingual teachers. In effect, they are encouraged to find their own 'voice' and then mentored on how to use this collective voice to affect change. With her kind manner, pleasing smile and warm hugs Mrs Segura encourages her faculty to work together; she provides them with many opportunities to experiment with innovative and new projects. Ms Herrera, the newest immersion faculty member comments, 'She [Segura] does not check on us all the time or tell us that we have to do this or that. She gives us liberty to perform, and that has really helped.' Mrs Segura is perceived as a nurturing person who cares about teachers, and is completely dedicated to the education of all children.

In a minor misunderstanding between an I/BT teacher and a parent, Mrs Segura was very supportive. The teacher describes her predicament as follows: 'I was crying; and the parent left, and I did not want to come back to the classroom; so I went to clean my eyes, and the principal saw me. I was not going to tell her; but since she asked me I told her. She is like my mother.' The teacher felt bolstered and loved by the principal. Mrs Segura is seen as a key supporter and advocate of the immersion/bilingual program.

Mrs Segura is in tune with the immersion bilingual program curriculum and philosophy. She is strongly in favor of the use of home languages in classrooms and the maintenance of home cultures. To that end she has become skillful at working with all of the teachers at Beamer. She is collegial and warm with all and motivates her faculty to grow professionally. In fact, she has mentored several of the I/BT faculty and encouraged them to pursue advanced degrees in educational administration so that in the future they can take on leadership roles in schools.

The magnitude of her impact was evident during her recent farewell activities. Over the course of several months faculty, students, staff and community members participated in dinners and retirement parties to recognize and acknowledge her important contributions over the years. The Hispanic community of Woodland showed their gratitude as well. Even the WJUSD Superintendent attended several farewell functions. Mrs Segura was perceived in the Hispanic community as an advocate for linguistically and culturally different students and a diplomatic and effective administrator.

The close faculty-staff relationships are maintained outside the classroom. They go to each other's homes, attend parties and socialize together. The I/BT faculty have a high sense of ethnic pride, and bring to the school a strong sense of cultural identity. Mr Gonzales, an I/BT teacher, said:

> I always thought I'd be the token Chicano or the sole minority in school. . . . In this school I am one minority out of twenty, so when a minority speaks here, he is not ostracized, or given these mean looks, because the minorities in the schools are not the minority numerically.

Another teacher said:

> At one level it frees me from being the all-encompassing bilingual minority, i.e., the translator, the pusher of this agenda, the expert; it frees me, I don't have to do menial things, I don't have to represent all the problems of the Chicano Latino community here; there are other people who can fill those positions freeing me to devote some time to the classroom to enhance my expertise, my training, more time to concentrate on my students. I am not wasting energy on negative experiences, i.e., defending bilingual education, defending cultural pluralism or diversity; it frees me up emotionally in terms of time; I can do other things.

Javier Gonzales, the fourth grade I/BT teacher made this remark:

> It means the right to self-determination, to determine what I want to teach, what I want to be, what I want to call myself; pride in who I am, where I come from, where my family and my community come from; pride in my community's contribution to society, the awareness of my history. I am committed and willing to act to help people in my community and others to achieve that feeling of pride, knowing where they come from, and knowing they can make it.

Liliana Herrera Comments:

> This is the school in which we do a lot of things that have to do with social problems in our curriculum, we talk about these things, we are teaching things to the students that they can relate to. Like in my class

I have a lot of students from Mexico; so I do a lot of things that have to deal with the Mexican culture; and I think that helps a lot when you build pride in your culture because if you don't you lose self-esteem . . . I invite parents from Mexico to talk to my students, so that the students can feel proud and [realize] that Mexicans are doing something good.

This pride is associated with their efforts in maintaining their language and culture, and helping students to do the same. The Spanish language is respected. A teacher who was dominant in Spanish when she immigrated to the US feels that in other schools you don't see the Spanish language being used with that status.

And in this school you do. So when you see that your language is spoken in a lot of classes in the school you become more confident about yourself as student. I do not know of any other school where so much emphasis is placed on second language; I don't see elsewhere the respect for each other that we see in this school. We do things to promote that [respect] . . . Yes the respect for diversity is clearly promoted.

Of paramount importance to this philosophy is the overwhelming consensus among the I/BT members that Beamer is a place where positive change can occur to benefit all of the children. In response to a long question about his impressions of being at Beamer, Javier Gonzales refers to the school as an oasis and comments:

I'm in heaven, this is an oasis for me, because first I have colleagues who share similar views, political views and educational views, who share pedagogical views, who share similar goals in terms of educating limited-English proficient students, educating non-white students, educating white students from a non-white perspective; in essence a multicultural education. Secondly, my culture is valued. My experience, my Chicano urban experience is valued. I'm in a position where my culture, my values, my upbringing is valued.

Gonzales suggests that at Beamer he feels pride in who and what he is and is secure enough to share his particular worldview in the classroom. He wants to be an effective educator with all of his students — the limited-English proficient students, minority students, and white students — what he refers to as a multicultural education for all students in his classroom. Beamer provides the opportunity for teachers to explore these themes in a safe and supported environment.

Voices of Teacher Empowerment

During the analysis of the I/BT teacher interviews it became apparent that specific themes were emerging from the teachers. Four clear and consistent themes ultimately surfaced:

1 Support and *esprit de corps* among the immersion/bilingual faculty;
2 Differential power and autonomy;
3 Redefinition of teacher role;
4 Teacher/student relationships.

An elaboration of these themes is necessary to better contextualize the process of empowerment being experienced by the I/BT teachers. The first of the themes, support and comradeship, refers to a perception among the teachers that their work environment is one in which they feel nurtured, recognized, acknowledged and supported, both professionally and personally. The corpus of the data indicated that the bilingual/immersion teachers felt an overwhelming amount of support at Beamer, both from colleagues and the administration, specifically the principal. The feeling of *esprit de corps* is a constant and strong thread in all of the interviews. Teachers felt autonomous and at the same time part of a larger schoolwide effort or cause (the immersion/bilingual program) and even of a broader community or societal effort — the promotion of cultural pluralism. Teachers we spoke with were self-confident and comfortable with themselves and their work at the school. Lillian Herrera states:

All of the teachers work together and the principal gives us the opportunity to do almost everything that we want, and she doesn't check on us all the time; she gives us liberty, freedom to perform and I think that this is something that has really helped us.

In reference to the collegiality and helpfulness of her colleagues during her first year of teaching, she explains:

There is no competition in who is going to teach a lesson or "I can't lend (materials) to other teachers." No, here it is different. This is my first year and I get a lot of ideas; they are willing to lend me the same activities to teach in my classroom or they are willing to teach me how; they are willing to collaborate. But I never see any competition, and in fact, that has made it very easy for me.

The principal and her staff provided an arena at Beamer where faculty could feel safe to experiment and explore new pedagogies and approaches to classroom delivery systems. The crucial principle is teacher cooperation and responsibility. Teachers redefine their roles to accomplish common goals, and thus become empowered to collaborate and support each other, in contrast with other schools where teachers feel isolated and in competition with each other. At Beamer teachers also feel the support of the principal and the freedom to pursue their own creative agendas. These agendas are clearly consistent with the linguistic and cultural resources children bring to school. Thus, teachers are encouraged to participate in training activities on campus and off, including literacy seminars as far as the University of California, Santa Cruz. The result is professional development through academic exercises oriented to stimulate creative and culturally congruent instructional strategies, as well as social activities that foster teacher unity, such as after-school clubs for the Beamer students (MESA or Chess Club), and the planning of the *menudo* (tripe stew) breakfast to generate funds.

One of the most salient characteristics of Hispanic teachers at Beamer is the level of awareness and sensitivity regarding their own cultural diversity. They use the themes of cultural diversity, equity and justice as part of their teaching content. Consequently, it is not unusual to find I/BT faculty developing lesson plans revolving around themes such as the following: César Chávez and the United Farm Workers Union, big business versus workers, social obligations in society, links between prejudice in school and society, injustice motivated by racism and sexism, and the need to make a better society for all through advocacy and changes of strategies.

Obviously, there is no change without conflict, and there is also conflict at Beamer. Articulate, bilingual, well-trained, opinionated young people, with a collective voice demanding change and innovative approaches often cause anxiety in faculty who are Anglo, monolingual and uncomfortable with the changes. The perception that the Hispanic faculty had a different world-view of schooling and the need for change brought a disparate opinion from several of the Anglo teachers who did not share either the knowledge or the sense of urgency to address issues of equity and pluralism.

Several conflicts came to the surface early in the 1990–91 school year. One important incident served as the impetus for a two month debate over US policy strategies and highlights the notion of differing views. During the Persian Gulf War there were fundamental differences of opinion among the faculty and staff about the role of US troops in the conflict; there were those for and against the war. This situation split the faculty and staff along ethnic lines. The I/BT faculty used the war and its impact to bring the information into their curriculum. The majority of the Anglo teachers thought that it inappropriate philosophically and pedagogically to address the Persian Gulf War in their classrooms. Mrs Segura supported and encouraged all faculty to address the issue as they thought best. It should be noted here that there was not unanimous support for either of the two camps. Some of the faculty and staff were undecided and some would vacillate from day to day. The result of this was that those opposed to the War would eat their lunches in the teacher/staff lounge while those who were pro-War removed themselves to the library area for their lunchtime. At the conclusion of the War all of the teachers and staff were again back in the lounge eating their lunches together.

Unique Program Activities

The Finding Out/*Descubrimiento* (FO/D) curriculum is a favorite of the teachers involved in the Immersion/Bilingual Program, because it is designed specifically for linguistically or culturally different children and incorporates cooperative learning strategies. Over the last five years the FO/D program at Beamer has become a model for other schools throughout the state of California. It is a visible and important benchmark curriculum in the school and the WUJSD as well. The FO/D curriculum is useful for curriculum activities in all grade levels, and has been well received by faculty in the Immersion/Bilingual Program, and the Gifted and Talented Education Program. In brief, the FO/D curriculum consists of guided, hands-on science and math cooperative activities for groups of four or five students, each with different assigned roles — for example, a recorder, a clean-up person, a facilitator, a materials person, and others. FO/D activities facilitate a great deal of student-generated involvement with the teacher role diminished. The teacher does no direct instruction or responses to questions, instead he/she assists students with their assigned tasks. Nine current teachers have received training in the FO/D curriculum and are, to date, very satisfied and comfortable with the approach. The objective is to complete a specific science (for example, basic chemistry experiments or a math activity described on laminated cards included in a materials kit) cooperatively and efficiently within a forty to fifty minute period. Some twenty-five FO/D complete kits (instruction cards, equipment, etc.) are available to teachers at Beamer and many have been translated from English to Spanish by volunteer immersion/bilingual faculty and the curriculum resource specialist with the purpose of making these instructional materials truly useful in the classroom. Cooperative education in the math and science content area, along with the development of higher order thinking skills (inquiry, analysis, synthesis, to name a few), are the underlying goals of the FO/D curriculum. The impetus to incorporate FO/D into the school was to create an opportunity to share knowledge across ethnic, gender, ability, and class groups and to simultaneously teach courtesy and respect for one another.

Another important activity that helped support and nurture the spirit of cooperation and respect among the students was the TRIBES Program. TRIBES encourages teamwork and serves as a self-esteem program that assists students to become better conflict resolvers and develop better communication skills. A part-time school district counselor was assigned to coordinate in-school TRIBES activities and facilitate twice weekly meetings in classrooms. Not all teachers participated in the TRIBES Program during the 1990–1991 school year; participation was strictly voluntary. It should be noted that all of the immersion/bilingual faculty participated in the program. A typical TRIBES meeting would allow students to bring to the floor their personal concerns or difficulties related to individuals in that classroom or in another classroom and resolve — with the help of the counselor and fellow students — their problem collectively. For example, during a recent lunchtime altercation a fifth grade student scuffled with a third grader. During the meeting (observed in the third grade classroom by the researcher) the fifth grade student was called over the intercom to come and face his third grade accuser. All students involved in TRIBES training are taught to present their concerns with clear and appropriate language (no name-calling or profane language, loud voices, etc.) and respect. Upon entering the room the fifth grade student responded and rebutted the accusations, while the counselor facilitated and guided the discussion until each student agreed upon an amicable, fair, and mutual resolution. During the discussion there was intervention from the other students in the circle. After a ten to fifteen minute group discussion and a proposed resolution the students involved in the conflict shook hands and the fifth grader was dismissed.

Unique Classroom Activities

One of the most poignant observations made during the Fall 1990 semester occurred during Thanksgiving celebration preparations. The Fall 1990 Thanksgiving celebration was prepared by teachers in advance. A visit to two classrooms the day before the Thanksgiving holiday was very revealing. In one of the non-immersion bilingual classrooms the teacher asked parents to bring traditional American Thanksgiving food items for an in-class dinner. There was a lot of food, and items included a large cooked turkey, stuffing, sweet potatoes, cranberry sauce, whipped cream, soft drinks, and several homemade pumpkin pies. In preparation for the feast, students prepared the room for a sit-down dinner complete with paper tablecloth, place mats, napkins, and plastic cups, forks, knives, and spoons. The teacher commented in passing that this was a good opportunity to teach the students how to use eating utensils appropriately. The mood of the students and the teacher was festive and excited as they readied themselves to eat.

I walked down the hall and entered an immersion classroom. In a marked and strong contrast to what I had just observed, I first noted five store bought pumpkin and apple pies (still in their plastic containers) off to the side on a small table and the teacher and the students involved in a complex and somber discussion about poverty throughout the world. The discussion centered around the plentiful bounty of US society and the rampant poverty in many European countries, in particular Poland (food shortages in Poland had been getting much media attention during this time). As the discussion concluded the teacher had several students go to the paper towel dispenser and begin tearing off medium-sized sheets of the brown paper and giving each student one. In the meantime, I was instructed to begin cutting the pies. After each student was given a sheet — ironically, I noted about placemat size — the instructor asked them to draw with their pencils a plate and utensils on the sheet. When everyone completed their drawing I dispensed a piece of pie to each student and strategically placed each slice on the their individual 'plates'. When this was completed the instructor then asked the students to stand, close their eyes, and pause for a minute of silence to give thought to those less fortunate. It was an incredibly emotional moment as a room of thirty primary students quietly participated in an alternative Thanksgiving celebration. At the conclusion of the pause the instructor invited the students to sit down and eat their pie slices with their hands; they did. Throughout the discussion the students called the others 'colega' (colleague), and the teacher would get the attention of the class by raising a closed fist in the air, as a sign of togetherness. Later, when I queried the teacher about why the celebration had been done in this manner he responded, 'I wanted them to understand the difference between those who have and those who don't; even though they are poor, they have more than other people have in other places in the world.'

Another unique and ongoing feature of many of the immersion/bilingual classrooms is the extensive use of thematic teaching strategies. The immersion/bilingual faculty as well as the non-immersion faculty have been trained in this approach, and many collaborate in cross-grade teaching assignments. Faculty meet in school during the weekends to prepare their units, and they share across the grade levels modifying accordingly. They conduct activities across grade levels; for example, a kindergarten class would prepare a unit on travel around the world, and a fifth grade would prepare a unit of Germany, Spain and France. The kindergarten would 'travel' through the fifth grade classroom to visit one of the other countries. They would be hosted by a fifth grader, and would receive pretend passports, partake of appropriate food, examine items brought to that class, and enjoy the experience of sharing knowledge with older students. A number of collaborative efforts across grades created a strong spirit of support and unity for all students; the sharing of teachers with each other resulted in teaching students to share and work together.

Noteworthy is the consistent infusion of multicultural themes K-6. The I/BT faculty made an effort to make the school curriculum truly multicultural. The principal and faculty know that multicultural education is the most important characteristic of the curriculum. It is important not only that the student and

teacher population is ethnoracially diverse, but that the curriculum reflects ethnic and cultural differences and capitalizes on the various cultures represented in the school, in content, analysis and overall learning experience. One experiences a multicultural environment.

The African American, East Indian and Hispanic students constitute the principal cultural groups. These groups are discussed throughout the year — not a multicultural education for the day — but integrated throughout the curriculum. Some examples include public display in classrooms of Martin Luther King (to celebrate his birthday), in January or of the Mexican flag during September (to celebrate the Mexican Independence). At Christmas, children carry banners depicting democratic themes, sing songs of liberation (in Spanish), world-wide freedom songs, songs celebrating mother earth, or Mayan music to celebrate Mayan myths with colorful costumes. *Cinco de Mayo* (May 5th Celebration of the freedom of Puebla from European troops) and *El Dia de las Madres* (Mother's Day) are celebrated with public dances organized with the help of the resource teacher. Students prepare for three months to perform folk dances that historically represent the significance of Cinco de Mayo for Mexicans living in Mexico and in the United States. Prior to the dance, information is given in the classrooms to explain the historical significance of that day.

Hispanic teachers are clearly effective in creating appropriate zone of proximal development (Vygotsky, 1962, 1978), culturally congruent learning environments (Au and Jordan, 1981), and have become aware that knowledge is power (Popkewitz, 1991; Apple, 1989, 1990), and that power does not change hands easily. The unique role of teachers working in such culturally diverse settings as Beamer presents challenges of reciprocal interaction and joint construction of knowledge through the creating of strong bonds between teachers and children

(Zeichner, 1992). The role of the home language in the emancipation of these teachers and their successful teaching for culturally diverse settings is remarkable (Trueba, 1988, 1989, 1991; Delgado-Gaitan and Trueba, 1991). No wonder Mexican children, like their Hispanic teachers, are growing aware of their capacity to play leadership roles in society, proud of their ethnic heritage, and willing to take responsibilities in school and society.

References

APPLE, M. (1989) *Teachers and Texts: A Political Economy of Class and Gender Relations in Education*, New York, NY: Routledge.

APPLE, M. (1990) *Ideology and Curriculum*, New York, NY: Routledge.

AU, K.H. and JORDAN, C. (1981) 'Teaching reading to Hawaiian children: Finding a culturally appropriate solution', in TRUEBA, H., GUTHRIE, G. and AU, K. (Eds), *Culture and Bilingual Classroom: Studies in Classroom Ethnography* Rowley, MA: Newbury House Publishers, Inc., pp. 139–52.

DELGADO-GAITAN, C. and TRUEBA, H. (1991) *Crossing Cultural Borders: Education for Immigrant Families in America*, London, England: Falmer Press.

POPKEWITZ, T.S. (1991) *A Political Sociology of Educational Reform: Power/knowledge in Teaching, Teacher Education and Research*, New York, NY: Teachers College, Columbia University.

SEGURA, L. (1990–91) *Beamer Park Elementary School: Consolidated Program Evaluation*, Beamer Elementary School Woodland, CA.

SEGURA, L. and ASSOCIATES (1991) *Demonstration of Restructure in Public Education*, Beamer Elementary School, Woodland, CA.

TRUEBA, H.T. (1988) 'Culturally-based explanations of minority students' academic achievement', *Anthropology and Education Quarterly*, **19**(3), pp. 270–87.

Trueba, H.T. (1989) *Raising Silent Voices: Educating Linguistic Minorities for the Twenty-first Century*, New York, NY: Harper & Row.

TRUEBA, H.T. (1991) 'Learning needs of minority children: Contributions of ethnography to educational research', in MALAVE, L.M. and DUQUETTE, G. (Eds), *Language, Culture and Cognition*, Philadelphia, PA: Multilingual Matters Ltd, pp. 137–158.

VYGOTSKY, L.S. (1962) *Thought and Language*, Cambridge, MA: MIT Press.

VYGOTSKY, L.S. (1987) *Mind in Society: The Development of Higher Psychological Processes*, in COLE, M., JOHN-TEINER, V., SCRIBNER, S. and SOUBERMAN, E. (Eds) Cambridge: Harvard University Press.

ZEICHNER, K. (1992) *Educating Teachers for Cultural Diversity*, National Center for Research on Teacher and Learning, Michigan State University, East Lansing, Michigan.

Chapter 7

Lessons Learned:
The Healing of American Society

Henry T. Trueba

It was not the brutal force of guns, or the roar of the masses demanding justice (as in the Russian and Chinese revolutions), nor the charisma of a single leader fighting for the emancipation of the people (as Hidalgo, Marti, Lincoln, and others), that pulled the low-income, farmworker group from its underclass status. The Mexican American community developed its own strategies for a collective, quiet action that changed the castelike position of the people to one of power and control of their own destiny. It was the cultural richness and resourcefulness of the entire community, but most of all its long-term commitment to maintain their language and culture and to survive a new land that explains the success of the Mexican American community in Woodland.

Understanding Success in Woodland

Success, as viewed by the Mexican community, is a better life for the new generation, a better education, a safe environment in which there is respect for elders, religious and civil traditions of the community, and a harmonious, cooperative, reciprocal exchange of services. The story of Chicanos in Woodland illustrates collective success in three domains, the cultural, economic and political:

1 *Cultural domain.* Chicanos managed to organize frequent, intensive cultural experiences that functioned to keep group unity, thus keeping the community together in their commitment to pursue their own welfare and cultural goals. Some examples will be given below.

2 *The economic domain.* Chicanos created a pool of economic resources by using family ties, friendship and *compadrazgo* (civil-religious relationship involving the care of the young). They also formed formal financial organizations based on economic interdependence in order to start new business or to develop community resources for the common good.

3 *The political domain.* Chicanos developed social networks that served as the infrastructure of their political activities and the training grounds for political campaigns. The examples provided here will give an idea of the nature of the linkages formed by community members.

Cultural traditions that started in Mexico were continued in Woodland. The organization of the *Comité Pro-Fiestas*, the *Comité de Guadalupanas* (originally a religious organization), and the Mexican cowboy (*charro*) associations, such as the *La Regional, Los Caporales* and the Folkloric dance groups functioned as the larger umbrellas within which Mexican families found the moral support and appropriate climate to maintain their cultural values, rituals, and the activities that enhanced their identity. The splendor and pleasure that cultural activities produced were the cement that bonded ethnic pride and a sense of belonging within the community. Under this general umbrella, newcomers found an opportunity to share important information about the resources available from the various members of the Mexican community, valuable in both practical terms to resolve daily problems, and symbolically to restore the psychological well-being often threatened by degrading experiences (racial prejudice, economic exploitation, exclusion from services and opportunities available to other citizens). Cultural activities also allowed the development of dyadic relationships and religious *compadrazgo* (civil and religious relationship between a godfather or godmother and a godchild — a child whose spiritual welfare is ritually and officially entrusted to a close friend or a relative).

The larger umbrella of cultural activities provides the entrance to the economic reciprocal exchanges in the form of loans, services, partnerships and other collaborative enterprises. It is common to establish economic relationships with individuals known over the years in the context of ritual (religious or civil) activities; for example, those with whom people celebrate *Fiestas Patrias* (*Cinco de Mayo*, or *Dia de la Independencia*) or religious events (Baptism of a child, confirmation, wedding; or *Fiesta de la Virgen de Guadalupe, Dia de los Muertos, Dia de Todos los Santos*, and others). The fine line between purely economic reciprocal relationships and exchanges resulting in mutual moral and spiritual support go back to the old Indian traditions in Mexico. Folk and Catholic traditions adopted early in the post-colonial period offer reciprocal exchanges that permeate the social, cultural, political and economic domains in rural Mexico. The classic case of the *Cargo* or *Cofradia* (often called cults of the saints) system in Indian villages has shown how the wealthy become responsible for the cost and organization of religious fiestas in honor of the patron saints of the village. The conspicuous expenditures provide them with status and political power and at the same time prevent them from accumulating excessive wealth. Thus, excess wealth is reinvested in the community.

Beyond the identification of rich sponsors to help pay for community activities, the Chicano community developed organizations similar to those well established in Mexico, such as the *Comité de Beneficencia Mexicana* which enjoyed the support of business owners (viewed as rich) and the general community. The *Beneficencia* establish common funds to be used in case of burials and emergencies. Reciprocal informal economic relationships are common within groups of Mexicans who came from the same state or area in Mexico, or who know each other well. Loans, advice, unsolicited economic assistance, food and shelter are exchanged between families or individuals, or they are requested, offered and/or accepted on behalf of individuals who have established reciprocal economic (and religious) relationships.

The isolation of new immigrants in a foreign country causes a great deal of insecurity and stress. The Mexican community of Woodland used cultural traditions to develop a strong economic network that provided relative economic security for all. Learning to become economically knowledgeable was as important as learning about the political system and how to demand equal opportunities for all the Mexican community. But beyond economic goals, much of the political activity developed in response to the educational needs of children.

The political sophistication of present Chicanos did not develop overnight. The organization of the Mexican American Political Association, the Mexican American *Concilio*, the United Chicano Student Organization, the *Movimiento Estudiantil Chicano de Aztlan*, the Brown Berets, and the *Latinos Unidos Para Mejor Educacion*, were the results of many years of effort and discipline. The learning process was long, painful and discouraged by years of failure. First, there was the lack of support within the Chicano community, out of fear of becoming penalized at work or socially by the mainstream community. Second, there was a lack of organizational experience to fund political campaigns; consequently individuals were unwilling to risk their lives and economic positions in order to run a doubtful campaign. The many efforts of Chicano activists who learned from their failures and persisted is a tribute to the entire community.

The success of Woodland Chicanos is more admirable considering that some of them have come from parents who were never involved in political activities. Chicano politicians must be able to communicate well in Spanish with recent Mexican immigrants whose cultural values were more traditionally passive in the face of economic abuse, and with young activists raised in this country (many of them English-speaking), and who are profoundly frustrated with the real or perceived racism. To bridge the political camps represented by previous generations of Mexicans, in contrast with the second or third generation US-born Mexicans, was a real challenge. Additionally, Mexican American politicians (or aspirants to become politicians) had to understand the American cultural values, the American political process, and had to communicate effectively with very diverse types of mainstream Americans, including those who were prejudiced or insensitive.

From the standpoint of research on minority empowerment it is rather difficult to explain the success of a Mexican community in the United States. The literature is rather biased against any collective success of Mexicans. The work by cultural ecologists (particularly by Ogbu, 1974, 1978, 1987, 1989) had clearly identified Mexican Americans as one of the groups classified as castelike, that is, a group who, in contrast with minorities, tends to fail in schools and society. Castelike persons are described by Ogbu as follows:

> *Castelike or involuntary minorities* are people who were *originally brought into United States society involuntarily* through slavery, conquest, or colonization. Thereafter, these minorities were relegated to menial positions and denied true assimilation into mainstream society. American Indians, black Americans, and Native Hawaiians are examples. In the case of Mexican Americans, those who later immigrated from Mexico were assigned the status of the original conquered group in the southwestern United States, with whom they came to share a sense of peoplehood or collective identity (Ogbu, 1987:321; emphasis in original).

Cultural ecologists argue that the reason that castelike minorities are unable to succeed is that they define their cultural identity in opposition to the cultural values of mainstream groups. So, if Anglo-American whites are characterized by school success, a Chicano, an African American, an American Indian or a Native

Hawaiian feels that becoming successful in school is becoming white, and there-fore, betraying his/her ethnic affiliation. Oppositional definitions of ethnicity are, in the views of cultural ecologists, a way of resisting oppression from dominant groups. The empirical evidence to generalize across ethnic or minority groups, or across historical periods is lacking. Furthermore, serious criticisms have been raised against the application of the castelike criticisms to entire ethnic or minority groups (or to most of the members of such groups) on the grounds that these groups are internally diversified, and do exhibit many different adaptive responses to American cultural and life-style. These responses depend on their pre-arrival experiences, socio-economic and educational background, and the support system they find in the new country. Here, however, we must accept the fact that the castification process has existed, and continues to exist, in American society. The recognition that most ethnic and minority groups (including those from European ancestry) who immigrated to the United States have been submitted to degradation incidents out of prejudice and have faced strong pressures to reject their home language and culture is an important contribution of cultural ecologists. In the case of Mexicans and their families, especially those who are undocumented, life is a nightmare where the simplest activities can become terrorizing and violent experiences. Castification does not have to be the result of intended deprivation of rights or systematic racism against a particular group. It can be the circumstances, the rigorous application of the letter of the law, and the subtle reflection of the hatred and disdain felt for a person or his or her ethnic community. Refugees crossing the Southern borders often arrived already traumatized. Chavez describes the experiences of Mexican migrants crossing the border:

> When one family member leaves for the United States, family left behind experience some justifiable anxiety about the potential dangers of the journey. . . . Crossing the border is filled with dangers. Bandits of both countries rob, rape and even kill unsuspecting migrants crossing the border over the hills and through canyons. . . . On May 18, 1990, a 12-year-old Mexican boy, on his way to his parent's apartment in Orange County, was gunned down as he and family members walked along a border hillside. A 23-year-old US citizen who lives in the area was charged with the murder. According to witnesses, the alleged killer, who was standing on the balcony of friend's apartment, said, "Let's shoot some aliens", and fired a hunting rifle toward a hillside where many undocumented border crossers were gathered. This same person was also charged with assaulting undocumented immigrants for 'beer money' earlier on the day of the murder . . . (Chavez, 1992:57).

According to Chavez, Border Patrol officers often chase undocumented workers into waterways, where they drown, or conduct raids which cause serious injuries or death to undocumented aliens:

> On February 15, 1988, in Madera, California, INS [Immigration and Naturalization Services][1] agents conducted a raid on a group of farm-workers, most of whom were Mixtecan Indians from Oaxaca. Most of the workers ran. But one 17-year-old was caught by a relatively large

agent who threw him on the asphalt, causing head injuries from which
he died a few days later . . . (Chavez, 1992:58).

There are innumerable accounts of abuse and trauma suffered by Mexican
immigrants who felt they had to risk their lives in order to maintain their families
back home. Many other Mexican immigrants either came with legitimate visas or
took advantage of amnesty, grace periods and other opportunities to obtain legal
residence in the United States. Unfortunately, their bad experiences never quite
end. They know, as those described in this study, that they are not respected or
wanted. The wounds and scars left in the minds of immigrants come to the
surface during daily life events as well as during such crises as death in the family,
poverty, unemployment, financial debts, confrontation with the policy, and
underpaid work subject to high stress.

The role of the ethnic community as the center of cultural, economic and
political activities becomes essential to the psychological and often physical survival of Mexican immigrants. It is precisely under the circumstances enjoyed by
Mexican immigrants in Woodland that immigrants can resist the castification
process and regain a sense of empowerment to succeed even in a difficult, foreign
society that seems to reject them. The complete confidence that being Mexican,
Mexican American, Chicano or Latino is something to be proud of, and something demanding a profound life-long commitment, is the immediate result and
the first step towards healing from the traumatic experiences of living in America.
The healing of American society, a nation of immigrants whose contributions
have maintained the ideals of democratic principles, deserves further discussion in
the next chapter. Some of the most important means to create a society in which
there is peace, harmony, respect for cultural differences and cooperation towards
common goals are developed in the school years through the influence of teachers
with vision and commitment to the democratic principles of American society.

The Role of Teachers in Success

We have evidence that the Chicano community had to contend with low expectations from teachers in the years when the schools hardly tolerated children
of color with white children in the same classroom. The work of Douglas (1949)
is a case in point. While there was no overt hostility, there were, in effect, mechanisms that tended to disempower young Mexican children. Having to break with
their language and culture and having to compete academically with white children in English was a very difficult task. The long-term efforts of the Mexican
parents to influence public opinion in order to develop instruction in Spanish and
English and to bring teachers who were competent and committed to cultural
diversity are the most important contributions of immigrants to Woodland.

Bilingual-bicultural teachers demonstrated:

1 cultural sensitivity and competence in using for pedagogical purposes the
   'cultural capital' of students, thus allowing students to develop their full
   potential;

2 a strong ethnic identity and commitment to help minority children develop a clear sense of their own ethnic identity and of their cultural values (Zeichner, 1992);

3 awareness of the dynamics of prejudice and racism, and the ability to prepare minority students to handle the manifestations of prejudice and racism, as well as to retain their self-respect and high self-esteem (Zeichner, 1992);

4 a cooperative spirit and the willingness and ability to teach children to work together with the teacher and with each other in the construction and acquisition of new knowledge;

5 appreciation for the value of cultural diversity and the skills and knowledge necessary to rectify the historical account often lacking in recording the contributions of ethnic and other minority groups;

6 competence in acquiring new professional skills and knowledge in order to improve their teaching performance;

7 ability and willingness to work with the families of ethnic minority children, and to involve these families in the academic and cultural activities of the school;

8 high expectations of children's achievement in school and outside the school;

9 creative approaches to instructional challenges, for example, in planning across grade level activities, and in using traditional American holidays to bring about social awareness about poverty in the world;

10 bicultural skills to assist children in their adjustment to school and society, especially in making clear to children the demands that school is going to make from them, and the commitment to deliver whatever is expected from them in school.

It is no wonder that the response of the community was overwhelmingly supportive and generous. The fact that teachers created strong support groups and that they demonstrate freedom from being a token minority teacher attempting to meet the multiple needs of the school, had a beneficial outcome in children; it taught them to defend their freedom and to depend on each other for support. Indeed, Woodland is a good example of how a school or school district can facilitate the adjustment of culturally different children to American society. Unfortunately, these gains for minority children have a price. The socialization of ethnic children in the free spirit of democratic principles tends to polarize teachers who differ philosophically about the role of schools and the role of minority communities.

The conflict between Hispanic and white teachers is common in many schools in which Hispanic teachers have reached a critical mass and become visibly supportive of ethnic languages and cultures. The cycle of intolerance for cultural diversity reached a high during the late 1980s and early 1990s. While during the mid 1980s the American public demonstrated their support to undocumented workers coming from Mexico by helping them to obtain American residency (often paying for the cost of legal aid and other expenses associated with the normalization of resident status), the last five years has seen increased vigilantism at the border with Mexico, and sheer cruelty in dealing with undocumented immigrants. The compassion shown in the 1980s to the aliens as they crossed the border has changed into organized brigades of citizens, who keep a night watch on key border areas, throwing their car lights onto the border in the hope of discouraging the thousands of Mexicans who try to cross to San Diego covered by the darkness of the night. As one of the undocumented immigrants put it:

> I had never thought about staying here in the United States. . . . You know how it is. One wants to improve the living standard and well-being of the family. . . . Here it is much better than over there [in Mexico]. It also depends on what kind of person you are. If you are not educated it is possible for you to fail in a good job over there. You are then obligated to find the means to live (Chavez, 1992:81).

Many immigrants never succeed in America. They lose their language, culture and self-respect; some lose even the hope of regaining the status they had in their home countries. Some become so frightened to be caught that never go out. They imagined the United States to be very different. The realization that life in the ghettoes, gangs, poverty, drugs, and alienation in the school in which ethnic youngsters learn hatred, violence and crime, comes too late to parents who have lost control over their children.

As American society becomes more complex socially, economically and culturally, it is becoming increasingly more polarized and divided. It is a common belief that traditional democratic principles led the United States to open its doors to immigrant groups from all over the world, and to create the conditions that permitted these individuals to succeed, precisely because as citizens, they had rights equal to those of US-born Americans. Ethnic group after ethnic group managed, over a period of time, to become an integral, functioning part of American social institutions. The civil rights struggles of the mid-twentieth century clarified interpretation of democratic principles, the true meaning of the American Dream, and the role of schools in inculcating American values to immigrant, refugee and minority groups in an effort to provide equal opportunities for learning and economic advancement.

The Need to Heal America

According to Dorothy Waggoner (1988:79–81) in 1980 there were in the US 34.6 million speakers of other languages than English, that is 15 per cent of the total population (one in seven). Of them, 2.6 million were children under age five, and approximately 8 million were school-age children. The largest group in 1980 was the Spanish speaking with 15.5 million people (45 per cent of all language minority people). Waggoner points out that in 1980, the French, German, Italian and Polish groups had at least 1 million people in the US, and that thirty other language groups had at least 100,000 each. She also states (1988:80) that in the same year 4.2 million children of Spanish language background constituted 52 per cent of the 7.9 million school-age children living in language minority families. The next group was the French with 685,000, the German with 594,000, and the Italian with 437,000. Groups that numbered between 100,000 and 200,000 were Filipino, Polish, Native American, Chinese, Greek and Portuguese.

In 1980, of the 7.9 million school-age children who were members of language minority families, 1.6 lived in California, 1.1 million in Texas, and 926,000 in New York. Overall, sixteen states had at least 100,000 language minority school-age children (Waggoner, 1988:81). Since 1980, at least 824,000 legal Spanish-speaking immigrants have come to the US to join the 15.5 million (Waggoner, 1988:105), and the analyses of the 1990 census data (not yet published) will probably put the total Spanish-speaking population, both legal and illegal around at 20 million.[2]

More recently, however, particularly after the war in Vietnam, the assassinations of John F. Kennedy, Robert Kennedy and Martin Luther King, and the disappointment with recent presidents, many Americans, from all socio-economic quarters and ethnic backgrounds, feel disenfranchised, angry, displaced and unhappy about public policies, public institutions (especially schools), ethnic relations, the differential use of tax monies for domestic purposes in contrast with its use for foreign purposes, and the overall role of America in the world. The infrastructure of the country, the quality of life in the cities in general, and the quality of urban schools in particular, is persuading the public that something is very wrong in America. American cultural values are changing in ways never anticipated before. Poverty of senior citizens, although condemned, was still rampant in the last few years; today, poverty of young families, and especially among school children of all ages and backgrounds — not only ethnic children, but also white children — demonstrate that Americans are neglecting their most precious resources for the future.

According to some, the overall feeling of disempowerment, expressed by educators in low-income neighborhoods which are plagued by drug dealers, homicide, prostitution, gang warfare, uncontrolled pollution and hunger, is only the tip of the iceberg. American culture is changing rapidly, and educators seem to be confused about what route to take, how to control the damage, how to heal our society, and how to protect our youngsters from abuse, neglect, poverty, ignorance and alienation.

In this scenario of dysfunctional inequity, or of 'savage inequalities' (as Kozol has described it in his recent book: *Savage Inequalities: Children in America's Schools*, 1991), social scientists speak about empowerment, conscientization, castification processes, and cultural therapy. Here we want to present and analyze some current anthropological thinking about the role of schools in healing American wounds and preparing our children to face the challenges of next century. Because many of our school-age children are from ethnolinguistic and racial minority and low-income backgrounds, we should focus on the nature of the problem of schools, from the perspective of educational anthropology which focuses on ethnicity, race, class and gender, but which examines school problems in its cultural context. This means that educational anthropology attempts to identify the schooling experience of children and the role of the family in children's education from the perspective of the home culture. More concretely, we may ask the following questions:

1   Is there a problem in schools? Does the schooling experience of many children ultimately result in disenfranchisement from school and society, and lead to disempowerment, that is, the inability to participate effectively in American institutions? If so, what is the nature of the problem?

2   Are the problems faced by school part of larger, systemic problems? Are the attempts to rectify the problems in the schools merely *reformist*, thus

ultimately doomed because they address only symptoms and not the root causes?

3 What are the current theoretical explanations of underachievement, disenfranchisement and disempowerment? Are these explanations adequate?

4 What is the solution to these problems? Is cultural therapy part of the solution? If so, how would cultural therapy work to empower teachers and students?

The United States is facing serious educational and economic problems. As in other industrial Western societies, immigration waves are seen with increasing anxiety. Scarcity of resources resulting in drastic school budget reductions and a troubled domestic and international economy provide the context for our discourse on educational reform. We need schools that capitalize on the talents and cultural heritage of all our children, that teach them to be proud of their ethnic, linguistic, and cultural background.

Educational reform is viewed with suspicion by the Right as an attempt to disperse funds provided by the tax payers on 'immigrant populations', while the Left disagrees with this strategy. The historical irony is that today, when the wave of intolerance for the instructional use of languages other than English is reaching its peak, is precisely when the use of Spanish in public is increasing most rapidly. Spanish-speaking children are only 11 per cent of the total US school-age population, but they represent 55 per cent of the total increase in child population in this country. The use of home languages (such as Spanish) and the low socio-economic status of ethnic groups are important factors of their isolation. Spanish-speaking children in America live in families with incomes that barely permit them to subsist. In the last ten years one million additional Latino (Hispanic) children joined the ranks of the poor (in a family of four members with less than $10,000 income). In 1989 2.6 million Hispanic children (out of the total 7.2 million Hispanic children) were poor, and most of them lived in urban and suburban areas (not in rural areas). In 1989, 48.4 per cent of all Puerto Rican children were poor, 37.1 per cent of all Mexican children were poor, and 26.1 per cent of Central and South American children were poor. The number of Hispanic children in poverty will grow because they cannot function in schools. They have either willingly given up or traded off their language and culture in hopes of pursuing the American Dream. Without their home language and culture they lack a bridge to reach the new language and culture of American schools and society.

Needs of Minority Children

The increase in poverty-stricken immigrants, in spite of their best efforts, is deplorable. Worse than poverty is the abandonment and permanent degradation associated with low income. Many families (particularly African American families) have been disregarded and forgotten by our society. Kozol describes a number of settings in Illinois (East St. Louis, Chicago), New York City and San Antonio, Texas). We could add to those setting many others in the Southwest (including some in California — East Los Angeles and Oakland, for example), in the Midwest (Detroit), and in the East — the Appalachian region). Take the following scenario (Kozol, 1991:7–39), for the purpose of discussion.

East St. Louis is a city with 98 per cent African American population, 75 per cent unemployment, no trash collection, a city clouded with toxic fumes from chemical companies, where one-third of the population earns less than $7500. The city had attracted a number of industries in the first two decades of this century. In 1917, in an attempt to bust the white unions, employers brought many African Americans from the South. During the depression most of these companies left town and created thousands of unemployed African American parents. A short-lived bonanza during World War II resulted in a peak population of 80,000 residents, which by 1970 had decreased to less than 50,000, and recently has now been reduced still further. Chemical companies have purchased entire blocks of homes to prevent potential lawsuits that could result from their frequent toxic spills. Once in a while the sirens will call for forced mass evacuations, the closing of the schools, and the hospitalization of residents. In 1989, 450 residents were taken to the hospital after 300 gallons of phosphorous trichloride were spilled. Upon release, each resident received $400 to exonerate the company from any liability.

East St. Louis has very sick children, and ranks among the highest in premature birth and fetal death in Illinois. The average daily food expenditure for children is only $2.40, and many children are not immunized for polio, diphtheria, measles, or whooping cough. As if the city's unhealthy environment was not enough, these children come to schools in deplorable condition. The schools within the city are not only dilapidated and grossly underfunded, but simply a risk to their health.

The science labs at East St. Louis High are 30 to 50 years outdated. John McMillan, a soft-spoken man, teaches physics at the school. He shows me the lab. The six lab stations in the room have empty holes where pipes were once attached. "It would be great if we had water." says McMillan (Kozol, 1991:27).

East St. Louis is filthy, backed up raw sewage often inundates school buildings, and it has become the theater of violent death, with one of the highest rates of homicide in the State of Illinois. Within this environment, pathos and misery are everyday experiences. Kozol summarizes his visit to a school as follows:

Before I leave the school, I take a final stroll along the halls. In a number of classrooms, groups of children seem to be involved in doing nothing. Sometimes there's teacher present, doing something at his desk. Sometimes there's no adult in the room . . . (Kozol, 1991:33)

Kozol goes to describe how in one of the unattended classrooms there were several students around a piano. Then, he says:

When I stick my head into the room, they smile and invite me to come in. . . . One of the students, a heavyset young woman, steps out just before the others. When she sings, her pure soprano voice transforms the room. "Sometimes I feel like a motherless child," she begins. The pianist gazes up at her with an attentive look of admiration (Kozol, 1991:33).

The most intriguing reflection of Kozol, invited by the comments of the superintendent, is:

The loveliness and aesthetic isolation of the singer in the squalor of the school and city bring to my mind the worlds of Dr Lillian Parks, the superintendent of the East St. Louis schools. Dr Parks says: "Gifted children are everywhere in East St. Louis, but their gifts are lost to poverty and turmoil and the damage done by knowing they are written off by their society. Many of these children have no sense of something they belong to. They have no feeling of belonging to America. . . . There is a terrible beauty in some of these girls — terrible, I mean, because it is ephemeral, foredoomed" (Kozol, 1991:33–34).

The 'terrible beauty' of many children in America has yet to be discovered in many other places of the country. How typical, how generalizable are the observations made by Kozol in East St. Louis, Chicago, New York and San Antonio? We do not know, but without encountering the extreme situations described by Kozol, educators seem to emphasize the same theme.

African American have had a long history of abuse and are tired of promises. They want to earn a decent living and to conduct their lives with dignity. They feel hopeless and abandoned. The lobbying power of heavy pollutant industries that have abused the environment and destroyed small communities such as East St. Louis have something in common with the political, social and economic machinery in California and other states. Those industries have chosen to ignore the suffering of African Americans, because they know that African Americans cannot muster the political, social and economic support from the government necessary to stop the abuse of their community. East Los Angeles gangs, who routinely abuse Hispanic and African American communities in Los Angeles, could have been easily stopped by the police during the April 29–May 2 riots in Los Angeles. The police let the beatings and burnings go on and on for hours. After a long seventy-two hours of destructive fires and an imposed peace by the National Guard, African American politicians, such as the ebullient lawyer Maynard Jackson, major of Atlanta, began to suggest remedies. Most of the African Americans would like to attract new businesses and go where the money is, that is, white capital. Jackson has been mayor since 1989. Now in his third term, he has been characterized (according to his critics) by a sobering realism that places civil rights at the bottom of the priorities. As Rev. Mckinley Youg of Big Bethel African Methodist Episcopal Church said: 'The dream of Martin Luther King has become a nightmare, because all it has done is make white businessmen richer and makes us poorer' (*Time*, May 11, 1992:39). While the African American politicians continued to prescribe economic remedies for Los Angeles, looters were taking their time in selecting merchandise from grocery stores, clothing stores, and a variety of small neighborhood shops, discouraged only by Korean owners and their friends who guarded the entrance to their stores with guns. Naturally, a few weeks after the riots, California imposed a substantial additional sale tax to cover the cost of the riots. However, one theme has received unanimous support — education for African American, especially for those from low-income areas.

Obviously, there are some problems with American education. The initiatives by the federal government speak to this issue. In a recent publication by the Secretary's Commission on Achieving Necessary Skills (SCANS) entitled *What Work Requires of Schools: A Scans Report for America 2000* (US Department of Labor, June, 1991) the Commission described its charge as follows:

1 Define the skills needed for employment.
2 Propose acceptable levels of proficiency.
3 Suggest effective ways to assess proficiency.
4 Develop a dissemination strategy for the nation's schools, businesses, and homes (US Department of Labor, 1991:xv).

Kozol is talking about *survival* and societal factors that create disenchanted and disenfranchised youth. In light of his graphic and deeply disturbing images, Government-sponsored reports seem hopelessly naive and unrealistic. The report was constructed from information gathered from business owners, public employees, union officials, workers, and from supervisors in shops, plants, and other organizations. A series of working groups were formed to look at the various kinds of jobs existing in the country. The presumed WASP and puritan work-ethic values are at the basis of the assumption that education and hard work lead to success. African American and other minorities know this is not true for them. WASP groups unanimously stressed the notion that 'good jobs will increasingly depend on people who can put knowledge to work' and that 'more than half our young people leave school without the knowledge or foundation required to find and hold a good job' (US Department of Labor, 1991:xv–xvi). What is particularly relevant to us here is that, according to many educators, those skills and qualities that are most needed by our job-seeking youth are precisely the ones lacking in many current teachers: basic skills, higher-order thinking skills, and personal qualities required to commit to work. Furthermore, that even if teachers had all the required skills, the WASP values that are assumed as the foundation of achievement cannot be taught in urban schools plagued with the problems outlined by Kozol. This reports talks about reading comprehension, writing skills, mathematical reasoning and computational skills, interpersonal skills to participate as a team member in learning settings, skills to search for information, evaluate, acquire and organize it, especially if information is to be obtained via computers; skills required to handle complex systems (including social, technological, and financial). The reason for raising these issues here is that the 'problem' of schools is described in entirely different terms by different groups of educators and analysts. There is no consensus of what the roots of the problem are. It may be the teachers, but it may also be the cultural disenfranchisement that has segregated ethnic and other minority student populations and communities from American institutions.

What is Wrong with America Today?

Overall, students that lack basic skills, higher-order thinking skills and personal qualities seem to share a common characteristic: they are socially marginal, isolated, and neglected youth. The questions arise: How do we explain this widespread phenomenon? Is the prevailing situation of youth lacking skills and personal qualities a reflection of a serious problem of social structure (government, organization of educational institutions)? Is there a more general neglect and abandonment of youth due to the lack of concern, thus expressing a change in socially-shared values of American culture? What is the full explanation for such a phenomenon?

Who or what are the main culprits? Is this problem new in American society? How do you explain this phenomenon?

The way a problem is described paves the way for proposed explanations and solutions. Educational anthropologists have emphasized cultural explanations of the problem. George and Louise Spindler, two of the founders of educational anthropology, since their early writings, stated the basic premise that they articulates in their later work (1991), that culture is 'in process, in everything that we do, say or think, in or out of school'. Furthermore, that in American society all of us are trapped in school as 'a mandated cultural process' in which the teacher is a cultural agent. This, of course, assumes that the role of teachers is to socialize children into American cultural values, to transfer American culture. They go a step further by looking at education — meaning schools — as 'a calculated massive interference with learning'. If my interpretation is correct, the Spindlers view today's schools as institutions that are systematically alienating children and creating cultural conflicts. These conflicts ultimately result in irreversible (permanent) marginalization of students in society.

The central theoretical premises that the Spindlers present are built around the concepts of self-identity. They distinguish (1991 and other writings) the concept of *enduring self* and *situated self*. The enduring-self is built during the early socialization stages and is retained by the individual for life. For George Spindler, the enduring self is the lakes, forest and landscape of Wisconsin, the elementary schools and the home where he spent his childhood, and the entire Midwest where German and Scandinavian cultures shaped the land, the minds and life-style of many hard-working Americans. The situated self reflects the changes resulting from new settings with diverse cultural values and life style. These two selves raise a number of questions. Does the enduring self live only in our minds? George and Louise state:

> The echoes of the past are faint and only the socio-political realities of the day seem alive. But is this feeling anything more than simple nostalgia for our own youth and reinforcement of the enduring self that we found there among the Menominee? (Spindler, G. and L., 1991:18)

Somehow, the living psychological reality of the enduring self is a powerful notion that helps us understand the lasting impact that schooling has on ethnolinguistic and racial minority persons. The alienation caused by schooling seems to suggest that many children can never successfully develop a situated self that permits them to participate effectively in American institutions. How is the situated self developed?

The situated self is constructed as an effort to adjust to new settings, to the immediate realities of modern life. George Spindler's situated self at Stanford took reality as he became a high achieving intellectual who played key roles in the American Anthropological Association, who published many books and articles, who, with Louise, guided (and controlled) the form and content of thousands of edited publications, who participated in public forums and professional conferences, and who taught thousands of students during their careers. In some sense, George Spindler was uprooted from the rural Midwest. In a similar way, many children have been uprooted from their countries of origin, or belong in families who were uprooted. As they attempt to adjust to a new sociocultural (and linguistic) school setting, they face intense feelings of marginality. Those feelings — the result of the cultural conflict between the home cultural environment that nourished the enduring self, and the new environments that required a situated self — are deeply embedded in George Spindler and in many of us too. The crises these children confront have been addressed in the anthropological literature under many rubrics. But ultimately, as the Spindlers suggest, they present an *endangered self*. This term, I believe, means that the essential cohesiveness of the personality is at risk, in danger, and that the individual cannot establish a healthy relationship between the enduring self and the situated self.

The explanations of minority failure (academic, as well as socioeconomic) have been consistently discussed by educational anthropologists for the last twenty years, and more recently, the debate over these explanations has focused on a number of theories, including cultural ecological theories of school failure and success. The work by DeVos and Wagatsuma (1966), DeVos (1973, 1983), J. Ogbu (1974, 1978, 1987, and 1989), M.M. Suarez-Orozco, (1989, 1990, 1991 — as editor, 1991a, and 1991b; M.M. Suarez-Orozco and C. Suarez-Orozco, 1991), Gibson (1987, 1988), and many others, illustrate the cultural ecological position, though with different nuances and emphases. These matters had been confronted by the work of George and Louise Spindler in psychological anthropology focused on acculturation, cultural transmission (continuities, discontinuities, and adjustment) through the use of Rorschach, interviews and other projective techniques among the Menominee, Blood and Mistassini Indians (see review by M.M. Suarez-Orozco, 1991a:281–291).

Cultural ecology, however, focused specifically on the process of castification, a process whereby ethnolinguistic, low-income or racial groups find themselves disempowered to function in American society (especially in schools). This process was explained both in terms of macro-sociological factors determining the status of these groups and their relative access to resources and other means of participation in mainstream institutions, and in terms of psychosocial mechanisms for the development of castelike ethnic identities. Concretely, the development of an ethnic identity which is defined in opposition to that of mainstream persons, creates a castelike person. The conflict embedded in such a definition results in viewing successful participation in mainstream societies (especially school achievement) as selling out or giving away one's own identity.

While cultural ecological explanations have been very instrumental in understanding the failure of some groups, they have been criticized for not explaining the success of other groups, as well as the differential performance within groups either synchronically or diachronically. Most scholars view the application of the castelike ethnic identity as stereotypic and problematic, particularly because castelike attributes vary within groups and even within families of the same group synchronically. The reservations about the application of this model, however, should not shadow the central contributions of cultural ecologists to our understanding of the role of macro-social factors (organizational structural features) that are used in a given culture to prevent full and successful participation of some individuals in the social institutions. The focus on structural and cultural factors causing differential participation has allowed scholars to study similarities in the processes of disempowerment across cultures, for example in European societies. For more detailed information on the comparability of the European and America situation, see *Different Cultures, Same School: Ethnic Minority Children in Europe*, by

Eldering and Kloprogge (Eds), 1989, and *Migration, Minority Status, and Education: European Dilemmas and Responses in the 1990s*, a theme issue of the *Anthropology and Education Quarterly* **22**(2) 1991, by M.M. Suarez-Orozco (Ed.).

Children Lose Their Voice and Self-Identity

The nature of the disempowerment of ethnolinguistic and racial minorities, however, is very complex and requires a multi-level analytical approach. If we examine the problem of academic low achievement as a sign of cultural mal-adjustment and disempowerment and look at high achievement as a sign of good adjustment and empowerment, we may be ignoring other more eloquent signs of relative failure or relative success. In other words, school failure may be, from the perspective of the students, the price of ultimate success. It may be a rational decision to drop out of school, or to reject assimilation, or to retain one's own language and culture in the face of pressure to reject it. Take, for example, the case of Richard Rodriguez, as analyzed by M.M. Suarez-Orozco and C. Suarez-Orozco (1991). Under certain conditions, and for reasons not understandable at the macro-social level, yet clear in the context of the family, community, and immediate peer group, schooling can be dysfunctional and destructive. In this context, what George Spindler had said earlier about schools being a massive interference in the process of learning makes some sense.

It is important to point out that the reason why disempowerment occurs in the context of rapid social, cultural and linguistic change in immigrant, refugee and other minority children is that many children experience a rapid loss of their home language; language is an essential instrument in the acquisition of self identity, for learning, and for adjusting to new situations. Sociolinguistic research and research on the ethnography of communication, emphatically argue for the significance of language in the communicative process, in the construction of new knowledge, and in the transmission of cultural values (Gumperz and Hymes, 1964, 1972; Hymes, 1971, 1974; Gumperz, 1971, 1982; Heath, 1983; Skutnabb-Kangas, 1984; Cook-Gumperz, 1986; and Hornberger, 1988a, 1988b). In a very real sense, the home language and culture become the survival kit for minority children. It is through language that they understand different scenarios and settings, different participation structures, the various usages and purposes of language, different instrumentalities and forms of communication (for example, text or face-to-face), the diverse genres (poetry, prayer, lecture, etc.) and the norms of communication associated with the various forms and usages.

We live in concrete linguistic and cultural environments created within the family, community, and social institutions. As we acquire language, we acquire the means to transfer our thoughts, values and attitudes. Speech communities (as defined by the ethnographers of communications (Hymes, 1971, 1974; Gumperz and Hymes, 1972, 1974, and others), families, and peer groups create settings that contextualize linguistic communication in such a way that we can make sense of messages. When those contexts are changed, we cannot communicate until we build new contexts. We are forced to reconstruct these contexts by facing continuous miscommunication and cultural misunderstandings. New knowledge is not acquired until we bridge previous knowledge through equivalent contexts that permit us to make sense of the content of communication.

The loss of the mother tongue before a new language is acquired can cause serious cognitive and emotional problems, as was the case of Richard Rodriguez. M.M. Suarez-Orozco and C. Suarez-Orozco (1991) are most insightful when they remark that Richard Rodriguez became very angry when his mother, advised by the teacher, stopped using Spanish in the home, and retaliated by hurting his parents in the way he corrected their English. Anger was replaced by guilt and shame, as when Rodriguez confessed 'I was not proud of my mother and father' (M.M. Suarez-Orozco and C. Suarez-Orozco, 1991; Rodriguez, 1982:52). The irony of these confessions is that, as Suarez-Orozco and Suarez-Orozco point out (1991), Richard Rodriguez became so isolated and lonely, that he sought intimacy with his unknown readers by sharing with them his most personal thoughts. Alienated from his family, his peers, his community, he attacks the use of home languages and views self-rejection as the means to become accepted by American society: 'To give up Spanish to acquire English represents a symbolic act of ethnic renunciation: it is giving up the mother tongue for the instrumental tongue of the dominant group' (M.M. Suarez-Orozco and C. Suarez-Orozco, 1991).

Is Richard Rodriguez a failure or a success? Is becoming upper-middle class, fluent in English and educated a clear sign of success? Did Richard Rodriguez have a choice? Probably he did not. The choices open to many who retain the home language and acquire a second, third and fourth language, thus being enriched culturally, were never open to Richard Rodriguez. Yet he is persuaded that self-rejection (via the rejection of the home language and culture) is the only way to success in American society. Is Richard Rodriguez empowered to participate in American social institutions? The psychological scars resulting from self-rejection and his break with his family and community are crippling factors that he will have to face for life. Could this tragedy and that of many other culturally-different school children be avoided? Could cultural therapy help? How could this be done?

Cultural Therapy and Empowerment

To describe the role of cultural therapy in contemporary American society, it is necessary to explore first the differential adjustment patterns of ethnolinguistic, racial and other minority groups to mainstream American culture. I will adapt some of the principles and acculturation typology of George and Louise Spindler (see their *Dreamers without Power: The Menomini Indians*, 1971; G. Spindler's 'Change and Continuity in American Core Cultural Values', in G.D. DeRenzo (Ed.) *We the People: American Character and Social Change*, 1977; G. Spindler's 'Beth Anne — A Case Study of Culturally Defined Adjustment and Teacher Perceptions' in his *Education and Cultural Process: Anthropological Approaches*, 1987; and one of their most recent books, *American Cultural Dialogue and its Transmission*, 1990). We take the concept of cultural therapy advanced by the Spindlers in the sources mentioned above, that is, the healing resulting from understanding one's own culture and the culture of those with whom we interact — the overall spiritual or psychological well-being we feel as members of a given society, nation or sociocultural group. The understanding of our own cultural identity, even when that understanding does not exist in others, is a function of a comparison between our values and those of other cultural groups and brings us into harmony with ourselves.

To explore how this understanding functions, we can briefly explore four basic types of adjustment responses to cultural conflict (that resulting from cultural contact with persons from other cultural groups, especially contact imposed and associated with oppression). While the scenario presented by the Spindlers for their typology (for example, Spindler and Spindler, 1990) is that of the American Indians in the face of conquest and forceful expropriation of natural resources, it remains valid in the context of modern ethnic minority groups adjustment.

1 *Nativistic*. A nativistic response is a rejection of any foreign cultural values as being incompatible with traditional home cultural values, the only ones to be recognized and accepted. This position is often accompanied by profound commitment to the maintenance of the home languages and cultures.

2 *Transitional*. A transitional response is a suspended support for any cultural values, a non-committal position with respect to both the cultural values associated with the home culture and the new cultural values associated with mainstream society.

3 *Assimilationist*. An assimilationist response is a rejection of the home values (including language and culture), and the acceptance of mainstream new cultural values.

4 *Multicultural*. A multicultural response accepts in principle the compatibility of cultural values from both the home and mainstream cultures. It is characterized by the willingness of individuals to acquire the language of mainstream members of society, without losing home languages.

While these four position are described from the perspective of ethnolinguistic, racial or other minorities, mainstream people can mirror their own responses. For example, a mainstream American can take a nativistic position by totally rejecting all other ethnic cultures as incompatible with the American way of life. This same person can reject American cultural values and remain unattached to the values of any other culture, thus becoming a transitional. There are examples of anthropologists and other persons who became completely assimilated into other cultures and felt they had to reject their American values. Lastly, there are many examples of mainstream Americans who have become multicultural by acquiring the language and culture of other communities.

Is this context of cultural contacts between mainstream persons and those from different linguistic and cultural backgrounds, the least conflictive position is taken by those persons who adopt multicultural responses. Yet, cultural therapy, as a means to compare and contrast cultural values and understandings, can enhance communication and resolve conflicts arising from misunderstandings in inter-ethnic, or intercultural exchanges. There are at least two main ways in which cultural therapy can help. First, it can help develop a strong personal identity based on a better known and better understood cultural background. Second, cultural therapy can also increase the ability to identify areas of value conflict, differences in interpretation of messages and expectations, range of acceptable etiquette, preferential protocol, and other expected behavioral responses.

A stronger personal cultural or ethnic identity is obtained by providing the individual with legitimacy and recognition for his or her enduring self. The psychological justification for retaining a personal framework for self-understanding and for self acceptance, the setting to which we feel attached as children — the quintessence of what we are in our own eyes, our enduring self — remains justified and unchanged regardless of other adjustments. This is the basis of deeper emotional peace and stability. In contrast, being forced to abandon this inner frame of the enduring self, especially when the home language is lost, isolates a child from the world of his dreams, the world of his affection. How can a child deal with two different worlds and transfer information from one to the other, if the bridge between the two (the language) is broken? How can a child retain a measure of psychological integrity if he is not allowed to reconcile conflicting values from home and school? How can a child enrich his home learning environment if going home is seen as degrading? How can a child seek emotional and cognitive support from parents who are seen as unworthy and despicable? Sooner or later, a child will comprehend that the rejection of one's own language and culture is ultimately the rejection of one's own self.

One of the embedded premises in the notion of cultural therapy is that it can enhance our ability to make appropriate adjustments during cultural contacts, and thus permit us the development of a new situated self. A strong cultural self identity is, by implication, viewed as necessary in order to adjust to new settings demanding a new behavioral repertoire and a life-style different from that associated with our enduring self. In other words, we are better able to adapt and change when there is something that remains consistent and which will always be part of our identity kit — the survival kit of our home language and culture. Perhaps, the development of instrumental competencies is linked to the strength of our enduring self and our ability to adopt new situated selves as required. G. Spindler's *instrumental competencies* may be interpreted basically as the knowledge, skills and experiences necessary to participate actively and effectively in social institutions of industrial societies, especially in school settings.

One could speculate that the development of these competencies is deeply linked to the opportunity children have to develop a strong enduring self and situated selves during their various cultural transitions. By implication, the nativistic, transitional and assimilationist responses of some minority children may be guided by lack of grounding in their home language and culture for the period necessary to develop a strong enduring self. The uprooting of these children may interrupt the process of self-identity.

Conclusion

What we have learned from the Chicano families in Woodland is that the commitment to maintain their language and culture led them to keep a keen sense of pride in being of Mexican ancestry, and permitted them to use cultural, economic and political mechanisms to transform the school from a white, Anglo institution that disenfranchises ethnic children, to an institution that values and celebrates ethnic diversity as a source of motivation to succeed. America should take pride in its ethnic diversity and commit resources to the education of all its children. For America to heal, that is, to recognize the neglect and destructive environment in which many of its children live, we Americans must invest additional resources in the proper education of America's highly diversified children, especially those who suffer poverty and isolation. The notion of cultural therapy has been used by the Spindlers for two decades, and it has encountered some resistance. Some of the problems of using the therapy language is that people assume there is something *personally* wrong with those in need of cultural therapy, and that the medical model (as used, for example in Special Education) is a very narrow one. Yet, in some very real sense, the acceptance of cultural therapy will make us recognize that collectively there is something that Americans must address: our need to better understand American culture, and to appreciate the cultural and linguistic resources of the United States.

In order for cultural therapy to function as an instrument of empowerment for all children and their teachers, we all need to take an active role as advocates of children's education. Indeed, teachers must redefine their role as advocates of minority children and change agents along the lines suggested by Cummins (1986, 1989). We should help schools create a learning environment in which teachers can develop and strengthen their own self-identity and thus become role models for their students; an environment that will not jeopardize their students' attachment to the home language and culture, their self-respect and ethnic pride. Schools can become genuinely exciting learning environments in which students become the primary engineers of their learning experience and make the full commitment to learn as much as possible. The requirements of such learning environments have been studied by a number of scholars using Vygotsky's socio-historical perspective of cognitive development (Vygotsky, 1962, 1978; Wertsch, 1981; Moll, 1990; Trueba, Jacobs and Kirton, 1990; Trueba, 1991a, 1991b, 1991c, 1991d). The increasing awareness of the linkages between, on the one hand, the strength or feelings of legitimacy of the self concept (in G. Spindler's enduring self) and, on the other, the adaptive strategies chosen by members of minority groups will allow us to look at the use of ethnic cultures as an asset in the teaching of minority groups, rather than an obstacle. The role of teachers in cultural therapy is essential. Teachers who are familiar with the culture of ethnic children and teachers who have a strong ethnic identity can find ways to use the cultural capital that their students present for pedagogical purposes. Instructional effectiveness requires high expectations of minority children and the ability to inspire them to work cooperatively in the acquisition of knowledge and to strengthen their linguistic and cultural resources.

Notes

1 The INS is called *La Migra* or *La Migración* by Chicanos and Mexicans.
2 A number of demographers (Professor Estrada from UCLA and Norm Gold from the California State Department of Education) feel that the undercount of census data must be rectified, and that the actual figures for Hispanics are much larger. (HT)

References

CHAVEZ, L.R. (1992) *Shadowed lives: Undocumented Immigrants in American Society*, in Spindler, G. and L. (Eds) *Case Studies in Cultural Anthropology*, New York, NY: Harcourt Brace Jovanovich College Publishers.
COOK-GUMPERZ, J. (Ed.) (1986) *The Social Construction of Literacy*, Cambridge, UK: Cambridge University Press.
CUMMINS, J. (1986) 'Empowering minority students: A framework for intervention', *Harvard Educational Review*, **56**(1), pp. 18–35.
CUMMINS, J. (1989) *The Empowerment of Minority Students*, Los Angeles, CA: California Association for Bilingual Education.

DeVos, G. and Wagatsuma, H. (1966) *Japan's Invisible Race: Caste in Culture and Personality*, Berkeley, CA: University of California Press.

Douglas, H.R. (1949) 'Intelligence quotients and achievement of Mexican American children in grades one through twelve', unpublished Master Thesis, Stanford University, CA.

Eldering, L. and Kloprogge, J. (Eds) (1989) *Different Cultures Same School: Ethnic Minority Children in Europe*, Amsterdam, The Netherlands: Swets and Zeitlinger.

Gibson, M. (1987) 'The school performance of immigrant minorities: A comparative view', *Anthropology and Education Quarterly*, **18**(4), pp. 262–75.

Gibson, M. (1988) *Accommodation Without Assimilation: Sikh Immigrants in an American High School*, Ithaca, NY: Cornell University Press.

Gumperz, J. (1971) *Language in Social Groups*, Palo Alto, CA: Stanford University Press.

Gumperz, J. (Ed.) (1982) *Language and Social Identity*, Cambridge, MA: Cambridge University Press.

Gumperz, J. and Hymes, D. (Eds) (1964) 'The ethnography of communication', special issue of *American Anthropologists*, **66**(6).

Gumperz, J. and Hymes, D. (1972) *Directions in Sociolinguistics: The Ethnography of Communication*, New York, NY: Holt, Rinehart & Winston.

Heath, S.B. (1983) *Ways with Words: Language, Life and Work in Communities and Classrooms*, New York, NY: Cambridge University Press.

Hornberger, N. (1988a) *Bilingual Education and Language Maintenance: A Southern Peruvian Quechua Case*, Dordrecht, Holland, and Providence, RI, Foris Publications.

Hornberger, N. (1988b) 'Iman Chay?: Quechua Children in Peru's School', in Trueba, H. and Delgado-Gaitan, C. (Eds) *School and Society: Teaching Content Through Culture*, New York, NY: Praeger, pp. 99–117.

Hymes, D. (1971) *On Communicative Competence*, Philadelphia, PA: University Pennsylvania Press.

Hymes, D. (1974) *Foundations in Sociolinguistics*, Philadelphia, PA: University of Pennsylvania Press.

Kozol, J. (1991) *Savage Inequalities: Children in America's Schools*, New York, NY: Crown Publishers, Inc.

Moll, L. (1990) *Vygotsky and Education: Instructional Implications and Applications of Sociohistorical Psychology*, Cambridge, MA: Cambridge University Press.

Ogbu, J. (1974) *The Next Generation: An Ethnography of Education in an Urban neighborhood*, New York, NY: Academic Press.

Ogbu, J. (1978) *Minority Education and Caste: The American System in Cross-Cultural Perspective*, New York, NY: Academic Press.

Ogbu, J. (1987) 'Variability in minority responses to schooling: Nonimmigrants vs. immigrants' in Spindler, G. and Spindler, L. (Eds), *Interpretive Ethnography of Education: At Home and Abroad* Hillsdale, NJ: Lawrence Erlbaum Associates, Publishers, pp. 255–78.

Ogbu, J. (1989) 'The individual in collective adaptation: A framework for focusing on academic underperformance and dropping out among involuntary minorities', in Weis, L., Farrar, E. and Petrie, H. (Eds) *Dropouts from School: Issues, Dilemmas, and Solutions*, Albany, NY: State University of New York Press, pp. 181–204.

Rodriguez, R. (1982) *Hunger of Memory: The Education of Richard Rodriguez, An Autobiography*, Boston, MA: David R. Godine.

Skutnabb-Kangas, T. (1984) *Bilingualism or Not: The Education of Minorities*, Clevendon, England: Multilingual Matters.

Spindler, G. (1959) *Transmission of American Culture*, The Third Burton Lecture, Cambridge, MA: Harvard University Press.

Spindler, G. (1963) *Education and Culture: Anthropological Approaches*, New York, NY: Holt, Rinehart and Winston.

SPINDLER, G. (1971) *Dreamers Without Power: The Menomini Indians* (with Spindler, L.). New York, NY: Holt, Rinehart and Winston. Republished by Waveland Press in 1984.

SPINDLER, G. (1977) 'Change and continuity in American core cultural values: An anthropological perspective. In DeRenzo, G.D. (Ed.) *We the people: American character and social change* (pp. 20–40). Westport: Greenwood.

SPINDLER, G. (1987) 'Beth Ann — A case study of culturally defined adjustment and teacher perceptions', in SPINDLER, G. (Ed.) *Education and Cultural Process: Anthropological Approaches*, 2nd Ed., Prospect Heights, IL: Waveland Press, Inc., pp. 230–44.

SPINDLER, G. (Ed.) (1955) *Anthropology and Education*, Stanford, CA: Stanford University Press.

SPINDLER, G. and SPINDLER, L. (1991) 'The processes of culture and person: Multicultural classrooms and cultural therapy', paper presented at the Cultural Diversity Working Conference, Teacher Context Center, Stanford University, October 4–6, 1991.

SPINDLER, G. and SPINDLER, L., with TRUEBA, H. and WILLIAMS, M. (1990) *The American Cultural Dialogue and its Transmission*, London, England: Falmer Press.

SUAREZ-OROZCO, M.M. (1989) *Central American Refugees and US High Schools: A Psychosocial Study of Motivation and Achievement*, Stanford, CA: Stanford University Press.

SUAREZ-OROZCO, M.M. (1990) 'Speaking of the unspeakable: Toward a psychosocial understanding of response to terror'. *Ethos*, **18**(3), pp. 353–83.

SUAREZ-OROZCO, M.M. (1991a) 'Dialogue and the transmission of culture: The Spindlers and the making of American anthropology', *Anthropology and Education Quarterly*, **22**(3), pp. 281–91.

SUAREZ-OROZCO, M.M. (1991b) 'Migration, minority status, and education: European dilemmas and responses in the 1990s', *Anthropology and Education Quarterly*, **22**(2), pp. 99–120.

SUAREZ-OROZCO, M.M. (Ed.) (1991) '*Migration, minority status, and education: European dilemmas and responses in the 1990s, Anthropology and Education Quarterly*, **22**(2), (Entire Theme Issue).

SUAREZ-OROZCO, M.M. and SUAREZ-OROZCO, C. (1991) 'The cultural psychology of Hispanic immigrants: Implications for education research', paper presented at the Cultural Diversity Working Conference, Teacher Context Center, Stanford University, October 4–6, 1991.

TRUEBA, H.T. (1991a) 'The role of culture in bilingual instruction: Linking linguistic and cognitive development to cultural knowledge', in GARCIA, O. (Ed.), *Festshcrift in Honor of Joshua A. Fishman*, Amsterdam, Holland: John Benjamins Publishing Co, pp. 43–55.

TRUEBA, H.T. (1991b) 'Learning needs of minority children: Contributions of ethnography to educational research', in MALAVE, L.M. and DUQUETTE, G. (Eds), *Language, Culture and Cognition*, Philadelphia, PA: Multilingual Matters Ltd., pp. 137–58.

TRUEBA, H.T. (1991c) 'Linkages of macro-micro analytical levels', *Journal of Psychohistory*, **18**(4), pp. 457–68.

TRUEBA, H.T. (1991d) 'From Failure to success: The roles of culture and cultural conflict in the academic achievement of Chicano students', in VALENCIA, R.R. (Ed.), *Chicano School Failure: An Analysis Through Many Windows*, London, England: Falmer Press, pp. 151–63.

TRUEBA, H.T., JACOBS, L. and KIRTON, E. (1990) *Cultural Conflict and Adaptation: The Case of the Hmong Children in American Society*, London, England: Falmer Press.

US DEPARTMENT OF LABOR (1991) *What Work Requires of Schools: A Scans Report for America 2000*, The Secretary's Commission on Achieving Necessary Skills (SCANS), Washington, DC: US Government Printing Office.

Henry T. Trueba

VYGOTSKY, L.S. (1962) *Thought and Language*, Cambridge, MA: MIT Press.

VYGOTSKY, L.S. (1978) *Mind in Society: The development of higher psychological processes*, COLE, M., JOHN-TEINER, V., SCRIBNER, S. and SOUBERMAN, E. (Eds). Cambridge, MA: Harvard University Press.

WAGGONER, D. (1988) 'Language minorities in the United States in the 1980s: The evidence from the 1980 Census', in MCKAY, S.L. and WONG, S.C. (Eds), *Language Diversity, Problem or Resource: A Social and Educational Perspective on Language Minorities in the United States*, New York, NY: Newbury House, pp. 69–108.

WERTSCH, J. (1981) *The Concept of Activity in Soviet Psychology*, New York, NY: M.E. Sharpe, Inc.

ZEICHNER, K. (1992) *Educating Teachers for Cultural Diversity*, East Lansing, MI: National Center for Research on Teacher and Learning, Michigan State University.

Chapter 8

Cultural Therapy in Action

Henry T. Trueba

Cultural therapy in action, that is, as applied in specific settings, such as school, community and the home, is a process of healing. What is unique to this process is that it focuses on the resolution of cultural conflicts that arise from racial or ethnic prejudice, from misunderstanding or trivialization of the cultural values and traditions of others, or from insensitivity to persons in a position of less power. Ultimately, cultural therapy attempts to prevent or cure the consequences of degradation incidents, which can be manifested as psychological insecurity, self-rejection, hopelessness, acceptance of abuse and failure, hatred and overall disenfranchisement.

The fundamental assumption in cultural therapy is that human interaction in ethnically, racially and socio-culturally diversified settings is inherently liable to misunderstandings and ethnocentrism. It is only human to attempt to impose on others our own values and world view. It is also a natural human reaction to suspect, dislike or reject the unknown. Xenophobic responses to racially different individuals can be as violent as the response to religious rituals considered evil, or eating, sleeping and interacting practices perceived (from an ethnocentric perspective) as indecent, inhuman, degrading, or otherwise unacceptable. Historical events have shaped our perceptions of other peoples and created stereotypes that govern our gut responses to such practices. Because human interaction is always jointly constructed, that is, it requires the participation of all persons involved in the interaction, the interpretation of other peoples' behavioral practices is guided by peoples' perceptions of each other's values.

Cultural therapy seeks to bring about an understanding of human behavior from the vantage point of other cultures, especially of the cultures of the persons involved in the interaction. How others view their actions and how they interpret ours is crucial to make sense of our interaction with them. In a broader context, cultural therapy provides us with a holistic understanding of why people do whatever they do, and how they interpret behavior in dealing with each other within and across groups. The basic claim of cultural therapy is that it raises our awareness of our own cultural values and our tolerance for the life-styles of others. From the standpoint of immigrant groups, the traumas and degradation incidents suffered (in their interpretation of events as experienced by them) requires a better understanding.

The essence of cultural therapy is to create internal harmony in each person by reconciling the enduring self and the situated self (see discussion in previous chapter). The cultural values that were inculcated during the early period of socialization must be integrated with the cultural values of the larger society, values that ultimately determine the adaptations which are translated into the series of situated selves that we become throughout our lives. Internal harmony between the early values we acquired in the home culture are represented in the enduring self (but values that continue to impact our lives), the values represented in our current situated self result from adaptive strategies we choose to cope with new cultural environments. This harmony is anchored in conscious reflection about our individual culture and the cultural knowledge we get from understanding better our roots, our ethnohistory, and our traditions. Knowledge and consciousness are not sufficient, however. There has to be a deeper linkage between knowing and feeling one's own values and adaptation strategies.

Anthropologists who dedicate their lives to studying other people's culture have significant insights into this consciousness and the acquisition of cultural knowledge. Often, they feel alienated from their own culture by engaging in interaction with persons from other cultures. They know from personal experience the psychic cost of cultural conflict and degradation experiences. They have felt the self-rejection that some minority persons experience as they attempt to cope with cultural conflict. The uprooting of oneself to understand others and the attempt to restructure one's own cognitive world in order to make sense of other people's world, is alluded to by many anthropologists describing their marginality in their own societies. Efforts in creating order of seemingly apparent cognitive chaos and of maintaining social and emotional distance in the fieldwork are part of the adaptive strategies that lead researchers to new situated selves, and thus to the experience of culture loss and social marginality.

There is a fine line between cultural therapy and psychological therapy. The former involves efforts at building the necessary cultural knowledge and understanding of one's own values, ethnohistory and enduring self. The latter deals with the psychological consequences of this knowledge and understanding, that is, with efforts to reconcile the cultural values and knowledge of the enduring self — with the reality of the world we must live in — a world in which we do not feel we fully belong, and one that demands a new cognitive and social order. Psychological therapy cannot function well without cultural therapy, and cultural therapy without facing its implications for psychological therapy is sterile.

What we propose in this chapter are exercises that can help all persons, mainstream and minority groups, low-income, middle-income and wealthy persons, to come to grips with their cultural conflicts; conflicts that remain unresolved, primarily because of lack of social awareness, conscious realization of the distance between the values consistent with our enduring self, and those in conflict with the enduring self which reflect the choice of current adaptive strategies, the way of dealing with our world of today, in brief, the values reflected in our situated self. Cultural therapy will help obtain cultural knowledge that guides informed judgment, providing contextual cultural knowledge of our own lives and of the people with whom we live or work. The realization that in our cultural world, the one in which we grew up, there is a measure of ethnocentrism, and that such ethnocentrism is reflected in value judgments about relative worth of life styles, persons and behaviors, is essential to find harmony in our lives.

The examples presented below illustrate possible scenarios and useful applications of cultural therapy; many others could fruitfully be developed. The focus will be on the following interactional settings: school, community, and home. In each of these scenarios we propose a series of tasks intended to produce a broader, deeper cultural knowledge of the value conflict between the enduring self and the situated self.

Cultural Therapy Exercises in School, Community and Work

Scenario #1: Mrs White, a middle-aged Anglo-Saxon 4th grade teacher, has never, in her ten years of teaching experience, worked with Mexican or low-income children. Just before the classes started three months ago, she discovered that fifteen of her twenty-eight students are migrant children, and that only two of them speak some English. The children are bused in from a ranch thirty miles away, and they seem unable to participate in classroom exercises. This is the third month of classes, and white students continue to make fun of the migrant children. They call them 'bins', 'tacos', 'smelly', 'wetbacks', 'greasers', and other names. There are frequent fights between white and Mexican children. The teacher is monolingual in English, and feels entirely hopeless in her attempts to teach these children. She feels that she is not prejudiced; she feels compassionate and caring, but she must demand discipline in order to teach. She feels that these children do not have the cognitive and social skills necessary to function in school, and that they cannot participate in classroom activities. As a consequence, she thinks these children cause some of the problems and try to take out their frustrations on the other students.

The teachers takes an introductory course in anthropology and she is encouraged to practice cultural therapy in her class. After consulting with her principal, and with his support, she obtains one half-day a week to engage in cultural therapy. What follows are examples of the tasks she is asked to do by her professor:

I. **Acquisition of New Knowledge about the Children and their Families**

1. Gathering General Information
   1 Visit children's camp and meet their parents. Bring an interpreter, and find time and opportunity to speak with the parents. Find out where they come from, where were they born, what the migration cycle is like, and what their dreams are for their children.
   2 Observe carefully where these children's families live, find out what they eat, how their parents manage on their income, and what the parents think about the school.
   3 With the help of an interpreter, collect from parents and children information about each child, his/her school experience in the various camps and schools attended, performance, and information about health, nutrition and other matters.
   4 Summarize the information per child/family, and your understanding of the lives of migrant families.

157

5   Articulate questions specifically related to the exposure of migrant children to reading and writing, mathematics, and other academic activities.

2. Reflecting on the Lives of Migrant Children
   1   What in the lives of these children do you find most difficult to understand, justify and accept?
   2   What are the most salient values you see in the way these children are raised at home?
   3   What do find in these values in clear contrast or conflict with your own values? That is, what do you find most difficult in the children or their families?
   4   What do you know about their place of origin in Mexico, their life-style there, their relatives, traditions and values?

3. Reflecting on your personal background and life-style:
   1   Do you know the ethnic, social and cultural background of your parents, grandparents and their ancestors?
   2   Do you keep in touch with your relatives? How often do you see them and what types of activities do you engage in when you see them?
   3   Has your life changed drastically since you became a teacher? In your view, do you still have the same values you had when you were younger — for example, after finishing college?
   4   Do you see any major contrast between your life style and that of your parents or other relatives?
   5   When you remember your early childhood, do you think of yourself in terms that contrast with your life-style? Are these contrasts disturbing to you?
   6   List and explain the most important lessons your parents and adult relatives taught you when you were a child.

4. Comparing and Contrasting your Values with those of Migrant Families:
   1   List side by side your view of their values and of your own values as taught to you when you were a child.
   2   Analyze the reasons why their values are less attractive to you, and the consequences of accepting them (rather than yours).
   3   List the lessons learned from continuing your study and observations of migrant families.
   4   Plan a joint activity of migrant and mainstream children to help both know more about each other.

II.   Implications for the Curriculum and for Life

1. Enriching your Class Experience with the Support of the Migrant Parents:
   1   With the help of your interpreter, continue to visit the migrant camp, and prepare some migrant parents to bring a

demonstration project to school: they could describe to all children their labor, their knowledge about crops, their cycles of migration, their cooking skills, their artistic talents (play guitar, dance, etc.) and their cultural traditions.

2 Have migrant children and their parents participate in the presentation of a special cultural activity on *Cinco de Mayo, Dia de los Muertos* or other important fiestas, with the purpose of enriching the entire class, and thus sensitizing Anglo-American children.

3 Continue to visit the camps and interview a woman close to your age. Write a life history of this woman, and discuss her options in life, her skills, challenges, and her problems.

2. Creating a Culturally Congruent Learning Environment

1 Knowing about your students a bit more, ask yourself if the content of the lessons in reading and other text materials is meaningful, or if it needs to be contextualized, explained or translated into experiences meaningful to migrant children.

2 Allow for flexible involvement of children in writing assignments that permit them to use their language and life experiences to share with you their inner thoughts.

3 Attract aides or parents who, in addition to knowing Spanish, are role models and school supporters. Have them mentor children and supervise special reading, writing and math activities.

4 Create combined groups of migrant and non-migrant children and let them propose joint writing projects and other cooperative efforts (art projects, inquiry about issues of interest of all children, or problem-solving efforts, etc.).

5 Have all children produce a project that includes a family history, the experiences of children, sport interests, and their dreams and aspirations. These projects could be combined with art exhibits and other public rewards.

3. Preparing a Summary of What you Have Learned about Yourself.

1 As you look as your life today, are there areas of internal unrest, doubts, untold conflicts, secret pain, self-rejection, insecurity? If so, write them (for yourself) and look at them squarely. Examining other peoples' lives has given you the strength and insights you need to examine your own life.

2 Describe the areas in which you would like to improve as a person and as a teacher. Specifically, what do you think you have learned through cultural therapy that will help you develop professionally.

3 Describe other areas of your life, outside of your teaching and private thoughts about yourself. What in your family and social life would you like to modify, in order to fully enjoy your cultural heritage, your family traditions, your skills and talents?

4 What plans do you have to keep enriching your cultural knowledge about your own home culture and your country?

Scenario # 2: Lyn Huan is a 12-year-old girl and fifth grade student from mainland China who arrived in Northern California two months ago. Her mother is getting her PhD in education, and her father, a former professor of physics in a main university, is learning English and conducting some experiments at the University of California. Yue Huan is a high-achieving child who can handle, in Chinese, mathematics equivalent to high school. She cannot speak a word of English. She is a gifted violin player; she is also studying piano. She avidly reads Chinese novels and other long books. Mr Jones, her teacher is an African American young man with relatively short teaching experience. The neighborhood school is highly diversified: about one third of the students are black, one third Hispanic and Asian, and one third white . . . Lyn Huan comes back from school very frustrated. She feels she is learning nothing in school. She cannot participate well, and hates English. She brought with her the fifth grade textbooks she would have used had she remained in China, and she works at home so she will not be left behind. She has no friends and lives in a low-income housing area. Sometimes she cries and complains that older kids stole her lunch or hit her. There is a large African American girl who intimidates her, hits her and then, when the teacher notices that Lyn Huan is crying, pretends not to know what happened. By the fifth month Lyn Huan is more fluent in English, but is still in shock and hates school. She is now enjoying English television and is advancing rapidly in English. You are a teacher-trainer responsible for organizing a school program involving the parents of non-English speaking children. Your job is to design a cultural therapy program for non-English speaking community (parents and children), and to sensitize teachers to cultural differences.

I. Acquisition of New Knowledge about the Community

1. Gathering General Information
   1 Consider the parents and children as your main resource. They will teach each other about their home countries, traditions and life-style. They will also help you, each other and the teacher to understand better the schools they came from in their home country and the kinds of activities they were used to in those schools.
   2 Organize meetings with the parents and some voluntary teachers. Make sure these meetings are in neutral territory, which may not necessarily be the school. It could take place in their housing area, for example, in a room used for social events in the community.
   3 The purpose of these meetings is to create working groups among parents and teachers that permit each cultural group to present and describe their home country.
   4 Encourage parents to bring pictures, clothing, slides, musical instruments, and anything else they want to share with the other parents.

    5 Encourage parents from the different groups to share description's of traditional rituals, fiestas or other family activities, and to explain their cultural meaning.

    6 Have children display their artistic and academic skills, and let them construct booklets, art projects, decoration objects in such a way that they can show their skills.

    7 The result of the above activities should be a substantial collection of artifacts, folklore, and other cultural objects, with some information about them.

2. Inviting Parents and Teachers to Reflect on what they Learned

    1 Let parents and teachers discuss their family values and traditions, and then share with them your own, or those values and traditions you are familiar with in the United States and other societies.

    2 Invite parents to explain in what ways coming to the US has changed drastically their lives and how they feel about it.

    3 Encourage parents to share their long-term plans with you and each other.

    4 Invite parents to share with each other, teachers and you their major problems: the acquisition of English, their ability to interact in school, in the bank, in the hospital, in other public places, etc.

    5 Encourage them to present to each other their strategies to cope with the above problems, and the results they observed.

    6 Have the teacher become a resource person for the parents, and to share with them information he or she thinks is appropriate.

3. Planning Maintenance of Home Language and Culture

    1 Have parents inventory their own networks and help them facilitate communication with other groups of the same culture and background.

    2 Encourage them to maintain communication with relatives and friends in their home country, and offer suggestions to increase and facilitate communication.

    3 Have parents from various language and culture groups establish a support parent group to assist each other in case of emergencies or other problems.

    4 Have them inquire about English classes for parents or other enriching experiences (including trips to visit museums, cities, and parks).

4. Planning Cultural Enriching Activities

    1 Have the school sponsor other activities to encourage parental participation in cultural activities.

    2 Encourage parents to seek help and public services when they face hardships.

    3 With the help of the school, plan matching of Anglo and ethnic parents in order to participate jointly in American

traditional festivities: Thanksgiving, Christmas, New Year, games, parades, fairs, etc.

4 Meet with ethnic parents and encourage them to share their interpretation of their experiences in America, their fears, their pleasant experiences, and their learning experiences.

5 The overall outcome of these enriching activities is to empower ethnic community parents to participate in American cultural activities more intelligently and to learn from them.

6 Encourage teachers and parents to provide you with direct feedback on the work, exercises and activities you have recommended.

II. Implications for Inter-Ethnic Relations and School Support

1. Learning from the Formation of Parents' Network

1 What can parents do now they could not before? In what way did the formation of friendships and networks played a key role to their becoming better adjusted to American society?

2 What new mechanisms were used by parents in order to resolve their problems and their children's problems at home and in school?

3 Are teachers satisfied with the inter-ethnic relations of their children? Are children and their parents more sensitive to cultural differences?

4 What are the main benefits of enriching the cultural experiences of parents by facilitating their social interaction and their experiences in American society.

5 Is the overall learning climate in school better as a result of cultural therapy? If yes, in what ways? If not, why not?

Scenario # 3: Juan Mendoza, Nelly Cheng and Frank Underwood are the three new faculty in the Department of Curriculum and Instruction. Juan is Chicano, Nelly is Chinese (from Taiwan) and Frank is African American. There are twenty-five faculty in total. The chair of the department is a white woman who is extremely supportive of all minorities. These three faculty were hired after many efforts to find minority candidates. The overall support of the faculty for the hiring was qualified by concerns about the ability of the new faculty to measure up to departmental expectations. In fact, the candidates had been interviewed in great detail and warned about the difficulties in getting tenure. The College of Education and the University in which these three faculty were hired is a prestigious, mostly white, institution with very few faculty and students from other ethnic and cultural groups. The faculty are highly polarized over race and gender issues. Some older faculty have never worked with non-whites and feel uncomfortable with the new faculty. The three new faculty are anxious and concerned about their future, but willing to face the challenge and happy to find mentors in some of the faculty. The student paper and local newspapers continue to emphasize school and city problems with the incoming of African Americans and Hispanics. Some professors have published articles in the papers accusing the current administrators of watering down standards in the selection of new faculty, and of imposing them on various departments. There is a general fear that attracting minority faculty will, in the end, destroy the quality of academic programs and that it will destroy the institution. Your job, as a consultant to the College of Education, is to develop a program of cultural therapy for the Department of Curriculum and Instruction.

I. Information and Reflection on Ethnicity and Academia in America

1. Becoming Aware of Ethnicity in American Academia
   1 Organize seminars, colloquia, conferences, classes and other academic activities for both faculty and students, with the purpose of gathering factual information about the current distribution of ethnic members of the faculty, staff and student bodies.
   2 Have white Anglo-Saxon faculty explore their roots and the ethnicity of their ancestors, and have them share with each other and the students their awareness and knowledge about their own ethnicity and family background.
   3 Have some of the sessions focused on the ethnohistory of the university, the College of Education, and the relative participation of, or isolation from, ethnic minority groups.
   4 Have faculty and students discuss their concerns about the future of academia in the face of inter-ethnic conflicts.
   5 Invite ethnic faculty and students to share their experiences in academia, and their personal dreams as professionals.
   6 Encourage faculty across ages and ethnic groups to share their dreams for their department, and their anxieties about ethnic diversity, the politics of ethnic conflicts, and equity issues.
   7 Inventory the concerns of faculty, their academic strengths, and their areas of common interests.
   8 Have a small group of faculty and students enrich and edit this inventory which will be used in the following exercise.

2. Developing Partnerships
   1 Working together in inter-ethnic teams, in the designing of research and teaching, as well as in joint interventions in local schools and community, can be very effective. Discuss this possibility with the faculty and students.
   2 Explore the possibility of a joint intervention short-term project to work with minority elementary or high schools, and have an inter-ethnic team develop the plan, propose it to the school authorities, and deliver it. This intervention may consist in after-school mentorship of high school students and teachers, in the organization of a play, a science project, an art exhibit or another activity that students themselves request.

3 Encourage faculty to develop inter-ethnic grant proposals to pursue curriculum research and development at the university, or to provide professional development workshops for local teachers, or to gather some basic data on problems affecting the local ethnic groups, such as poverty, drugs, and isolation.

4 Have the faculty propose to the dean of the college and the central administration a program to involve, in a non-threatening environment, a candid discussion of problems related to ethnicity. Invite members of ethnic studies programs, and other experts in the anthropology, sociology and psychology of low-income and minority groups. What is important is to start cooperative efforts — even the start may seem difficult, divisive and draining.

II. Implications of Knowledge for Academic Policies and Practices

1. Reflecting on Current Policies and Practices

    1 Organize, with the assistance of the dean or departmental chair of college and central administration, a departmental study group (interethnic, composed by both faculty and students) whose responsibility it is to gather and analyze policies and practices associated with hiring and promotion. This group may take the form of a blue ribbon committee or task force, and should be given a clear mandate with deadlines and expected outcomes.

    2 Upon completion of task, have this group discuss with the entire department their findings and recommendations.

    3 Have their recommendations passed to other department chairs and student groups for possible reactions and suggestions.

    4 Have the dean and departmental chairs react to the findings in terms of the accuracy of factual data, the wisdom of data analysis, and the feasibility of recommendations.

    5 Provide insights and feedback to dean and chairs from the perspective of the ethnic and minority faculty, and invite them to look into long-term effects of policies and practices for the welfare of the entire college of education and its global mission in a democratic society.

    6 Discuss the need to recognize the assets of American society as a multicultural democratic society that respects and values its rich cultural heritage.

    7 Discuss the place of many cultures and ethnic groups in the university and its value in the education of all students who will live in a democratic society.

Methodological Training for Cultural Therapy

The fundamental philosophy underlying cultural therapy is intimately related to the methodological and theoretical framework used by anthropologists in cross-cultural research. In essence, cultural therapy requires ethnographic approaches to gather and analyze information about cultural values and behavioral interpretations. Ethnographic approaches are useful because they bring about information and reflection about real life issues, and identify the deepest rationale for acting the way we do. This is the reason why ethnographic research has become widespread. In fact, ethnographers observe with mixed feelings the recently acquired popularity of qualitative research methods in various kinds of research designs and applied projects. They see qualitative approaches as relatively unstructured and, at times, irrelevant to the main issues of a study. Ethnographers have noticed the differential expertise and sophistication exhibited by researchers and project directors. There seems to be an imbalance between our technological advances to gather and analyze data and our ability to investigate issues from the perspective of the persons involved. Inter-ethnic conflict and multicultural issues are cases in point. Is modern ethnography compatible with advocacy research? Can such studies become biased by advocacy concerns, or in the opposite corner by racial prejudice? Is modern ethnography instrumental in gathering data for cultural therapy exercises? Indeed, it is, not only because it is a powerful means of creating awareness about cultural differences, but also of developing plans for a more harmonious interethnic interaction. Ethnography can become an instrument of social and cultural change beyond its value as a heuristic tool helping us understand better the world in which we live.

Ethnographers, even those who are not interested in cultural therapy, cannot escape the responsibility that comes from documenting social phenomena. They develop theoretical constructs in order to explain inequity, oppression, differential access to resources, school failure, racial prejudice, and the nature of decision-making; they study mechanism for upward mobility of women and minorities in educational institutions. Ethnographic research as a part of cultural therapy must be expanded to serve functions other than the gathering of scientific knowledge for science's sake alone. This is a strong feeling on the part of new researchers who are members of ethnic and minority groups.

To discuss methodological tools (modern ethnography) in a political or theoretical vacuum, that is, in the absence of appropriate socio-political and theoretical contexts and frameworks, is unrealistic and futile. Research designs are meaningful, or useful, or dangerous, or irrelevant, or stimulating precisely because they have a specific value within these contexts. Ethnographic research becomes significant historically when its contribution is to shed some light on the power of ideas and the need to preserve the freedom to share these ideas, especially in academia, even if such ideas are less acceptable to those in power.

Any ethnographer or apprentice to ethnographer that engages in gathering data (especially in the context of cultural therapy exercises) must be guided and trained. It is not sufficient to know something about methodological techniques from research approaches: interviews, video-taping, audio-taping, photography, life histories, case-students, vignettes, journals, participant observations, unobtrusive observations, note-taking, linguistic text analysis, historical accounts, archival documents, and others can be very instrumental in a number of different designs and research approaches. Training in such techniques is useful and can expedite the tasks of the researcher. Researchers need to go beyond ethnographic research and become reflective agents of change through a deeper understanding of cultural values and inter-ethnic conflict based on value differences. The explicit purpose of ethnographic research in cultural therapy exercises is to help people understand cultural conflict, resolve it and heal. Healing is viewed as the psychological adjustment of understood value differences.

There are a number of approaches that ethnographic data gathering can take. The choice of approach is a function of the specific project and the persons involved in the cultural therapy project. The following types can help understand such diversity:

1   Ethnohistorical approaches are used to conduct studies focused on the emic reconstruction of history, both those studies based primarily on oral history of particular sociocultural groups via interviews, as well as those based on archival research, and/or research on existing monuments, cemeteries, and/on archaeological monuments.

2   Ethnolinguistic approaches are used to conduct studies focused on language groups and linguistic behavior congruent with social and economic strata. These studies, for example, could focus primarily on linguistic behavior in the context of cultural contacts, or on cultural patterns and values associated with given linguistic groups. The methodology is based on linguistic analysis with some emphases of the cultural context of language use. The use of the ethnography of communication, a tool that has become fashionable since the early 1960s in the United States, has now become extremely important in interactional analysis as conducted by sociolinguists and anthropological linguists (see the work of Gumperz and Hymes).

3   Ethnomethodological approaches, those used to conduct research on patterns of interaction, are often part of larger studies of social strata (structural analysis). Such studies conducted by micro-sociologists require linguistic analysis of either oral and written language. Such analysis is intended to reveal the meaning of face-to-face interaction, as well as to lead to structural characteristics of social organizations. Thus, these studies can be linked to larger macro-sociological studies of institutional change that affects individual behavior at various structural levels. Federal changes in health service policies — for example, in the need for justification of specific types of services — may drastically change doctor-patient relationships and patient treatment.

4   Anthropological (ethnographic) approaches are those used to conduct studies characterized by their emphasis on the cultural dimensions of behavior; that is, studies of human interaction with the intent of understanding why and how people do what they do. Cultural explanations of behavior, in contrast with psychological or sociological, provide an understanding of the shared cultural values leading to certain behaviors. While ethnographic approaches are used within a number of disciplines and theoretical frameworks, they retain important theoretical and methodological characteristics that will be discuss below.

Classic ethnographic studies are, at least ideally, long-term oriented, grounded in empirical evidence collected through field-based methodological techniques (included those alluded to above). Most importantly, *all ethnographic studies are fundamentally interpretive*, they rely on the judgment of the investigator who gathers the data through his/her cultural lenses. One of the main purposes of ethnographic research is to interpret the meaning of behavior by providing the appropriate social and cultural context in which behavior takes place. However, the social and cultural context often becomes understandable in a cross-cultural comparison and perspective, that is, with reference to comparable behaviors in other cultural groups. This is a particularly stringent requirement for ethnographic studies designed by anthropologists, but it has also proven useful to psychologist, linguists (psycholinguists and sociolinguists), ethnographers of communication, ethnomethodologists and other social scientists. A simple superficial analysis of behavior and cultural values does not constitute an ethnographic research; a more systemic and long-term study is needed. Indeed many scholars want to distinguish further between ethnographic studies (those which have an ethnographic component) and ethnographies (cohesive, comprehensive, holistic studies of human behavior framed in the appropriate ethnohistorical and socio-cultural contexts).

Different disciplinary frameworks provide different direction to modern ethnographies. Not every aspect of human behavior is equally important across disciplines. Psychological frameworks often focus on cognitive processes, motivation, or developmental issues. Neo-Vygotskian researchers, for example, conducting ethnographic studies with the purpose of empowering minorities, belong here (Diaz, Moll and Mehan, 1986; Moll, 1990; Cole and D'Andrade, 1982; Cole and Griffin, 1983; Cole and Scribner, 1974). Sociolinguists, ethno-methodologists and ethnographers of communication, in turn, may focus on the use of language to make inferences about institutional structures in society, about group boundaries, interactional patterns reflective of social status, or about the use of opportunity structures and closure structures via the use of class privileges (Cook-Gumperz, 1986; Gumperz, 1982, 1986; Gumperz and Hymes, 1964, 1972).

It is precisely the methodological plasticity and compatibility of ethnographic research, with a number of potential theoretical frameworks, that have attracted large numbers of applied researchers, action researchers, and scholars interested in using their skills to heal society. When ethnographic research is applied to study equity, cultural diversity, multicultural settings, class and caste structures, ethnicity, academic achievement, performance in schools and society, minority status and success, and other issues that affect our lives, it becomes a potential instrument for cultural therapy. While the many and complex dimensions of behavior in pluralistic societies are accessible from a variety of approaches, modern ethnographic research has provided unique insights because it is one of the best instruments to get at the heart of psycho-social behavioral phenomena and the motivation behind them. Ethnographers cannot assume stability of behavioral patterns. The interpretive process brings the ethnographer closest to the dynamics of social change. *This is the reason why the actual data gathered impacts continuously the research goals and the nature of the inquiry itself which are restructured with the new information obtained.* New questions must be asked in order to get to the bottom of explanations, or at the configuration of experiences, and consequently, new research goals must be constructed as they promise to be relevant to the new line of inquiry. Inquiry is guided, in turn, by promises of yielding emically significant insights, that is, functionally relevant explanations from the perspective of the persons under study, that help the ethnographer understand the relationship between cultural values and behavior.

There are other reasons why modern ethnography, in spite of its inherent difficulties and requirements (being a long-term, intensive time investment, an interpretive and persistent, but flexible inquiry process), continues to attract large number of socially-minded scholars. We cannot accept simplistic answers to the complex behavioral issues involved in the study of many human phenomena such as substance abuse, rape, physical and verbal abuse, other types of violence, teenage suicide, teenage pregnancies, child pornography, destructive social behavior, failure in school, oppressive economic policies in business, abuse of male power in academic institutions, and others. We search for contextual information and sociocultural explanations because we need to understand and to make sense of such behaviors in their essential components and genesis.

References

COLE, M. and D'ANDRADE, R. (1982) 'The influence of schooling on concept formation: Some preliminary conclusions', *The Quarterly Newsletter of the Laboratory of Comparative Human Cognition*, **4**(2), pp. 19–26.

COLE, M. and GRIFFIN, P. (1983) 'A socio-historical approach to re-mediation', *The Quarterly Newsletter of the Laboratory of Comparative Human Cognition*, **5**(4), pp. 69–74.

COLE, M. and SCRIBNER, S. (1974) 'Culture and thought: A psychological introduction', New York, NY: Basic Books.

COOK-GUMPERZ, J. (Ed.) (1986) *The Social Construction of Literacy*, Cambridge, MA: Cambridge University Press.

DIAZ, S., MOLL, L. and MEHAN, H. (1986) 'Sociocultural resources in instruction: A context-specific approach', in *Beyond Language: Social and Cultural Factors in Schooling Language Minority Students*, Sacramento, CA: Bilingual Education Office, California State Department of Education, pp. 187–230.

GUMPERZ, J. (Ed.) (1982) *Language and Social Identity*, Cambridge, MA: Cambridge University Press.

GUMPERZ, J. (1986) 'International sociolinguistics in the study of schooling', in COOK-GUMPERZ, J. (Ed.) *The Social Construction of Literacy*, Cambridge, MA: Cambridge University Press, pp. 45–68.

GUMPERZ, J. and HYMES, D. (Eds) (1964) 'The ethnography of communication', Special issue of *American Anthropologists*, **66**(6).

GUMPERZ, J. and HYMES, D. (1972) *Directions in Sociolinguistics: The Ethnography of Communication*, New York, NY: Holt, Rinehart and Winston.

MOLL, L. (1990) *Vygotsky and Education: Instructional Implications and Applications of Sociohistorical Psychology*, Cambridge, MA: Cambridge University Press.

Chapter 9

Annotated References for Cultural Therapy

Henry T. Trueba

The person conducting cultural therapy must select a series of reading materials, video cassettes, movies, and other materials that can help those involved in the exercise. The main purpose of these readings and materials is to invite reflection, discussion and comparisons focused on specific aspects of cultural diversity, multiculturalism, language differences, interethnic conflict, self-concept, cultural values, culture change, and other important themes often alluded to in such exercises. In addition to materials related to theoretical content and ethnographic descriptions, it is important to discuss the methods used in collecting the ethnographic description and other information. What follows is only a brief listing of reading materials with short annotated comments.

AMERICAN COUNCIL ON EDUCATION (1986) *Minorities in Higher Education*, Washington, DC: Office of Minority Concerns, Fifth Annual Status Report.

AMERICAN INSTITUTES FOR RESEARCH (1977a) *Evaluation of the Impact of ESEA Title VII Spanish/English Bilingual Education Program*, I: *Study Design and Interim Findings*, Palo Alto, CA.

AMERICAN INSTITUTES FOR RESEARCH (1977b) *Evaluation of the Impact of ESEA Title VII Spanish/English Bilingual Education Program*, II: *Project Descriptions*, Palo Alto, CA.

The three sources above present a number of specific findings on the education of minority students. The first study focuses on the scarce numbers of African American and Hispanics in doctoral programs, especially those on natural sciences and mathematics. The two 1977 reports are the controversial reports on the quality of bilingual education. These reports are often criticized as being biased against the instructional use of the home languages. For more accurate and recent work consult the chapter by W.G. Secada (1989, and 1992), and Trueba (1989, 1991a, 1991b, 1991c).

ANICK, M.C., CARPENTER, T. and SMITH, C. (1981) 'Minorities and mathematics: Results from the national assessment of educational progress', *Mathematics Teacher*, Oct. 1981, pp. 560–66.

An important source to understand the differential achievement of minorities in math. Secada (1992) has also discussed this topic and provides additional explanations for underachievement.

APPLE, M. (1979) *Ideology and Curriculum*, London, England: Routledge & Kegan Paul.

APPLE, M. (1982) *Cultural and Economic Reproduction in Education*, New York, NY: Macmillan.

APPLE, M. (1989) *Teachers and Texts: A Political Economy of Class and Gender Relations in Education*, New York, NY: Routledge.

APPLE, M. (1990) *Ideology and Curriculum*, New York, NY: Routledge.

Michael Apple's many important books have been translated into many languages and have had an international impact far beyond academic discourse. Apple deals with fundamental philosophical issues linking class, economic status and quality of teaching. In a democracy sharing knowledge and values in schools affects the status and quality of life of students and their families. The quality of schooling mirrors social stratification and class biases. His fundamental theories about social science research reveal a profound commitment to equity through teaching and research, and the application of democratic principles within academic circles.

AU, K.H. (1980) 'Participation structures in a reading lesson with Hawaiian children: Analysis of a culturally appropriate instructional event', *Anthropology and Education Quarterly*, **11**(2), pp. 91–115.

AU, K.H. (1981a) 'The comprehension-oriented reading lesson: Relationships to proximal indices of achievement', *Educational Perspectives*, **20**, pp. 13–15.

AU, K.H. and JORDAN, C. (1981) 'Teaching reading to Hawaiian children: Finding a culturally appropriate solution', in TRUEBA, H., GUTHRIE, G., AU, K. (Eds), *Culture and the Bilingual Classroom: Studies in Classroom Ethnography*, Rowley, MA: Newbury House Publishers, Inc., pp. 139–52.

AU, K.H. and KAWAKAMI, A.J. (1982) 'A conceptual framework for studying in the long-term effects of comprehension instruction', *The Quarterly Newsletter of the Laboratory of Comparative Human Cognition*, **6**(4), pp. 95–100.

AU, K. and MASON, J.M. (1981) 'Social organizational factors in learning to read: The balance of rights hypothesis', *Reading Research Quarterly*, **17**(1), pp. 115–52.

The work of Au, Jordan and others to be discussed below (Boggs, Gallimore, Tharp, etc.) represents a high quality research conducted in the Kamehameha Schools of Hawaii. The seminar work of pioneers in the research of 'talk story' such as Karen Watson-Gegeo, impacted many other scholars searching for cultural congruence through discourse patterns. The application of cultural congruence principles to reading research has some limitations, and much of the success in Kamehameha reading programs could be explained by principles of reciprocal interaction (Zeichner, 1992) or by the joint construction of knowledge (see Cook-Gumperz, 1986 and Gumperz, 1971, 1986, etc. below).

BARTH, F. (1969) *Ethnic Groups and Boundaries*, Boston, MA: Little, Brown.

One of the classic pieces in anthropology dealing with ethnicity and the mechanism to determine ethnic boundaries in different social and political contexts is the central contribution of this source.

BEACH, W.G. (1932) *Oriental Crime in California*, Palo Alto, CA: Stanford University Press.

Among other sources that shatter the 'model minority' applied to all Asians is this book. The reality of differential achievement and selected cultural ways to adapt to American society forces scholars to distinguish intragroup differences. See below (Trueba, Jacobs and Kirton (1990), and Trueba, Cheng and Ima (1993).

BIDWELL, C. and FRIEDKIN, N. (1988) 'The sociology of education' in SMELSER, N. (Ed.) *The Handbook of Sociology*, Newbury Park, CA: Sage Publications, pp. 449–71.

One of the most enlightening historical reviews of the theoretical development of the sociology of education is presented in this chapter. The authors, in a terse and forceful style, take the reader back to struggles between Left and Right sociologists, macro- and micro-sociologists, and present a cohesive view of how education has been viewed by American sociologists in the last half century.

BILINGUAL EDUCATION OFFICE, CALIFORNIA STATE DEPARTMENT OF EDUCATION (1984) *Handbook for Teaching Cantonese-speaking Students*, Sacramento, CA: Author.

BILINGUAL EDUCATION OFFICE, CALIFORNIA STATE DEPARTMENT OF EDUCATION (1986) *Handbook for Teaching Filipino-speaking Students*, Sacramento, CA: Author.

BILINGUAL EDUCATION OFFICE, CALIFORNIA STATE DEPARTMENT OF EDUCATION (1983) *Handbook for Teaching Vietnamese-speaking Students*, Sacramento, CA: Author.

BILINGUAL EDUCATION OFFICE, CALIFORNIA STATE DEPARTMENT OF EDUCATION (1983) *Handbook for Teaching Korean-speaking Students*, Los Angeles, CA: Evaluation, Dissemination and Assessment Center, California State University, Los Angeles.

BILINGUAL EDUCATION OFFICE, CALIFORNIA STATE DEPARTMENT OF EDUCATION (1987) *Handbook for Japanese-speaking students.* Sacramento, CA: State Department.

The collection of handbooks on the various ethnic groups has enriched the knowledge of many teachers over the years. California has played a leadership role in the nation both in bringing a deeper understanding of multicultural education, and in developing effective instructional program for ALL Americans, especially those from low-income, ethnic minorities and alienated white Americans.

BOGGS, S.T. (1972) 'The meaning of questions and narratives to Hawaiian children', in CAZDEN, C.B. JOHN, V.P. and HYMES, D. (Eds), *Functions of Language in the Classroom*, New York, NY: Teachers College Press, pp. 1–28.

BOGGS, S.T. (1985) *Speaking, Relating and Learning: A Study of Hawaiian Children at Home and at School*, Norwood, NJ: Ablex Publishing Corp.

See discussion on Kamehameha above, with reference to Au and associates, p. 170. Boggs was one of the pioneers in the sociolinguistic approach to reading research in Hawaii.

BOOS-NUNNING, U. and HOHMANN, M. (1989) 'The educational situation of migrant workers' children in the Federal Republic of Germany', in ELDERING, L. and KLOPROGGE, J. (Eds) *Different Cultures Same School: Ethnic Minority Children in Europe*, Amsterdam, The Netherlands: Swets & Zeitlinger, pp. 39–59.

The ongoing research in Europe (see p. 178) Eldering and Kloprogge, 1989) has provided a comparative view that helps one to understand the struggles of underclass and castelike minorities throughout the world. Consult below the work of Roosens, Suarez-Orozco and the Spindlers. Boos-Nunning and Hohmann bring important data on the conflicting educational policies of the Germany before the merging of East and West Germanies into one. The serious difficulties faced by Turks and other people of color have worsened in the last few years.

BORISH, S. (1988) 'The winter of their discontent: Cultural compression and decompression in the life cycle of the Kibbutz adolescent', in TRUEBA, H. and DELGADO-GAITAN, C. (Eds) *School and Society: Teaching Content Through Culture*, NY: Praeger, pp. 181–99.

Borish, trained under the supervision and with the support of George and Louise Spindler, is a superb ethnographer who has produced many insightful pieces. His main point here is the paradox of socialization stages during adolescence, and the struggle with decisions as young adults have to face military service and high risks. The compression-decompression cycles are a powerful analogy created by the Spindlers.

BRONFENBRENNER, U. (1978) 'Who needs parent education?', *Teachers College Record*, **79**(4), pp. 767–87.

BRONFENBRENNER, U. (1979) *The Ecology of Human Development: Experiments by Nature and Design*, Cambridge, MA: Harvard University Press.

Bronfenbrenner has championed the role of parents in education, and the idea of empowering the family. His main contribution is to provide a realistic social context for the education of adults in working America.

BROWN, A., CAMPIONE, E., COLE, M., GRIFFIN, P., MEHAN, H. and RIEL, M. (1982) 'A model system for the study of learning difficulties', *The Quarterly Newsletter of the Laboratory of Comparative Human Cognition*, 4(3), pp. 39–55.

The seminal work of Brown and Campione has capitalized on the Neo-Vygotskian research conducted by Michael Cole and associates at the Laboratory of Comparative Human Cognition, University of California at San Diego. Their efforts have helped revise concepts and processes related to learning disabilities, and the role of social and cultural factors affecting the cognitive development of those classified and treated as learning disabled.

BROWN, G., ROSEN, H., HILL, S. and OLIVAS, M. (1980) *The Condition of Education for Hispanic Americans*, Washington, DC: United States Department of Education, National Center for Educational Statistics.

BROWN, S.V. (1987) *Minorities in the Graduate Education Pipeline*, Princeton, NJ: Educational Testing Service.

BROWN, S.V. (1988) *Increasing Minority Faculty: An Elusive Goal*, A Research Report of the Minority Education Project. Graduate Record Examinations Board and Educational Testing Service, Princeton, NJ: Educational Testing Services.

The three studies above are examples of the efforts made by scholars to assemble empirical data showing the reality of inequality in American education. At the rate of progress minorities are making, it will take a very long time to open doors in universities and industries to give minority persons the opportunity to develop and fully use their talents. The social and economic infrastructure of educational institutions continues to block the entrance and successful completion of minority students.

CALIFORNIA STATE DEPARTMENT OF EDUCATION (1981) *Schooling and Language Minority Students: A Theoretical Framework*, Los Angeles, CA: California State University, Evaluation, Dissemination and Assessment Center.

CALIFORNIA STATE DEPARTMENT OF EDUCATION (1983) *Basic Principles for the Education of Language-minority Students: An Overview*, Los Angeles, CA: California State University, Evaluation, Dissemination and Assessment Center.

CALIFORNIA STATE DEPARTMENT OF EDUCATION (1984) *Studies on Immersion Education*, Los Angeles, CA: California State University, Evaluation, Dissemination and Assessment Center.

CALIFORNIA STATE DEPARTMENT OF EDUCATION (1986) *Beyond Language: Social and Cultural Factors in Schooling Language Minority Students*, Los Angeles, CA: California State University, Evaluation, Dissemination and Assessment Center.

These four volumes are an excellent example of the importance of California in contemporary American thinking regarding multiculturalism. Important and substantive articles guide the reader through very complex social, cognitive and historical issues related to the education of language minority students and other students who have been disenfranchised. They form a must in the readings of both beginners and sophisticated readers.

CARDENAS, J.A., ROBLEDO, M. and WAGGONER, D. (1988) *The Undereducation of American Youth*, San Antonio, TX: Intercultural Development Research Association, Center for the Prevention and Recovery of Dropouts.

CARTER, T. (1970) *Mexican Americans in School: A History of Educational Neglect*, New York, NY: College Entrance Examination Board.

CARTER, T.P. and SEGURA, R.D. (1979) *Mexican Americans in School: A Decade of Change*, New York, NY: College Entrance Examination Board.

These three volumes discuss Hispanic education — or the neglect of their education. (Additional sources presented below can be useful. See San Miguel, 1987.) Mexican

American children account today for over 55 per cent of the entire growth in the minority student population. In many cities, Hispanics are now reaching 60 or 65 per cent (or even more) of the urban student population.

CAUDILL, W. and DE VOS, G. (1956) 'Achievement, culture and personality', *American Anthropologist*, (**58**), pp. 1102–26.

The work by De Vos will discussed below.

CAZDEN, C. and MEHAN, H. (1989) 'Principles from sociology and anthropology: Context, code, classroom, and culture', in REYNOLDS, M.C. (Ed.), *Knowledge Base for the Beginning Teacher*, Oxford, England: Pergamon Press.

CAZDEN, C., JOHN, V. and HYMES, D. (Eds) (1972) *Functions of Language in the Classroom*. New York, NY: Teachers College Press.

The work of Cazden and Mehan is highly respected because it deals with the extremely complex problem of how to teach children from many home language and culture environments in a single classroom or school. They emphasize the need to translate the cultural knowledge acquired in interaction with a multicultural classroom into pedagogical strategies. The nature of reciprocal interaction (Zeichner, 1992), in which communication (teaching) is jointly constructed by both children and teacher. This is particularly appropriate from the perspective of a Neo-Vygotskian conception of cognitive development.

CHAN, K.B. (1983) 'Resettlement of Vietnamese-Chinese refugees in Montreal, Canada: Some socio-psychological problems and dilemmas', *Canadian Ethnic Studies*, **15**, pp. 1–17.

CHAN, K.S. (1983) 'Limited English-speaking, handicapped, and poor: Triple threat in childhood', in MAE, C.C. (Ed.) *Asian- and Pacific American Perspectives in Bilingual Education: Comparative Research*, New York, NY: Teachers College, Columbia University.

The sources related to Asian Americans placed in this short list are often of different quality, depth and come from different theoretical perspectives. Empirical research and theoretical efforts to consolidate understanding of Asian Americans in schools and society requires a more serious long-term effort on the part of educational researchers.

CHAVEZ, L.R. (1992) *Shodowed Lives: Undocumented Immigrants in American Society. Case Studies in Cultural Anthropology*, SPINDLER, G. and L. (Eds). New York, NY: Harcourt Brace Jovanovich College Publishers.

This short book is an extremely powerful and well-documented source that brings us close to the reality of the undocumented Hispanics crossing by the thousands the Southern borders. It is a shocking account of the lack of compassion and racism that guides much of the hostility against these people whose only sin is attempting to survive. The book tells us a great deal about current American values, and the cycles of intolerance for culturally and racially different persons that come to America. Chavez, trained under George Spindler at Stanford, collected materials that only a most competent Chicano, with high level of fluency in Spanish and great determination, could collect and analyze.

CHENG, L. (1989) 'Service delivery to Asian/Pacific LEP children: A cross-cultural framework', *Topics in Language Disorders*, 9(3), pp. 1–14.

CHILCOTT, J.H. (1987) 'Where are you coming from and where are you going? The reporting of ethnographic research', *American Educational Research Journal*, 24(2), pp. 199–218.

This piece of Chilcott attacks serious and difficult methodological problems that for generations have been worrying scholars in anthropology and sociology. See comments below on the methodological contributions of the Spindlers (pp. 185–6) and the review by Suarez-Orozco (1991a) of the Spindlers' work.

COLE, M. and GRIFFIN, P. (1983) 'A socio-historical approach to remediation', *The Quarterly Newsletter of the Laboratory of Comparative Human Cognition*, 5(4), pp. 69–74.

Another significant contribution of New-Vygotskians to our understanding of mediation in cognitive development, or the need for an assisted instruction for children.

COOK-GUMPERZ, J. (Ed.) (1986) *The Social Construction of Literacy*, Cambridge, UK: Cambridge University Press.

See comments on sociolinguistic research below, in the context of the work by Gumperz and Hymes.

CUMMINS, J. (1976) 'The influence of bilingualism on cognitive growth: A synthesis of research findings and explanatory hypotheses', *Working Papers on Bilingualism*, 9, pp. 1–43.

CUMMINS, J. (1978) 'Bilingualism and the development of metalinguistic awareness', *Journal of Cross-cultural Psychology*, 9(2), pp. 131–49.

CUMMINS, J. (1979) 'Linguistic interdependence and the educational development of bilingual children', *Review of Educational Research*, 49, pp. 222–51.

CUMMINS, J. (1980) 'The cross-lingual dimensions of language proficiency: Implications for bilingual education and the optimal age issue', *TESOL Quarterly*, 14, pp. 175–87.

CUMMINS, J. (1981) 'The entry and exit fallacy in bilingual education', *National Association for Bilingual Education Journal*, 4(3), pp. 26–60.

CUMMINS, J. (1981) 'The role of primary language development in promoting educational success for language minority students', in *Schooling and Language Minority Students: A Theoretical Framework*, Los Angeles, CA: California State

University at Los Angeles Evaluation, Dissemination and Assessment Center, pp. 3–49.

CUMMINS, J. (1983) *Heritage Language Education: A Literature Review*, Toronto, Canada: Ministry of Education, Ontario.

CUMMINS, J. (1984) *Bilingual special education: Issues in assessment and pedagogy*, San Diego, CA: College Hill Press.

CUMMINS, J. (1986) 'Empowering minority students: A framework for intervention', *Harvard Educational Review*, **56**(1), pp. 18–35.

CUMMINS, J. (1989) *The Empowerment of Minority Students*, Los Angeles, CA: California Association for Bilingual Education.

The many important contributions of Cummins are well known in psychology, sociology and bilingual education. His contribution has been to stress the role that the home languages play in the cognitive development and second language acquisition of minority children. His clear commitment to the education of ALL children has taken him to propose a radically different role for teachers. Rather than teachers being simple dispensers of intellectual goodies (sharing knowledge) he wants teachers to become advocates for children and their families. His contributions have implications for special and bilingual education. Cummins is perhaps one of the best known scholars linking cognitive research and bilingualism.

D'ANDRADE, R. (1984) 'Cultural meaning systems', in SHWEDER, R.A. and LEVINE, R.A. (Eds) *Culture Theory*, pp. 88–119.

A cognitive anthropologist, who has written extensively about cognitive processes in a cross-cultural perspective, proposes here a deeper and more comprehensive notion of culture that includes not only cognitive codes, but normative and emotional dimensions. For a comparative view of culture see the work of the Spindlers (pp. 185–6).

DELGADO-GAITAN, C. (1990) *Literacy for Empowerment: The Role of Parents in Children's Education*, London, England: Falmer Press.

DELGADO-GAITAN, C. and TRUEBA, H.T. (1991) *Crossing Cultural Borders: Education for Immigrant Families in America*, London, England: Falmer Press.

These two examples of the work of Delgado-Gaitan explore the relation between the home and the schools, and the impact of one on the other. The role of parents, even those who do not know English, is crucial in the development of children's cognitive skills, reasoning and inquiry strategies, and their overall ability to deal with reading comprehension. The umbrella of empowerment links her work to that of Freire and Apple.

DEVOS, G. (1967) 'Essential elements of caste: Psychological determinants in structural theory', in DEVOS A. and WAGATSUMA, H. (Eds) *Japan's Invisible Race: Caste in Culture and Personality*, Berkeley, CA: University of California Press, pp. 332–84.

DeVos, G. (1973) 'Japan's outcastes: The problem of the Burakumin', in Whitaker, B. (Ed.) *The Fourth World: Victims of Group Oppression*, New York, NY: Schocken Books, pp. 307–27.

DeVos, G. (1980) 'Ethnic adaptation and minority status' *Journal of Cross-Cultural Psychology*, **11**, pp. 101–24.

DeVos, G. (1983) 'Ethnic identity and minority status: Some psychocultural considerations', in Jacobson-Widding, A. (Ed.) *Identity: Personal and Socio-cultural*, Upsala Sweden: Almquist & Wiksell Tryckeri AB, pp. 90–113.

DeVos, G. and Wagatsuma, H. (1966) *Japan's Invisible Race: Caste in Culture and Personality*, Berkeley, CA: University of California Press.

DeVos has made many important contributions to our knowledge of ethnicity and achievement. His work on socialization across cultures, his discussion of degradation incidents and differential strategies (culturally determined) to deal with conflict are based on a complex methodological combination of protective techniques used in conjunction with historical and ethnographic data analysis. His work was pivotal for the scholars who developed cultural ecological positions (Ogbu, Gibson, Suarez-Orozco, etc.).

Diaz, S., Moll, L. and Mehan, H. (1986) 'Sociocultural resources in instruction: A context-specific approach', in *Beyond Language: Social and Cultural Factors in Schooling Language Minority Students*, Sacramento, CA: Bilingual Education Office, California State Department of Education, pp. 187–230.

These authors, originally colleagues at the Laboratory of Comparative Human Cognition in San Diego, make the important point that students, regardless of the antecedents of underachievement (poverty, exploitation, conquest, oppositional self-concept, i.e., self-concept in contrast with mainstream students who see themselves as successful) achieve according to the nature of the schooling experience. The immediacy of the context-specific variation in achievement requires an explanation. This paper was presented in response to the cultural ecological position of Ogbu, who did not attribute much influence to home-language development in school or outside the school, or for that matter to any school intervention. Ogbu's position has changed somewhat.

Eldering, L. and Kloprogge, J. (Eds) (1989) *Different Cultures Same School: Ethnic Minority Children in Europe*, Amsterdam, The Netherlands: Swets & Zeitlinger.

See discussion of European research below, along with the work of Roosens and Suarez-Orozco. Eugeen Roosens, the Director of the Center for Social Anthropology at the University of Leuven, Belgium, has developed an exchange program, for faculty involved in research, with the University of California at Los Angeles, Berkeley and San Diego. Marcelo Suarez-Orozco is the liaison person in the United States who facilitates this program. Over the last fifteen years scholars from America and Belgium have been visiting each other and sharing the results of their research. The main results are described in the writings of both Roosens and Suarez-Orozco (see discussion associated with these names later on in this chapter).

ERICKSON, F. (1982) 'Taught cognitive learning in its immediate environments: A neglected topic in the anthropology of education', *Anthropology and Education Quarterly*, **13**(2), pp. 149–80.

ERICKSON, F. (1984) 'School literacy, reasoning, and civility: An anthropologist's perspective', *Review of Educational Research*, **54**(4), pp. 525–44.

ERICKSON, F. (1986) 'Qualitative methods in research on teaching' in WITTROCK, M.C. (Ed.) *Handbook of Research on Teaching*, New York, NY: Macmillan Publishing Co., pp. 119–58.

ERICKSON, F. (1987) 'Transformation and school success: The politics and culture of educational achievement', *Anthropology and Education Quarterly*, **18**(4) pp. 335–56.

ERICKSON, F. and MOHATT, G. (1982) 'Cultural organization of participation structures in two classrooms in Indian students' in SPINDLER, G. (Ed.) *Doing the Ethnography of Schooling: Educational Anthropology in Action*. New York, NY: Holt, Rinehart and Winston, pp. 132–75.

Erickson is an internationally recognized scholar whose methodological and other substantive contributions have shaped the field of educational anthropology. His strength has been in the use of focused ethnographic studies (criticized by Ogbu and others as 'micro-ethnographic' and consequently myopic or decontextualized). His mastery of the sociolinguistics and his use of interview materials to pursue issues of differential interpretation of norms, rules and values, is highly regarded.

FISHMAN, J. (1956) *Language Loyalty in the United States*, The Hague, The Netherlands: Mouton Co.

FISHMAN, J. (1976) *Bilingual Education: An International Sociological Perspective*, Rowley, MA: Newbury House.

FISHMAN, J. (1977) 'Bilingual education: The state of social science inquiry', *Papers in Applied Linguistics, Bilingual Education series*, Arlington, VA: Center for Applied Linguistics.

FISHMAN, J. (1978) 'A gathering of vultures, the 'Legion of Decency' and Bilingual Education in the USA', *NABE*, **2**(2), pp. 13–16.

FISHMAN, J. (1979) 'Bilingual Education: What and Why?', in TRUEBA, H.T. and BARNETT-MIZRAHI, C. (Eds) *Bilingual Multicultural Education and the Professional from Theory to Practice*, Rowley, MA: Newbury House, pp. 11–19.

Fishman has produced many and more recent monumental contributions to the sociology of language and bilingualism. His esoteric knowledge of dialects, macro-linguistic processes, cross-cultural comparisons of linguistic factors affecting change and language policy, are unsurpassed today. The above examples are just a taste of his acumen and broad perspectives.

FREIRE, P. (1973) *Pedagogy of the Oppressed*, New York, NY: Seabury.

Freire has won the minds and heart of people all over the world, and his ideals on the role of social consciousness, awareness and commitment to social justice, have made him the hero of applied researchers and scholars working for democratic principles. His long exile ended in glory, and Brazil has now seen him as the Minister of Education eager to bring reforms that open opportunities for all. Literacy and social literacy are seen by Freire as the gate to freedom and meaningful political participation in society.

FUJITA, M. and SANO, T. (1988) 'Children in American and Japanese day-care centers: Ethnography and reflective cross-cultural interviewing' in TRUEBA, H. and DELGADO-GAITAN, C. (Eds), *School and Society: Teaching Content Through Culture*, New York, NY: Praeger, pp. 73–97.

Also trained under the tutelage of George and Louise Spindler, these authors have adapted several instruments developed by the Spindlers, including the 'reflective cross-cultural interview' that permitted them to compare day care centers in America with those of Japan. Through the use of these instruments the authors unveiled different cultural values underlying behavioral contrasts between the Japanese and American teachers.

GIBSON, M. (1987a) 'Playing by the rules', in SPINDLER, G. (Ed.) *Education and Cultural Process: Anthropological Approaches*, Second Edition. Prospect Heights, IL: Waveland Press, Inc., pp. 274–83.

GIBSON, M. (1987b) 'The school performance of immigrant minorities: A comparative view', *Anthropology and Education Quarterly*, **18**(4), pp. 262–75.

GIBSON, M. (1988) *Accommodation Without Assimilation: Sikh Immigrants in an American High School*, Ithaca, NY Cornell University Press.

Gibson has worked closely with Ogbu and has applied his theoretical 'cultural ecological position' to her work among the Punjabi of Northern California. Her main claim is that the Punjabi, in contrast with the Mexicans, their neighbors, have become high achievers in school (without losing their language and culture), and that perhaps the home culture is somewhat responsible for such achievement. This book discusses the cultural value compromises that appear in the adaptation process of the Punjabis.

GOLDMAN, S. and TRUEBA, H.T. (Eds) (1987) *Becoming Literate in English as a Second Language*, Norwood, NJ: Ablex Corporation.

This book presents a series of essays related to the differential approaches to second language learning and the various strategies used for that purpose.

GOLDMAN, S. and McDERMOTT, R. (1987) 'The culture of competition in American schools', *Education and Cultural Process: Anthropological Approaches*, Second Edition, Prospect Heights, IL: Waveland Press, Inc., pp. 282–89.

An insightful piece on high school competition as taught and enforced by teachers. The reader is faced with the reality of high school work and its implications for the crises faced by young adults in the schools.

GRANT, C.A. and SLEETER, C.E. (1986) 'Race, class and gender in education research: An argument for integrative analysis', *Review of Educational Research*, **56**, pp. 195–211.

Grant's work in this joint piece is pursued in several important books and articles. Racial prejudice is compounded by class consciousness and sexist biases. Their analysis is forceful.

GUMPERZ, J. (1971) *Language in Social Groups*, Palo Alto, CA: Stanford University Press.

GUMPERZ, J. (1981) 'Conversational inference and classroom learning', in GREEN, J. and MALLAT, C. (Eds) *Ethnography and Language in Educational Settings*, Norwood, NJ: Ablex.

GUMPERZ, J. (Ed.) (1982) *Language and Social Identity*, Cambridge, MA: Cambridge University Press.

GUMPERZ, J. (1986) 'Interactional sociolinguistics in the study of schooling', in COOK-GUMPERZ, J. (Ed.) *The Social Construction of Literacy*, Cambridge, MA: Cambridge University Press, pp. 45–68.

GUMPERZ, J., and HYMES, D. (1972) *Directions in Sociolinguistics: The Ethnography of Communication*, New York, NY: Holt, Rinehart & Winston.

GUMPERZ, J. and HYMES, D. (Eds) (1964) 'The ethnography of communication', Special issue of *American Anthropologists*, **66**, 6.

The birth of sociolinguistics and of the ethnography of communication owes a great deal to Gumperz and Hymes. Their continued productivity continues to enlighten complex interactional processes with an analysis of chains of meaning constructed between interactors in context-specific settings. A profound understanding of cultural and linguistic contexts permits Gumperz get at the heart of misunderstanding in interethnic understandings.

HAKUTA, K. (1986) *Mirror of Language: The Debate on Bilingualism*, New York, NY: Basic Books.

The author's work on bilingualism is informed by a philosophical position congruent with cultural democratic principles. His subsequent work is congruent with his premise of the nature of bilingualism and the importance of the home language for cognitive development and active participation in American institutions.

HEATH, S.B. (1983) *Ways with Words: Language, Life and Work in Communities and Classrooms*, New York, NY: Cambridge University Press.

The seminal work of Heath is probably one of the best known in anthropological linguistics. Teachers from all over the world have used her book to explore the linkages between linguistic (cultural) knowledge and pedagogical reform. Her critics often express concerns that linguistic changes and the acquisition of white discourse patterns alone cannot bring about equity, effective learning and participation in American society for the people of color.

HORNBERGER, N. (1988a) 'Iman Chay?: Quechua Children in Peru's Schools', in TRUEBA, H. and DELGADO-GAITAN, C. (Eds) *School and Society: Teaching Content Through Culture*, NY: Praeger, pp. 99–117.

HORNBERGER, N. (1988b) *Bilingual Education and Language Maintenance: A Southern Peruvian Quechua Case*, Providence, RI: Foris Publications.

HYMES, D. (1971) *On Communicative Competence*, Philadelphia, PA: University of Pennsylvania Press.

The work of Hornberger, inspired by that of Hymes and other ethnographers of communication, is of rare quality. The quality of the data gathered, the depth of her analysis, and her total fluency in Spanish and Quechua permits her to walk the reader through complex bilingual interactional events that she uses to make a major point: the significance of the home language in the instructional process.

MACIAS, J. (1987) 'The hidden curriculum of Papago Teachers: American Indian strategies for mitigating cultural discontinuity in early schooling'. SPINDLER, G. and SPINDLER, L. (Eds) *Interpretive Ethnography of Education: At Home and Abroad*, New Jersey: Lawrence Erlbaum Associates, Publishers, pp. 363–80.

McDERMOTT, R. (1977) 'Social relations as contexts for learning in school', *Harvard Educational Review*, **47**(2), pp. 198–213.

McDERMOTT, R. (1987) 'Achieving school failure: An anthropological approach to illiteracy and social stratification', in SPINDLER, G. (Ed.) *Education and Cultural Process: Anthropological Approaches*, Second Edition, Prospects Heights, IL: Waveland Press, Inc., pp. 173–209.

McDermott, senior to Macias, has in common with him the fact that both were students of George and Louise Spindler, and that both were well-trained in ethnographic research methods. Macias' topical interest and grounded analysis carries issues of cultural continuity and discontinuity in the study of the Papago school children. McDermott has made important methodological contributions on the nature of ethnographic research in contrast with other approaches. He has also made the forceful point that failure is achieved and is a sociological fact created by structural and cultural arrangements of American society; therefore, failure is not just a matter of personal choice and responsibility.

MEHAN, H. (1984) 'Language and schooling', *Sociology of Education*, **57**, (July): pp. 174–83.

See comments on Cazden p. 174.

MERCER, J. (1973) *Labeling the Mentally Retarded*, Berkeley, CA: University of California Press.

MERCER, J. (1979) 'In defense of racially and culturally non-discriminatory assessment', *School Psychology Digest*, **8**, pp. 9–115.

Mercer has examined the consequences of assessment processes and instruments that are insensitive to children of other languages and cultures. She has strongly advocated for alternative assessment and approaches that recognize linguistic and cultural diversity. Her work is closely associated with that of Rueda (see p. 184).

MOLL, L. (1990) *Vygotsky and Education: Instructional Implications and Applications of Sociohistorical Psychology*, Cambridge, MA: Cambridge University Press.

MOLL, L. and DIAZ, E. (1987) 'Change as the goal of educational research', *Anthropology and Education Quarterly*, **18**(4), pp. 300–11.

The work of Moll, based on the socio-historical approaches of Vygotsky, has moved theoretical advances to practical educational settings. He has advocated for the notion that the ethnic community has a considerable cultural capital that should be used by educators and researchers.

OGBU, J. (1974) *The Next Generation: An Ethnography of Education in an Urban Neighborhood*, New York, NY: Academic Press.

OGBU, J. (1978) *Minority Education and Caste: The American System in Cross-cultural Perspective*, New York, NY: Academic Press.

OGBU, J. (1981a) 'Origins of human competence: A cultural-ecological perspective', *Child Development*, **52**, pp. 413–29.

OGBU, J. (1981b) 'Education, clientage and social mobility: Caste and social change in the United States and Nigeria', in BERREMAN, G.D. (Ed.) *Social Inequality: Comparative Developmental Approaches*, New York: Academic Press, pp. 277–306.

OGBU, J. (1982) 'Cultural discontinuities and schooling', *Anthropology and Education Quarterly*, **13**(4), pp. 290–307.

OGBU, J. (1983) 'Minority status and schooling in plural societies', *Comparative Education Review*, **27**(2), pp. 168–190.

OGBU, J. (1987a) 'Variability in minority responses to schooling: Nonimmigrants vs. immigrants', in SPINDLER, G. and SPINDLER, L. (Eds) *Interpretive Ethnography of Education: At Home and Abroad* Hillsdale, NJ: Lawrence Erlbaum Associates, Publishers, pp. 255–78.

OGBU, J. (1987b) 'Variability in minority school performance: A problem in search of an explanation', *Anthropology and Education Quarterly*, **18**(4), pp. 312–34.

OGBU, J. (1989) 'The individual in collective adaptation: A framework for focusing on academic underperformance and dropping out among involuntary minorities', in WEIS, L. FARRAR, E. and PETRIE, H. (Eds) *Dropouts from School: Issues, Dilemmas, and Solution*, Albany, NY: State University of New York Press, pp. 181–204.

OGBU, J. and MATUTE-BIANCHI, M.E. (1986) 'Understanding sociocultural factors: Knowledge, identity and school adjustment;, in *Beyond Language: Social and Cultural Factors in Schooling Language Minority Students*, Sacramento, CA: Bilingual Education Office, California State Department of Education, pp. 73–142.

The work of John Ogbu has been mentioned frequently in this volume and needs no additional discussion. Suffice it to say that Ogbu is one of most important scholars working with African American and other minority persons. His theoretical position has been well received by most, and his contributions recognized internationally. Some of the limitations of his theory of differential achievement are mentioned by Trueba (1988a, 1988b).

PESHKIN, A. (1978) *Growing up American: Schooling and the Survival of Community*, Chicago, IL: Chicago University Press.

This author is a classic ethnographer of middle America. Perhaps no other modern ethnographer has conducted such a systematic and detailed study of American small towns, their schools and their cultural values. He has many other books.

POPKEWITZ, T.S. (1991) *A Political Sociology of Educational Reform: Power/knowledge in Teaching, Teacher Education and Research*, New York, NY: Teachers College, Columbia University.

As a philosopher of education profoundly concerned with reform, Popkewitz provides an analysis of the complex nature of educational reform, and of the consequences of structural changes for the reorganization of power relationships. The depth of his analysis and the impact of his work are remarkable.

ROOSENS, E. (1989) *Creating Ethnicity: The Process of Ethnogenesis*, Newbury Park, CA: Sage Publications.

ROOSENS, E. (1989a) 'Cultural ecology and achievement motivation: Ethnic minority youngsters in the Belgian system', in ELDERING, L. and KLOPROGGE, J. (Eds) *Different Cultures Same School: Ethnic Minority Children in Europe*, Amsterdam, The Netherlands: Swets & Zeitlinger, pp. 85–106.

ROOSENS, E. (1989b) *Creating Ethnicity: The Process of Ethnogenesis*, in BERNARD, H.B. (Series Editor) *Frontiers of Anthropology*, 5. Newbury Park, CA: Sage Publications.

Roosens is the dean of anthropological research on ethnicity in Europe. He is the director of the Center for Social Anthropology at the University of Leuven in Belgium. His team of researchers have, with the support of the Belgian government, conducted detailed, long-term studies on Moroccans, Turks, Spaniards, Italians, and many other groups all over Europe. His major personal contributions deal with the development and maintenance of ethnic boundaries, and the linguistic, legal, cultural, social and psychological implications of those boundaries. He was highly instrumental in establishing contacts with American scholars at the University of California in Berkeley, San Diego, Santa Barbara and Davis. His work has inspired DeVos, Suarez-Orozco, Trueba, Hansen and others to pursue cross-cultural comparative analyses of ethnic groups.

RUEDA, R., RODRIGUEZ, R. and PRIETO, A. (1981) 'Teacher's perceptions of competencies for teaching bilingual/multicultural exceptional children', *Exceptional Children*, **48**, pp. 268–70.

On the basis of Vygotskian premises, but with unique interdisciplinary skill in psychology, linguistics and sociology, Rueda has dealt with Special Education issues, assessment, cognitive development and bilingual education.

SAN MIGUEL JR., G. (1987) *'Let all of them take heed': Mexican Americans and the Campaign for Educational Equality in Texas, 1910–1981*. Austin, TX: University of Texas Press.

Along with other Chicano educational historians, after years of tedious and detailed research, San Miguel has made important contributions to our understanding of the educational neglect of Hispanics. He provided a rich political context (national and local) to explain the differential use of resources and quality in Chicano education.

SCRIBNER, S. and COLE, M. (1981) *The Psychology of Literacy*, Cambridge, MA: Harvard University Press.

This classic piece brought to psychologists, educators and other social scientists the realization that Vygotskian theories had much to contribute to our understanding of literacy (and literacies). The authors describe the different uses of text in different languages for different purposes, some ritual, other economic, other for interpersonal communication. They stress the need to understand the different type of literacy associated with languages of wider communication, in contrast with languages used for religious purposes across tribal groups, or for communication within tribal groupings.

SECADA. W.G. (Ed.) (1989) *Equity in Education*. London, England: Falmer Press.

SECADA, W.G. (1992) 'Race, ethnicity, social class, language and achievement in mathematics' in Grouws, D. (Ed.) *Handbook of Research on Mathematics Teaching and Learning*, New York, NY: Macmillan.

The extensive reviews of bilingual education policies, theories and practices has made Secada one of the top experts in the field. His earlier work (which is again pursued) is on mathematics education, specifically for children of different language groups. The depth of Secada's analysis reflects a vast knowledge of the field of mathematics, psychology, linguistics and curriculum.

SKUTNABB-KANGAS, T. (1984) *Bilingualism or Not: The Education of Minorities*, Clevendon, England: Multilingual Matters.

The author has produced one of the classics in bilingual education and advocacy for the home languages. Her subsequent research on the maintenance of mother tongues and bilingualism is essential to understand why certain bilingual education programs fail.

SPINDLER, G., with SPINDLER, L. (1971). *Dreamers Without Power: The Menomini Indians*, New York, NY: Holt, Rinehart and Winston. (Republished by Waveland Press in 1984).

SPINDLER, G. (1974) 'Schooling in Schoenhausen: A study of cultural transmission and instrumental adaptation in an urbanizing German village', in SPINDLER, G. (Ed.) *Education and Cultural process: Toward an Anthropology of Education*, New York, NY: Holt, Rinehart & Winston, Inc., pp. 230–71.

SPINDLER, G. (1977) 'Change and continuity in American core cultural values: An anthropological perspective' in DERENZO, G.D. (Ed.) *We the People: American Character and Social Change*, Westport: Greenwood, pp. 20–40.

SPINDLER, G. (1987) 'Why have minority groups in North America been disadvantaged by their schools?', in SPINDLER, G. (Ed.) *Education and Cultural Process: Anthropological Approaches*, Second Edition, New York, NY: Holt, Rinehart & Winston, pp. 160–72.

SPINDLER, G. (1987a) 'Beth Ann — A case study of culturally defined adjustment and teacher perceptions', in SPINDLER, G. (Ed.) *Education and Cultural Process: Anthropological Approaches*, Second Edition, Prospect Heights, Illinois: Waveland Press, Inc., pp. 230–44.

SPINDLER, G. (Ed.) (1978) *The Making of Psychological Anthropology*, Berkeley, CA: University of California Press.

SPINDLER, G. and SPINDLER, L. (Eds) (1987a) *The Interpretive Ethnography of Education: At Home and Abroad*, Hillsdale, NJ: Lawrence Erlbaum Assoc.

SPINDLER, G. and SPINDLER, L. (1989) 'Instrumental competence, self-efficacy, linguistic minorities, and cultural therapy: A preliminary attempt at integration', *Anthropology and Education Quarterly*, **10**(1), pp. 36–50.

SPINDLER, G. and SPINDLER, L. with TRUEBA, H. and WILLIAMS, M. (1990) *The American Cultural Dialogue and its Transmission*, London, England: Falmer Press.

Rather than provide here a detailed analysis of the work of the Spindlers, we would recommend that you read Suarez-Orozco (1991a, see p. 186) which does that in an exemplary fashion. Some remarks are in order, however. The Spindlers have created a number of concepts and theories that are now the cornerstone of ethnography. They originated and articulated concepts of cultural continuity and discontinuity, cultural transmission, cultural adaptation, and cultural therapy. To them we owe hundreds of written and/or edited volumes, articles, book chapters and book reviews. Educational anthropology, a discipline that counts many thousands of members, has been the child of the Spindlers since its birth in the early 1950s. Probably there is no other anthropologist on earth that knows as much about ethnographic studies throughout the entire world as George Spindler. His productivity and originality are internationally recognized (and perhaps envied by some).

SPRADLEY, J. (1979) *The Ethnographic Interview*, New York, NY: Holt, Rinehart & Winston.

This is just an example of the many and important methodological contributions made by this author. The entire collection of his works are recommended for scholars who teach ethnographic research methods.

SUAREZ-OROZCO, M.M. (1989) *Central American Refugees and US High Schools: A Psychosocial Study of Motivation and Achievement*, Stanford, CA: Stanford University Press.

SUAREZ-OROZCO, M.M. (1990) 'Speaking of the unspeakable: Toward a psychosocial understanding of responses to terror', *Ethos*, **18**(3), pp. 353–83.

SUAREZ-OROZCO, M.M. (1991a) 'Dialogue and the transmission of culture: The Spindlers and the making of American anthropology', *Anthropology and Education Quarterly*, **22**(3), pp. 281–91.

SUAREZ-OROZCO, M.M. (1991b) 'Migration, minority status, and education: European dilemmas and responses in the 1990s, *Anthropology and Education Quarterly*, **22**(2), pp. 99–120.

The work of Suarez-Orozco is intimately related to that of DeVos and Ogbu. His own cultural background, however, his immigrant experience, character and creative spirit mark each of his many works. In a short time, this young scholar has reached the wisdom and analytical depth that many senior researchers aspire to. His insights into the experience of other immigrants, their castification, experience of terror, degradation and poverty are elegantly presented in solid theoretical frameworks and in interdisciplinary and broad cross-cultural perspectives. The strengths of Suarez-Orozco are precisely the scope of his view in contrasting South American, Central American, Mexican and North American empirical data on ethnicity or psychological adjustment, with data from Europe and Asia. He can combine detailed psychological accounts with ethnohistorical accounts, with sociolinguistic analysis in his effort to build a theoretical model explaining complex behavioral processes.

THARP, R. and GALLIMORE, R. (1989) *Rousing Minds to Life: Teaching, Learning and Schooling in Social Context*, New York, NY: Cambridge University Press.

An outstanding use of Neo-Vygotskian theory, clearly explained to teachers, for the purpose of organizing instruction in culturally and psychologically appropriate ways.

TRUEBA, H.T. (1983) 'Adjustment problems of Mexican-American school children: An anthropological study', *Learning Disability Quarterly*, **4**(4), pp. 395–415.

TRUEBA, H.T. (Ed.) (1987) *Success or Failure: Linguistic Minority Children at Home and In School*, New York, NY: Harper & Row.

TRUEBA, H.T. (1988a) 'Culturally-based explanations of minority students' academic achievement', *Anthropology and Education Quarterly*, **19**(3), pp. 270–87.

TRUEBA, H.T. (1988b) 'English literacy acquisition: From cultural trauma to learning disabilities in minority students', *Journal of Linguistics and Education*, **1**, pp. 125–52.

TRUEBA, H.T. (1989) *Raising Silent Voices: Educating Linguistic Minorities for the 21st century*. NY: Harper & Row.

TRUEBA, H.T. (1990a) 'The role of culture in literacy acquisition', *International Journal of Qualitative Studies in Education*, **3**(1), pp. 1–13.

TRUEBA, H.T. (1991a) 'The role of culture in bilingual instruction: Linking linguistic and cognitive development to cultural knowledge', in GARCIA, O. (Ed.), *Festshcrift in Honor of Joshua A. Fishman*, Amsterdam, Holland: John Benjamins Publishing Co, pp. 43–55.

TRUEBA, H.T. (1991b) 'Linkages of macro-micro analytical levels', *Journal of Psychohistory*, **18**(4), pp. 457–68.

TRUEBA, H.T. (1991c) 'From failure to success: The roles of culture and cultural conflict in the academic achievement of Chicano students', in VALENCIA, R.R. (Ed.), *Chicano School Failure: An Analysis Through Many Windows*, London, England: Falmer Press, pp. 151–63.

TRUEBA, H.T. and DELGADO-GAITAN, C. (Eds) (1988) *School and Society: Learning Content Through Culture*, New York, NY: Praeger Publishers.

TRUEBA, H., CHENG, L. and IMA, K. (1992). *Myth or Reality: Adaptive Strategies of Asian Americans in California*, London, England: Falmer Press.

The work of Trueba, Cheng and Ima is but a simple attempt to invite additional research into topics abandoned in educational and anthropological research. The physical characteristics as well as the cultural characteristics of the Asian people must be emphasized. The linguistic and cultural diversity of Asian groups within countries such as China, Japan, Korea, Indochina, and the Pacific is overwhelming. Members of Western societies tend to oversimplify this diversity and lump together groups that may have some historical connections but today are entirely different, such as the Hawaiian Chinese, the Japanese Koreans, the Chinese Vietnamese, and others. This diversity of Asians is present in America. We have recent immigrants from Indochina with roots in China, France and America; we have Cambodians, Hmong, Khmer, and Vietnamese. We also have Filipinos, Pacific Islanders, and Central Americans with Asian ancestry and some physical characteristics similar to some of the Chinese groups. Asian Americans are very diverse culturally, socially, and educationally. Pacific Island Chinese, for example, have a different culture from those born in Taipei or Beijing. Some Asians are educationally disadvantaged when they come to the US, yet, some are achieving so highly that they have displaced their competitors for entrance to science and math programs in graduate schools.

TRUEBA, H.T., JACOBS, L. and KIRTON, E. (1990) *Cultural Conflict and Adaptation: The Case of the Hmong Children in American Society*, London, England: Falmer Press.

The author and his associates have pursued ethnographic research with minority communities, schools and students in order to explore the relationships between language and culture, as well as to make more understandable the differential achievement of ethnically diverse persons. Their focus on cultural conflict and views on culture have been deeply impacted by the work of George and Louise Spindler. They are interdisciplinary in their analysis, and favor combinations of Neo-Vygotskian theory with sociolinguistic and cultural explanations of behavior.

Vygotsky, L.S. (1962) *Thought and Language*, Cambridge, MA: MIT Press.

Vygotsky, L.S. (1978) *Mind in Society: The Development of Higher Psychological Processes*, in Cole, M., John-Teiner, V., Scribner, S. and Souberman, E. (Eds) Cambridge, MA: Harvard University Press.

The comments made in the work by Brown, *et al.*, 1982; Cole and Griffin, 1983; Moll, 1990; and Moll and Diaz, 1987 serve to summarize the impact of the work of the late Vygotsky. His impact has been explored by Cole and his associates at the Laboratory of Comparative Human Cognition.

Wagatsuma, H. and DeVos, G. (1984) *Heritage of Endurance: Family Patterns and Delinquency Formation in Urban Japan*, Berkeley, CA: University of California Press.

See comments on DeVos' work pp. 177.

Wolcott, H. (1988) '"Problem Finding" in qualitative research', in Trueba, H.T. and Delgado-Gaitan, C. (Eds), *School and Society: Learning Content Through Culture*, New York, NY: Praeger Publishers, pp. 11–35.

Trained with the Spindlers, this author has made many contributions to our understanding of the requirements of a genuine ethnography in the context of other qualitative research efforts. His ethnographic accounts are exemplary.

Zeichner, K. (1992) *Educating Teachers for Cultural Diversity*, National Center for Research on Teacher and Learning, East Lansing, MI: Michigan State University.

This author has a broad interdisciplinary knowledge including sociology, anthropology, linguistics, and psychology. He is one of the best known scholars in teacher education, and is now an advocate for the preparation of teachers to work in culturally diverse settings. His national and international reputation is based on solid, profound research on the complex process of teaching and learning, from a democratic perspective.

Index